FRENCH AND FRANCOPHONE STUDIES

*At the Border*

# At the Border: Margins and Peripheries in Modern France

Edited by
*Henrice Altink and Sharif Gemie*

UNIVERSITY OF WALES PRESS
CARDIFF
2007

**British Library Cataloguing-in-Publication Data**
A catalogue record for this book is available from the British Library.

ISBN 978–0–7083–2076–1

Typeset by Florence Production Ltd, Stoodleigh, Devon
Printed in Great Britain by Antony Rowe Limited, Chippenham

*To Margaret Majumdar,*
*for her support and inspiration*

# Contents

Series editors' preface     ix

Acknowledgements     xi

List of contributors     xiii

A note on the texts     xvii

Introduction: Borders: ancient, modern and
post-modern: definitions and debates
*Henrice Altink and Sharif Gemie*     1

**Part I: France's Geographic Borders**

Chapter one: France as periphery? The challenge
of change
*Alistair Cole*     25

Chapter two: The making of the eastern frontier:
the French–German border, 1815–70
*François Roth*     40

Chapter three: Algeria and the Mediterranean frontier:
a hostile horizon?
*Marianne Durand*     58

**Part II: Between the Centre and the Margin:
the French Regions**

Chapter four: From the other side of the mirror:
the French–German border in landscape and memory:
Lorraine, 1871–1914
*Didier Francfort*     79

Chapter five: Between borders: the remembrance
practices of Spanish exiles in the south west of France
*Scott Soo*                                                                96

Chapter six: Otherness, invisible borders and
representations of identity in the Midi, 1920s
*Laure Teulières*                                                          117

**Part III: The Margins Within**

Chapter seven: Insecurity and no-go areas
*Cathérine Levy*                                                           137

Chapter eight: The Maghrebian community in France:
defining the borders
*Dawn Marley and Judith Broadbridge*                                        153

Chapter nine: Solidarity in pariahdom? Oppression
and self-oppression in gay representations in France
*Owen Heathcote*                                                           175

Index                                                                      191

# Series editors' preface

This new series showcases the work of new and established scholars working within the fields of French and francophone studies. It publishes introductory texts aimed at a student readership, as well as research-orientated monographs at the cutting edge of their discipline area. The series aims to highlight shifting patterns of research in French and francophone studies, to re-evaluate traditional representations of French and francophone identities and to encourage the exchange of ideas and perspectives across a wide range of discipline areas. The emphasis throughout the series will be on the ways in which French and francophone communities across the world are evolving into the twenty-first century.

This volume analyses the nature of French society and culture in the context of globalization and other challenges to the internal and external borders of the French nation-state.

Sharif Gemie and Claire Gorrara

# Acknowledgements

The editors would like to thank the following individuals, organizations and institutions who made possible the 'At the Border' conference and this subsequent publication.

The French Embassy, the French Consulate at Cardiff, the Department of Humanities, and the Association for the Study of Modern and Contemporary France, for their generous financial support and advice.

Gemma Jones and all the staff at the Glamorgan Business Centre, for their help in organizing the conference.

Richard Hand and Mike Wilson for directing a one-act play at the conference.

Julia Gemie, for her design of the conference poster.

Christophe Viriot, who designed the map that appears in Chapter two.

Steve Jones and Rebecca Edwards for their useful advice on particular papers.

Kath Oakwood, Susanna Schrafstetter and Danu Reid for their assistance with the conference organization.

Ian Wiblin, for his help in organizing the commemorative display for Eric Cahm.

Sally Davison, for her editorial advice.

Ashley Drake, for his encouragement and enthusiasm.

Chris Meredith, who wishes to make it clear that he had nothing, absolutely nothing, to do with the translation of the doggerel in Chapter six.

The contributors, for their patience.

From Sharif: special thanks to Patricia, as always.

# Contributors

HENRICE ALTINK was a lecturer in American/Caribbean history at the University of Glamorgan while working on this volume; she moved to the University of York in September 2004. She is an executive member of the Society for Caribbean Studies, and the South West of England and South Wales Women's History Network. She has published work on representations of Jamaican slave women and the Jamaican apprenticeship system, and is currently studying the construction of gender ideologies in post-emancipation Jamaica. Her publications include: 'Slavery by Another Name: Apprenticed Women in Jamaican Workhouses 1834–8', *Social History,* 26:1 (2001), '"An Outrage on all Decency": Abolitionist Reactions to Flogging Jamaican Slave Women, 1780–1834', *Slavery and Abolition,* 23:2 (2002); and 'Retain or Remove: The Border Question in St. Martin in the 1990s', *Journal of Eastern Caribbean Studies,* (24:4) 2003.

JUDITH BROADBRIDGE is Deputy Registrar at St Martin's College, Lancaster. Her PhD was on Alsatian language and identity, and she has published several articles and book chapters on this subject. She has also published on Boris Vian, the subject of her MPhil.

ALISTAIR COLE is a professor in the School of European Studies at Cardiff University. His recent publications include *An Introduction to French Politics and Society* (London: Longman, 2004); (with Michèle Breuillard) *La Gouvernance locale du changement éducatif en Angleterre et en France* (Paris: l'Harmattan, 2003); (with Peter John) *Local Governance in England and France* (London, Routledge: 2001); *Franco-German Relations* (Harlow, Longman:

2001); and *François Mitterrand: a Study in Political Leadership* (London: Routledge, 1997, 2nd ed.).

MARIANNE DURAND is a historian specializing in colonial Algeria. She is currently completing a PhD thesis on 'The Causes and Consequences of May 1945 in Algerian History' in the Centre for European Studies Research at the University of Portsmouth. *marianne.durand@port.ac.uk*

DIDIER FRANCFORT is Professeur d'histoire contemporaine at l'Université Nancy 2. His first research topic was sociability and associational life among Italian immigrants in Lorraine and in their home region, Frioul. He then studied cultural history, concentrating mainly on musical sources – firstly in Italy and then in Central Europe. His comparative work on nationalism and musical traditions in Europe 1870–1914 was published in 2004 by Hachette Littératures. *Arrivefrancfort@aol.com*

SHARIF GEMIE is Reader in History at the University of Glamorgan. He has previously published *Women and Schooling: Gender, Authority and Identity in the Female Schooling Sector, France, 1815–1914* (Keele University Press, 1995); *French Revolutions, 1815–1914: An Introduction* (Edinburgh University Press, 1999); *A Concise History of Galicia* (University of Wales Press, 2006); and *Brittany, 1750–1950: the Invisible Nation* (University of Wales Press, 2007). He is currently working with Dr Fiona Reid on refugees and the Second World War. *sgemie@glam.ac.uk*

OWEN HEATHCOTE is Honorary Visiting Reader in Modern French Studies at the University of Bradford. He researches the relationship between violence, gender and representation in French literature and film and has published widely on such writers as Balzac, Duras, Guibert, Guyotat, Jourdan and Wittig. He has edited/co-edited *Gay Signatures: Gay and Lesbian Theory, Fiction and Film in France* (Berg, 1998); *Forty Years of the Fifth French Republic: Actions, Dialogues and Discourses* (Peter Lang, 1999); and *Negotiating Boundaries: Identities, Sexualities, Diversities* (Cambridge Scholars Publishing, 2007); and special journal issues of *South Central Review* (Violence in French Literature and Film) and *Modern and Contemporary France* (Gays and Lesbians in Contemporary France). He is currently preparing a monograph on violence in Balzac.

CATHÉRINE LEVY is a sociologist at the Centre national de la recherche scientifique. She has researched the topics of strike and labour conflicts, and the re-structuring of the iron and steel industry. She is co-author (with Katia Vladimirova) of *Statuts d'emploi, contrats de travail et sécurité* (Paris: Maison des Sciences de l'Homme, 2004). *catherine.m-levy@wanadoo.fr*

DAWN MARLEY is a senior lecturer in French at the University of Surrey. Her research interests focus on the relationship between language and identity in France and the role of French language and culture in the Maghreb. She has published on language policy and the role of French in Morocco (in the *International Journal of Francophone Studies* and *Language Policy*, among others). She is currently working on the issue of language and identity among French people of Maghrebian origin, and on francophone women's magazines, particularly in Morocco. *d.marley@surrey.ac.uk*

FRANÇOIS ROTH is Professeur d'histoire contemporaine at l'Université Nancy 2. His principal previous works include *La Guerre de 70* (Hachette, 2005); *L'Histoire de la Lorraine et des lorrains* (Serpenoise, 2004); and a biography of Raymond Poincaré (Fayard, 2001). He is currently researching on Robert Schumann and on the history of the construction of the EU. *roth.francois@tiscali.fr*

SCOTT SOO is a lecturer in French studies at the University of Southampton. His recent publications include 'Putting memory to work: A comparative study of three associations dedicated to the memory of the Spanish republican exile in France', *Diasporas: Histoires et Sociétés*, 6 (2005); and 'Ambiguities at work: Spanish Republican exiles and the Organisation Todt in Occupied Bordeaux' in *Modern and Contemporary France*, 15, 4 (2007). He is currently preparing a book on the history of the Spanish Republican refugees in south-west France. *ssoo@soton.ac.uk*

LAURE TEULIÈRES is Maître de conférence en histoire at the Université Toulouse II – le Mirail. She is a specialist in cultural history and the history of social representations, and also in the history of immigration to France. She is on the editorial board of *Diasporas: Histoire et sociétés* and has previously published

*Immigrés d'Italie et paysans de France (1920–44)* (Toulouse: Presses Universitaires du Mirail, 2002); 'Mémoires de migrations, *Diasporas* (2005); and 'Patrimoine et immigration', *Les Cahiers de Framespa* (2007). *laure.teulieres@univ-tlse2.fr*

# A note on the texts

These papers all originate from the Conference of the Association for the Study of Modern and Contemporary France at the University of Glamorgan, held in August 2002. Each has been revised, edited and expanded. Furthermore, four of the papers have been translated. Sharif Gemie was responsible for translating the papers by Didier Francfort, François Roth and Laure Teulières; Sharif Gemie and Margaret Majumdar translated the paper by Cathérine Levy.

# Introduction

# Borders: ancient, modern and post-modern: definitions and debates

*Henrice Altink and Sharif Gemie*

Tap the word 'border' into the Google search engine and you will get 3.76 million hits. The phrase 'border studies' gets you just less than 1 million hits. Working through some of these websites, one notes the extraordinary elasticity of the term 'border': it refers not only to territorial divisions between nations and invisible lines separating classes, genders and races in a society but also to the rim around a piece of sewing, the edge of a printed text, forms of deviant sexuality, marginalized types of literature and culture, a commercially successful bookstore and media chain, a Scottish television channel, an Australian paper, a type of dog, a Swedish independent music production service, changes in juvenile justice, networks in international politics and so on.

The papers presented at the Association for the Study of Modern and Contemporary France (ASM&CF) conference 'At the Border: Margins and Peripheries in Modern France', held at the University of Glamorgan in August 2002, were not quite as diverse, but still examined many varied themes. The participants not only applied the term to France's external borders and the borders separating its various regions, but also to the art of Fernand Léger[1] and André Techine, to the storytelling of Breton fishermen, and to the political and cultural marginalization of homosexuals and blacks in French society and culture. This volume contains a selection of the papers presented. Its purpose is two-fold: to show the wide variety of work undertaken on France's many borders, and to illustrate some recent trends in the area of border studies. This introductory chapter provides a framework for the papers: it explores some of the border-related concepts that are examined in detail by the contributors. It does this first by discussing the rise of Border Studies as an academic discipline and considering the various questions that the discipline addresses. And second, it provides a genealogy of the term 'border' and an overview of the major shifts in Europe's borders from the Roman Empire to the present.

While some of this volume's nine chapters concentrate on France's external borders and the borders that separate its various regions, most focus on cultural borders within France; that is, the visible and invisible lines that separate the classes, ethnicities, and races. For example, the chapter by Owen Heathcote uses the term 'border' in a metaphorical sense; namely, as denoting the difference between accepted and unaccepted norms of good taste. He analyses what Emily Hicks has called 'border writing': literature that emphasizes 'the differences in reference codes between two or more cultures'.[2]

What the following chapters suggest, then, is that there is a continuum of borders, running from the apparently 'real' (a line in the sand separating states or regions) to the more obviously metaphorical. To date, scholars have concentrated more on the first category and less on the latter. Amongst them are not only geographers but also anthropologists, sociologists, political scientists and historians. The following section sets out the questions that each of these disciplines has brought to the study of territorial borders.

## 1. Border Studies

The last decade has not only witnessed a burgeoning output of scholarly articles on territorial borders but also the publication of specialized journals, such as the *Journal of Borderlands Studies,* and the establishment of professional bodies. In addition, various universities worldwide have recently set up research centres on borders. Not surprisingly, many are located in regions with a past of border struggles, such as the Centre for International Border Research at Queen's University Belfast and the Centre for Inter-American and Border Studies at the University of Texas in El Paso. A number, however, have also been set up in regions with a history of cross-border co-operation, like the Centre for Border

Research at the Catholic University Nijmegen in The Netherlands. Most of these centres are interdisciplinary and carry out empirical case studies and comparisons. They tend to concentrate on state borders and the land stretching away from the border and pay less attention to regional borders and the cultural borders within a society. The Centre for Border Studies (CBS) at the University of Glamorgan concentrated on the Welsh-English border and, more widely, on European borders.

Two factors explain the recent growth in Border Studies: the fall of the Berlin Wall in 1989, and globalization, a trend that came to public notice in the 1970s. The fall of the wall was a step in the dissolution of the USSR, which in turn reawakened nationalism in some parts of Europe (e.g. the Czech Republic), triggered conflict (e.g. Yugoslavia) and also led to closer cooperation between Western European states. These trends led, on the one hand, to a weakening of state borders (e.g. the Schengen treaty) and on the other, to the creation of new or the revival of old borders (e.g. the reunification of Germany and the division of Czechoslovakia). They also led to the reinforcement of existing borders or, more precisely, to the growing importance of certain borders, such as the European Union's external border. The first chapter by Alistair Cole provides an introduction to some French responses to this new context, showing in particular the effects it has had on the traditional French model of politics. Not surprisingly, many borders studies centres examine the shape and nature of the 'new' Europe that is forming to the east.[3]

Globalization, here understood as the accelerated movement of capital, commodities, information and labour across state boundaries, has had a similar impact on state borders. It has made some borders less important in order to facilitate the flow of capital, goods and people; for example, the Caribbean Community (CARICOM) and the North American Free Trade Agreement (NAFTA). But equally, in some parts of the world, there have been negative effects stemming from the free movement of capital, goods, culture and peoples, leading in turn to a strengthening of borders.[4] One of these negative effects, some claim, is the influx of labour migrants who are seen to take away resources from a large part of the population. Some nations have tried to counteract this trend by issuing stricter immigration controls. To cite one example, the Dutch, French, and other governments have negotiated a treaty which allows visitors to the French-Dutch Caribbean island of St. Martin from the European Union (EU), the USA, Canada and New Zealand to visit for a limited time without visas, but requires visitors from other countries to obtain a visa. This treaty aims to reduce the influx of migrants from Haiti, the Dominican Republic and other Caribbean islands, who undertake low-paid and unskilled work in the tourist sector and are largely held responsible for the rise in crime in the island.[5] In other words, globalization and the withering away of borders do not necessarily do away with differences between states. On the contrary, these processes can actually reinforce differences and contain potential for both conflict and isolation.

One of the most prominent and innovative disciplines in Border Studies is anthropology. This discipline concentrates on the culture of border regions and the identities (national or ethnic) that are constructed and maintained there.[6] The term 'border region', it needs to be noted, like the term 'border' itself, has a variety of meanings. It generally refers to the areas immediately alongside a state's external border or straddling it, such as the French-Spanish Basque country. It can, however, also mean the administrative regions abutting a border whose centres are physically and socially distant from that border, such as Aquitaine, of which the French Basque country is only a small part. Some border regions may have an underlying cultural unity not congruent with the state borders, but their *raison d'etre* may be the very border that divides them.[7] The regional unity of the US/Mexico border region, for example, stems from the use of the border to exploit opportunities such as wage/price differentials. This particular border region has for a long time dominated anthropological work on borders. More recently, however, anthropologists have shifted their attention to other border regions. Hastings Donnan, for example, has carried out field work in South Armagh, searching for visible markers of sub-national identity in this region's landscape.[8]

The work undertaken by anthropologists has encouraged other scholars to move away from 'an interest in what a boundary encompasses to an interest in the boundary itself'.[9] Geographers are no longer so interested in the questions of why and where state boundaries are drawn; they have moved on to consider the functions they serve. Meanwhile, political scientists and sociologists have adopted the anthropologists' focus on border regions. Political scientists are primarily interested in the question of how state policies, especially those relating to environment, immigration and crime, affect people in border regions and how these people help to shape such policies. Sociologists, on the other hand, have grown more interested in the identity that people in border regions construct. Supported by evidence collected from case studies on minority groups, they have argued that these people are pulled in two ways as a result of economic, cultural and linguistic factors.[10]

History was not as quick as the other social sciences to shift its focus from borders to border regions. For years it followed an approach to borders inaugurated by Frederick Turner in his paper at the 1893 convention of the American Historical Association, in which he argued that the expanding frontier had had a unique influence on American democracy by providing a safety valve for pressure within American society.[11] Historians focused, in other words, on the question of what role borders had played in the formation of nations and states and considered the land alongside the border almost as a passive entity, exercising very little influence on the construction of the nation and state. Recently, however, historians have also studied social forces in border regions and the effects they have exerted locally and beyond. Peter Sahlin's work on the Pyrenean valley region of Cerdanya, for example, shows that this region, divided between France and Spain, has a shared culture and has managed to retain its distinctive identity irrespective of state policies on both sides of the border to impose national cultures by reinforcing otherness.[12]

The foregoing shows, then, that the field of Border Studies has pioneered the study of border regions and has begun to unravel the complex relationships between territory, sovereignty and identity. It presents borders as both processes and institutions. In the first case, it indicates that borders are shaped by the interaction between the state and the people in the border region, and by numerous other factors, and so they change over time. Or, in the words of Donnan and Wilson:

> *Borders are continuously negotiated and reinterpreted through the dialectics of every day life among all people who live at them, but to a lesser extent, by those who cross them, and by those people within a state's border who feel in contact with or threatened by outsiders.*[13]

Borders are also processes in the sense that they make meaning; that is, they help to define the nation-state and frame the related internal borders, such as those demarcating a state's internal divisions, as in a devolved system of local or provincial government (e.g. the UK).[14]

In the second case, borders carry meaning. They reflect the governance of a place – in particular its rigidity and openness – and its associated social system. People's first impression of a state is often through their encounter with its border. Many tourists who travelled along the 'iron curtain' in West Germany before 1989, for example, often gained the impression from the armed guards on the watchtowers that the state on the other side was ruthless in its methods of controlling its population. Borders such as the Berlin Wall embody history; they mark and limit the sovereignty of a government and the rights of its citizens; they indicate the relation between a state and its neighbours; and they define the constituency or electorate.

Border Studies analyses borders as social rather than political constructions. It sees them as motive forces in the development of nations and states, and treats them as zones of cultural contact that often extend some distance away from a borderline. Border Studies has, however, not only debunked the myth that borders are places fixed in time and space but also the idea that borders are simple. It has shown that borders are inherently contradictory, problematical and multifaceted.[15] As the following chapters will illustrate, borders can be at once gateways and barriers; zones of contact and zones of struggle; places of co-operation and places of competition. They also indicate that the identities of people in border regions are often highly ambivalent.

## 2. The origins of the border: a history of definitions

In their pioneering work, Donnan and Wilson make two significant points concerning the definition of the term 'border'. First, they stress the importance of differentiating between a border (i.e. a politically constructed line) and a frontier (i.e. the land that stretches away from the borderline).[16] Second, the two authors show some reluctance to accept studies of 'borders-as-metaphors' as serious, dismissing them as 'efforts to be fashionable or persuasive'.[17] While – obviously – any scholar would welcome the conceptual clarity that the two authors' work suggests, there is some reason to question the approach they present.

A number of different terms are used to describe the edges and limits of state power. The current English-language term 'border' appears to have an early medieval origin in either Old German or Frankish:

**Old German, ninth/tenth century**
*bort*: edge, rim (*Einfassung*)
*borto*: trimming, braid (*Borte*)[18]
*bort*: edge, side of a ship, plank
*borda*: edge, braid[19]

Significantly, the term does not appear to have Latin roots: a point to which we will return. The concept of the side of a ship is certainly provocative: it suggests a sharp differentiation between an inside and an outside, between the wet and the dry. But the clinker-built ships of the early medieval period were anything but permanently intact: constantly leaking, the maintenance of the ship's integrity required continual bailing and frequent repairs. In other words, what might initially appear as an image of permanent and reliable solidity, was actually an evocation of a constant effort to maintain a boundary.

Alongside the term *border*, there is the linked term *frontier*, from the Latin *frons*, meaning – originally – forehead, brow, or front. Spanish is a more Latinate language than English: significantly, the term *frontera* is usually applied in the place of any term resembling the English *border*.

> Frontero, -ra – *The limits or border of a state, kingdom or land: the totality of the forts and positions which defend a land. From the Latin frons., frontis.*[20]

French, like Spanish, has made use of the Latin-derived term.

> Frontière – *A limit which naturally marks out the extent of a territory or which, by convention, separates two states; any type of barrage, or obstacle.*
> *c.1213, the front of an army*
> *1292, a fortified place facing an enemy*[21]

Despite the probable Old German origins of the term 'border', this word is not currently used by Germans. The German-language term for *both* border and frontier is *Grenze,* which may be German, Polish, Russian or Czech in origin. Once again, the adoption of this term involved the application of a metaphor: it appears to have been derived from the term *gran,* meaning the edge of something. This remains the standard term for border in modern Russian, from which a variety of technical and administrative terms is derived; for example, *pereiti granitsu,* to cross the border; and *pogranichnik,* border guard. Significantly, the term also has many contemporary metaphorical uses, such as *pogranichnoye povedeniye,* a psychiatric term for liminal behaviour.[22]

Modern Arabic also makes no distinction between frontiers and borders. A single term, *hadd,* means border, limit and obstacle. The number of terms associated with this single word is extraordinary, including the edge of a knife, the boundaries of orthodox religious faith, and mourning rituals or *hedad.* Acts that are considered immoral or forbidden may be termed *hadded.* Lastly, a sharp-witted or eloquent person is described as *hadeed.*[23]

These points suggest that Donnan and Hastings's neat conceptual distinction between borders and frontiers may need some reconsideration: it certainly can be noted that it draws specifically on an English-language vocabulary, and that it is far less easy to set up this clear division in other languages. Secondly, the authors' reluctance to treat seriously studies of 'borders-as-metaphors' appears contradictory, for it seems likely that the coining of both the terms 'border' and 'frontier' to signify political-territorial boundaries was originally based on the use of metaphors. It therefore seems inconsistent to distinguish a 'real' metaphor from a merely 'symbolic' one.

### 3. Borders in the Roman Empire

It is significant that the English-language term 'border' is not drawn from Latin. The Roman Empire had no clear concept of distinct external borders, for the simple reason that at that time maps were extremely rare. Thus the type of semi-visual conceptualization evoked by our contemporary sense of the term 'border' – a distinct line surrounding a particular territory – was not available to most inhabitants of the Roman Empire.[24] Instead, the term which the Romans have left to contemporary political discourse, and which was popularized by Frederick Turner, is 'frontier', a word used to describe a mobile, military force, perhaps best understood as enforcing the domination of a zone. The frontier was not so much the end of the empire, as its beginning or its vanguard. Indeed, as Daniel Nordman notes, the term 'frontier' evokes the aggression of one state against an enemy; it suggests the threat of war. The term 'border', on the other hand, evokes the agreement of two states; it suggests a condition of peace.[25]

British readers may be surprised by these points: after all, what of Hadrian's Wall? Was that not a clear, permanent border? Others might also raise the question of the *limites*, the line of military defences that protected the Roman Empire. These issues are important and merit a few moments' debate. Throughout most of the seven centuries of Rome's long rise, domination and decline, frontiers were merely the place 'where the last campaign ended': they were temporary, provisional areas.[26] Rome was never defeated: the next year, its military forces would return, and push these frontiers further forward. The turning point was the rise of Emperor Augustus, following a protracted civil war in 31 BC. Augustus's priority was to de-militarize the Roman polity. He disbanded thirty-two of the sixty legions, and then sent the rest away from Rome, to the frontiers. As Derek Williams has suggested, this was a potentially dangerous strategy. In simple military terms, it was far more effective to maintain a centralized military force, and then mobilize them along roads to meet an attacker, than it was to disperse Rome's forces along its boundaries.[27] Augustus was, however, motivated by political considerations: Rome's armies were placed along its frontiers, which became militarized zones, rarely visited by civilians.

Its technicians and military experts then adapted to the new strategy: tents were exchanged for forts, landscapes were studied, natural features – the Rhine, the Danube – were identified as elements within a defensive line. In many areas, however, the defensive line ran along roads and tracks. These markers demonstrate Roman thinking: the *limites* was not a solid impermeable wall that mapped out, square inch by square inch, the extent of Rome's territory. Instead, it was a zone of force, prepared and adapted for military use. Roads and tracks were ideal for this as they allowed the defenders to move more quickly than the attackers. To cite Williams once more: the *limites* was, 'a manned obstacle whose purpose . . . was less against attack than as an aid to

patrolling and a deterrent to infiltration . . . [it was] not a method
of boundary marking but a strategy'.[28] Rome's long-term aim was
the peaceful occupation of territory, for 'a peaceful province was
one which did not need a frontier'.[29] In many areas, however,
peaceful occupation was not possible and so, for example, the
Rhine-Danube line developed: 310 miles long, with its sixty forts
and 900 signal towers.[30]

Hadrian's Wall developed as a consequence of Emperor
Claudius's botched invasion of the British Isles and the resulting
seventy-five-year-long search for an effective frontier. There were
some precedents for this type of construction: in the Iron Age,
dykes and earthworks had marked out territories, and in Classical
Greece, walls had been built to protect cities. Aristotle noted
on this point that, 'deliberately to give cities no walls at all is
like choosing an easily attacked position and clearing away the
surrounding high ground'.[31] More distantly, it is possible that
knowledge of the Great Wall of China may have reached Rome.[32]
But none of these earlier initiatives really anticipated Hadrian's
Wall. It was almost 75 miles long, between 8 and 10 feet wide and
between 15 and 20 feet high, with a small fort every mile and a
watchtower every third of a mile. A hundred gates ran through
it, and some thirty million bricks were used in building it, with
some twenty million gallons of water used in making its mortar.
Soldiers as far away as Caerleon, in south Wales (about 15 miles
south east of the site of our conference), marched for three weeks
up to Scotland each year in order to build it. It needed a constant
garrison of approximately 20,000 soldiers – 160 for each mile of
the wall. Finally, the entire edifice was regularly whitewashed, a
sign of the importance of its visual impact.[33]

This remarkable monument can be seen as the precursor of
other politicized and fortified walls in the world, ranging from
the Berlin Wall and the 'Peace Wall' in Belfast to the walls
closing in on the Palestinians in the Occupied Territories today.
It should be noted, however, that Hadrian's Wall was not typical
of Roman policies. It was a *unique* boundary, enormously expen-
sive, unnecessary (it was never attacked) and a fitting symbol for
the decadence of Imperial Roman power, for it represented the
'knowledge barrier' and the 'cultural quarantine' with which
the declining Roman power sought to protect itself.[34] Rather than
adding to the cultural development of the world, Rome's rise may

well have had the long-term effect of preventing communication and innovation within Europe.[35] Hadrian's Wall is therefore the exception that proves the rule: it shows that the practices of Roman Empire did not create the modern concept of the 'border'.

## 4. Borders in medieval and early modern Europe

During the early medieval period any large-scale political stability achieved by the Roman Empire rapidly faded. Europe became a patchwork of overlapping jurisdictions, which included fair-sized monarchies, ecclesiastical domains, independent cities, autonomous duchies and irregular micro-territories. The map of the Holy Roman Empire is a good illustration of this type of political mixture. One point that never fails to amaze students is that no researcher can say with any certainty exactly how many polities composed this mass (though current estimates seem to suggest approximately 300).[36] In looking at this map, however, we need to bear in mind once more that this visual conceptualization distorts a complex political reality. Very few members of the Holy Roman Empire would ever have thought of their territory in this unified manner. Indeed, there was only the vaguest concept of 'Europe', intermittently evoked as Christian identity in opposition to the Muslim 'other' to the east and south.[37]

The nature of this visual distortion can, perhaps, be better understood if we consider a single town, particularly as portrayed in those countless pen and ink city portraits that were printed in the sixteenth and seventeenth centuries. At first sight, the town's borders seem clearly, even emphatically, represented by its walls. At this point, however, it should be remembered that these types of city portraits were often commissioned by the city councillors themselves. Their aim was to represent the solidity of the city and the strength of its walls, and thus to affirm the city's independence against a potentially hostile outside world. Machiavelli registers their importance in his *The Prince*:

> *The cities of Germany are wholly independent, they control only limited territory, and obey the emperor only when they want to. They fear neither him nor any neighbouring power, because they are so fortified that everyone knows it would be a protracted, difficult operation to reduce them. This is because they all have excellent moats and walls; they have adequate artillery; they always lay in public stocks of drink, food, and fuel to last a year.*[38]

Significantly, there was an important debate concerning the
manner in which to represent a town visually. Critics often claimed
that a 'bird's-eye-view' perspective failed to represent adequately
the most honourable elements of a city, because it gave equal space
to the hovel and the mansion, the brothel and the church, the
slum and the square. It would be more appropriate, argued such
status-bound critics, to commission a representation of the city as
a vertical-cross section, from the principal gates, through the main
streets, the greatest buildings and the central square.[39]

Such debates reveal an important aspect of the conceptualization of internal borders during the medieval period. The most
significant urban boundaries were not necessarily those that were
solidly affirmed by the bricks and mortar of the city walls. There
were also rigidly enforced systems of internal borders in most
towns: the no-go areas running along particular streets, developing
according to the irregular and invisible rhythms of power and
authority, such as the Jewish quarter in some of the main European
cities. The fact that such borders were intangible does not detract
from their force.

There can be no doubt that the territorial borders created by
medieval authorities were fragile and often ineffective. Established
authorities, whether royal, aristocratic or religious, held power at
the centre of their realms. The further one travelled from their
courts or *châteaux*, the weaker their power became. The exact
point at which their jurisdiction ended and the power of another
authority was enforced was always subject to debate and dispute.
Nevertheless, efforts were made to mark out such lines of power.
The well-known French medievalist, Bernard Guenée, noted
amongst others the following: crosses at crossroads, hedges, trees,
rivers and streams, bridges, ditches, and sticks.[40] Such efforts to
symbolize the border, however, often appeared absurd for two
reasons. First, rival powers were not usually separated by neat
lines, but by rambling zones or marches. These zones were places
of both conflict and contact. During the medieval period, for
example, ritual tournaments were often held in these zones, which
helped to institutionalize and tame potentially violent rivalries.
In troubled zones, the marches could grow ever larger: between
the thirteenth and sixteenth centuries, approximately one-half
of the territory of modern Wales took the form of marches.[41]
Second, during the medieval period, power was understood as a

personal, contractual relationship that tied subject to master, not as a form of territorial domination. Whether this patch of land or that marsh belonged to one master or another mattered little to medieval authorities: what really counted was their domination of particular people. For these reasons, then, the most effective way to enforce borders was not by forms of abstract symbolism, but through the active participation of the ruler or his representatives. Kings, for instance, would lead their itinerant courts along the lines of their territories, and once a year local priests would lead their parishioners in the tramping of the parish boundaries.

Like the *bort*, medieval frontiers were fragile, flexible and shifting, adapting to currents of power and the developments of authority. The Spanish *Reconquista*, which lasted from the ninth to the fifteenth centuries, is perhaps the most striking example of this. It epitomizes the Europe-wide rise of 'military landed elites', whose heavy cavalry, castles and new Gregorian Christianity structured a common pattern of rule, and who used these instruments to '*faire frontière*'.[42] It is important to note that even at their most fierce, the armed disputes between Christians and Muslims never created 'a true religious, linguistic or economic barrier' dividing the peoples of Spain.[43] Alongside kidnapping, cattle-rustling, robbery and reprisals – structured according to a semi-formal code of honour – there were also ideals of 'good neighbourliness'. Paintings depicting scenes from the legends of Tristan and Isolde and the Arthurian cycle were painted on three domes in the Hall of Justice of the Alhambra in Granada, the last great monument of Arab civilization in medieval Spain.[44] The lasting memory of the *Reconquista*, however, is that of the battles and disputes between Christians and Muslims that it inspired. While kings came and went, the conflict appeared permanent: the legend of the frontier created its own laws, its own 'system', its own reality.[45] It is no surprise that it was in this zone of conflict and contact that the modern passport was invented.[46]

## 5. Borders in the age of nationalism

In the seventeenth and eighteenth centuries, the diocese of Strasbourg stretched over the border between the kingdom of France and the Holy Roman Empire: one-third of its territory lay east of the Rhine. It contained Lutherans and Catholics, and French

speakers and German speakers. Its bishop was a *seigneur* in his
own right, a prince of the Holy Roman Empire and a servant of
the French Crown.[47] This approximate, shifting, informal approach
to borders was ended by the rise of nationalism. How could France
exist as a moral community if its parishes and towns showed such
divided loyalties? As many commentators have noted, nationalism
demands homology: a state formation should be attached to a
nation, a nation to a people, and a people to a territory.[48] Border
conflicts with neighbouring states became almost a normal part
of state-craft, as illustrated in François Roth's paper (Chapter two)
on the French-German border between 1815 and 1871. But the
nation-states that developed in Europe in the nineteenth century
were also inherently suspicious of all forms of internal borders,
whether visible or invisible. They aimed to create a polity that was
'one and indivisible'. They therefore worked to eradicate all
internal borders, while emphasizing ever more strongly the importance of external, territorial borders, which were increasingly
policed and even fortified.

Most new nation-states witnessed a public debate about minorities
and 'others'. On the one hand, this debate called for greater
integration. Demands were made for integrative programmes, such
as mass schooling, social security and health care, which were
supported by principles such as legal equality and even the concept
of human rights. This call for integration was exemplified in two
developments: a shift in symbolic representation of the external
border, from the monarch's presence to the passport or identity
card, and the influx of labour migrants needed to develop emerging
industries.[49] The papers by Francfort and Teulières (Chapters
four and six) stress the importance of migrant labour for the
French economy in the late nineteenth and early twentieth
centuries. They show that Italians migrated to Lorraine and to the
Midi, and that the latter region also witnessed an influx of Spanish
migrants.

On the other hand, the new nations' debates led to the
identification of 'others' who refused to recognize, or – worse still
– were unable to recognize the honour of the nation. One clear
example of this is the changing fate of refugees. The Huguenot
refugees of the seventeenth century were seen as potentially
valuable additions to kingdoms and polities as is demonstrated by
the rivalry between British and German polities to receive them.

By the early nineteenth century, however, attitudes had changed: political refugees were now seen as misfits and troublemakers, aliens who would be unable to fit into the newly forming national communities.[50] Soo, in Chapter five, details the hostility Spanish republican refugees faced in France after 1939, and the strategies they adopted to cope with this. The most tragic example of this tendency, however, is the fate of the European Jews, who were identified as 'anti-national nomads'.[51]

Under these circumstances, there was a protracted effort by nationalists to treat external borders as key defining characteristics of any nation. Their symbolism worked to override all other forms of cultural or social allegiance: a point neatly illustrated by the Italian fascists' references to Italy as a 'proletarian nation', a term which suggested the collapsing of social class into the schema of national self-identity.

Yet while nationalists were re-conceptualizing the nature of the border, people in the border regions were learning some other aspects of these newly affirmed boundaries. One obvious advantage was the possibility of smuggling: one could rework Blake's observation that, 'brothels are built with bricks of religion' to argue, more prosaically, that, 'smuggling was created by state borders'. Such illicit trades obviously transgressed the new, neat rules of a state-directed economy. They are, however, but one of a range of transgressive activities, which also included political subversion, religious dissidence and cultural experimentation. Rather than these new boundaries functioning as distinct, impermeable limits to a nation-state's politics, culture and economy, they instead acquired a certain relative autonomy.[52] Like the marches of the medieval period, they became zones of debates and communication, rather than zones of closure and limits. And they did not only mark the existence of the nation-state, but also the limits of the nation-state's territorial projects: they inspired challenges and provocations.[53]

## 6. Borders in a post-modern era

Skilled and perceptive observers have sensed a fundamental shift in political/territorial structures in the twentieth century. For J. H. Elliott, the 1919 Treaty of Versailles marked the triumph of nationalism, after which it began its decline.[54] According to Jürgen

Habermas, the Allied victory in 1945 marked the long-term victory of Enlightenment universalism over its last enemy, fascism.[55] And for Liam O'Dowd, the four decades from 1945 to 1995 were the zenith of the nation-state system, offering a period of unprecedented international stability.[56] The shape and structure of the world and its borders following this triumph, this zenith, is still uncertain and the unhappy neologism 'post-modern' is probably the most evocative term to capture the sense of change.

In this new situation, globalization, a revolution in mass communication, the increase in mobility and mass tourism, and various other processes have both diminished the significance of geographical borders, *and* have made borders become more salient or have even led to the construction of new borders. While after 1992 the territorial border posts and checkpoints were abandoned in France, 'a thousand shifting borders are set up within the national territory of France'.[57] For example, since the 1997 attack on an Réseau Express Régional (RER) train at the Port Royal station, the RER has been policed: soldiers conduct extensive identity checks on those who 'look' foreign. As Derrida notes, in these new circumstances we are moving to a position of 'police without borders'.[58] Cathérine Levy's paper (Chapter seven) concerning the eradication of human rights in certain problem areas, presents a similar analysis of a new form of neo-colonialist exploitation developing *within* the French mainland. Other countries that have experienced a large influx of migrants have witnessed what Van Houtum has described as 'the social production of spaces of difference and indifference'; that is, anything 'beyond the self-defined differentiating border of comfort (difference) is socially made legitimate to be neglected (indifference)'.[59] Marianne Durand's paper (Chapter three) analyses attempts in contemporary Algeria to adapt to these changing circumstances and suggests that this country's troubled past may provide it with some valuable lessons for the challenges of the future.

Post-modern identities are no longer so solidly constructed around borderlines. Post-modern cultures are shaped – for Benedict Anderson – by the 'long-distance nationalism' of permanent exiles and – for Arjun Appadurai – by diasporic public spheres, informed by a post-national imagination, inspired by a nostalgia without memory.[60] Didier Francfort's study of a line where the border used to be (Chapter four) shows how nostalgia, memory and history can leave their traces in both a culture and a landscape. Other initiatives suggest the re-formation of new forms of non-national borders. Ruba Salih's revealing study of Moroccan women migrants in Italy gives a good example of such processes. These women forge a new, transnational Islam, 'cleared from local variations and traditional performances', and construct a de-territorialized community with their *hijab* and their satellite televisions.[61] Elsewhere, within France, new micro-nationalisms are revived, reinvented and reimagined. The 'soldier-singers' of Corsica resurrect 'traditional' polyphonic singing as a vehicle for an assertion of local neo-nationalism; in Brittany, French-speakers campaign for the right of their children to learn Breton. As Marley and Broadbridge show in their paper (Chapter eight), the use of Arabic plays a central role in the construction of a Maghrebian identity by children from first- and second-generation Maghrebian migrants.[62]

## Conclusion: 'At the Border'

This volume is divided into three sections: Part I, 'France's geographic borders'; Part II, 'Between the centre and the margin: the French regions'; and Part III, 'The margins within'. Although they leave unaddressed many borders in French society, such as that between the private and the public, these chapters show us how borders, both external and internal, are constructed and maintained. In addition, they examine the functions that borders fulfil in social life, such as the regulation of social and political life and the differentiation between various groups of people. They furthermore suggest possible items on the research agenda of Border Studies. Levy's chapter, for instance, calls for a stronger focus on the ways in which internal borders can lead to immobilization of large segments of society; while Soo's study asks scholars to regard the process of identity construction of migrants as ongoing, and Francfort's essay highlights the need to explore the role that physical markers of former borders play in identity construction.

The nine contributions to this volume provide a sample of recent work on France's borders. They show that questions concerning *how* and *why* borders are created and maintained still fascinate scholars. Alongside these, there are new issues, such as how borders can be transgressed, and what role borders play in the construction of personal and collective identities. While some contributions, such as those of François Roth and Alistair Cole, have followed earlier approaches in Border Studies by concentrating on external borders, others have adopted more cross-disciplinary approaches. Those by Soo, Teulières, and Marley and Broadbridge, for example, study the movement of people across national borders; and the contribution by Cathérine Levy examines the construction of new internal borders after Schengen. Whichever approach they adopt to the study of borders, each contribution demonstrates that borders are both processes and institutions. The nine chapters not only show that France's territorial and cultural borders have changed over time, but also that they were, and still are, highly ambivalent, acting as both zones of conflict and contact.

## Notes

1   Unfortunately, for reasons of space, we have not been able to include Maureen Shanahan's paper on Fernard Léger. Readers can, however, consult her essay, 'Male Ga(y)zes: Rolf de Maré and Fernand Léger's partnership', in Irene Eynat-Confino and Eva Sormova (eds), *Patronage, Spectacle and the Stage* (Prague: Theatre Institute, 2006).

2   As cited in M. G. Henderson, 'Introduction: borders, boundaries, and frame(works)', in M. Henderson (ed.), *Borders, Boundaries, and Frames: Cultural Criticism and Cultural Studies* (New York/London: Routledge, 1995), p. 3.

3   See, for example, James Anderson and Liam O'Dowd, 'Borders, border regions and territoriality: contradictory meanings, changing significance', *Regional Studies*, 33:7 (1999), pp. 593–604 (pp. 600–2).

4   Anderson and O'Dowd, 'Borders, Border Regions and Territoriality', pp. 597–600. For a good introduction into globalization's effects on state borders, see the following studies by Zygmunt Bauman: *Life in Fragments: Essays in Postmodern Morality* (Oxford: Blackwell, 1995); *Globalization, The Human Consequences* (New York: Columbia University Press, 1998) and *Liquid Modernity* (Oxford: Polity Press, 2000).

5   J. H. Lake Jr, *The Republic of St. Martin* (Philipsburg: The House of Nehesi, 2000), p. 13. The negotiations started in 1994. As a result of pressure exerted by local residents who expect a downturn in trade and tourism if implemented, the Dutch government has thus far refused to ratify the treaty. For more information on the treaty, see H. Altink, 'Remove or retain?: The border question in St. Martin in the 1990's', *Journal of Eastern Caribbean Studies*, 24:4 (2003), pp. 26–55.

6  For a good overview of the work undertaken by this discipline in recent years, see H. Donnan and T. M. Wilson, *Borders: Frontiers of Identity, Nation and State* (Oxford: Berg, 1999), pp. 4–6.

7  Anderson and O'Dowd, 'Borders, border regions and territoriality', p. 595.

8  Hastings Donnan, 'Material identities: fixing ethnicity in the Irish borderland', paper delivered at the opening of the Centre for Border Studies, University of Glamorgan, October 2003.

9  Donnan and Wilson, *Borders*, p. 21.

10  Donnan and Wilson, *Borders*, pp. 45, 54, and 59.

11  For more information on Turner's thesis, see William McNeill, *The Global Condition: Conquerors, Catastrophes and Community* (Princeton: Princeton University Press), pp. 5–12.

12  Donnan and Wilson, *Borders*, 49; Peter Sahlins, *Boundaries: The Making of France and Spain in the Pyrenees* (Berkeley: University of California Press, 1989).

13  As cited in L. O'Dowd and T. M. Wilson (eds), *Borders, Nations and States* (Aldershot: Avebury, 1996), p. 8.

14  Anderson and O'Dowd, 'Borders, border regions and territoriality', pp. 594–5.

15  Anderson and O'Dowd, 'Borders, border regions and territoriality', concentrate mainly on the dichotomies presented by borders.

16  Donnan and Wilson, *Borders*, pp. 15–16.

17  Donnan and Wilson, *Borders*, p. 41.

18  Jochen Splett, *Althochdeutsches Wörterbuch* (Berlin: De Gruyter, 1993).

19  Ge. Köbler, *Wörterbuch des althochdeutschen Sprachschatzes* (Paderborn: Schöningh, 1993). The authors would like to thank Susanne Schrafstetter for help with this section.

20  *Enciclopedia Universal Ilustrado* (Madrid: Espasa-Calpe, 1924).

21  *Trésor de la Langue Française*, CNRS (1980).

22  The authors would like to thank Viktor Postilnikov of the Institute of Electrodynamics, at the Ukrainian Academy of Sciences, for his help with this section.

23  The authors would like to thank Fouad Gemie for his help with this section.

24  See Josep Fontana, *The Distorted Part: A Reinterpretation of Europe* (Oxford: Blackwell, 1995), pp. 12–15.

25  Daniel Nordman, 'Des limites d'Etat aux frontières naturelles' in P. Nora (ed.), *Les Lieux de Mémoire*, vol. I (Paris: Quarto/Gallimard, 1997), pp. 1125–46 (p. 1137).

26  Derek Williams, *The Reach of Rome: A History of the Roman Imperial Frontier, 1st–5th Centuries AD* (London: Constable, 1996), p. 2.

27  Williams, *Reach of Rome*, p. xvii–xviii.

28  *Reach of Rome*, pp. 50–2 (p. 36).

29  *Reach of Rome*, p. 41.

30  *Reach of Rome*, 46.

31  *The Politics*, translated by T. A. Sinclair (Harmondsworth: Penguin, 1962), p. 279.

32   *Reach of Rome*, p. 98.
33   *Reach of Rome*, pp. 100–9.
34   *Reach of Rome*, p. 299.
35   On this point, see Klaus Randsborg, 'Barbarians, Classical Antiquity
     and the Rise of Western Europe: an Archaeological Essay', *Past and
     Present*, 137 (1992), pp. 8–24.
36   See Michael Hughes, *Early Modern Germany, 1477–1806* (London:
     MacMillan, 1992).
37   Peter Burke, 'Did Europe exist before 1700?', *History of European
     Ideas* 1 (1980), pp. 21–9.
38   Niccolò Machiavelli, *The Prince*, translated by George Bull (Harmonds-
     worth: Penguin, 1999 [originally written 1513]), p. 35.
39   See Daniel Roche, *The People of Paris: An Essay in Popular Culture in
     the Eighteenth Century*, translated by Marie Evans (Leamington Spa:
     1987), pp. 11–13.
40   Bernard Guenée, 'Des limites féodales aux frontières politique' in
     P. Nora (ed.), *Les Lieux de Mémoire*, vol. I (Paris: Quarto/Gallimard,
     1997), pp. 1103–24 (p. 1105).
41   Rees Davies, 'Frontier arrangements in fragmented societies: Ireland
     and Wales' in R. Bartlett and A. McKay (eds), *Medieval Frontier Societies*
     (Oxford: Clarendon, 1989), pp. 77–100 (p. 82).
42   Robert Bartlett, 'Colonial aristocracies of the High Middle Ages', in
     Bartlett and McKay, *Medieval Frontier Societies*, pp. 23–48 (p. 24);
     Guenée, 'Limites féodales', p. 1112.
43   Marie-Claude Gerbet, 'Los Españoles de la "Frontera"', translated by
     B. Hervàs, in P. Bonnassie, P. Guichard and M.–C. Gerbet (eds), *Las
     Españas medievales* (Barcelona: Crítica, 2001), p. 196.
44   Angus MacKay, 'Religion, culture and ideology on the late medieval
     Castilian-Granadan frontier', in Bartlett and MacKay, *Medieval Frontier
     Societies*, pp. 217–43 (pp. 222–3).
45   Manuel González Jiménez, 'Frontier and settlement in the kingdom
     of Castile (1085–350)' in Bartlett and MacKay, *Medieval Frontier Societies*,
     pp. 49–74.
46   Darren O'Byrne, 'On passports and border controls', *Annals of Tourism
     Research* 28:2 (2001), pp. 399–416 (p. 400).
47   Louis Chatellier, 'Frontière politique et frontière religieuse: l'example
     du diocèse de Strausbourg (1648–1790)', *Annales de l'Est*, numéro
     spécial, 2003, pp. 103–26.
48   On this point see, for example, Donnan and Wilson, *Borders*, 10; and
     Stuart Woolf, 'Introduction' to his *Nationalism in Europe, 1815 to the
     Present* (London: Routledge, 1996), pp. 1–40 (p. 10).
49   O'Byrne, 'On passports and border controls'; Saskia Sassen, *Guests
     and Aliens* (New York: The New Press, 1999), pp. 41 and 58.
50   See Sassen, *Guests and Aliens*, pp. 11–34.
51   See Neil MacMaster, *Racism in Europe, 1870–2000* (Houndsmill:
     Palgrave, 2001), pp. 92–4.
52   This point is argued most persuasively by Sahlins in *Boundaries*.
     See also Sharif Gemie, 'France and the Val d'Aran: politics and

nationhood on the Pyrenean border, c.1800–25', *European History Quarterly* 28:3 (1998), pp. 311–45, and in Teulière's contribution to the present volume.

53  Anderson and O'Dowd, 'Borders, border regions and territoriality'.

54  J. H. Elliott, 'A Europe of composite monarchies', *Past and Present* 137 (1992), pp. 48–71.

55  Jürgen Habermas, *Après l'état-nation; une nouvelle constellation politique*, translated by Rainer Rochlitz (Paris: Fayard, 2000), pp. 22–3.

56  Liam O'Dowd, 'The changing significance of European borders', in J. Anderson, L. O'Dowd and T. M. Wilson (eds), *New Borders for a Changing Europe* (London: Frank Cass, 2003), pp. 13–36.

57  Laurent Dubois, '*La République métisée*: citizenship, colonialism and the borders of French history', *Cultural Studies* 14:1 (2000), pp. 15–34.

58  Jacques Derrida, *On Cosmopolitanism and Forgiveness*, translated by M. Dooley and M. Hughes (London: Routledge, 2002), p. 14.

59  H. van Houtum and T. van Naerssen, 'Bordering, Ordering and Othering', *Tijdschrift voor Economisch en Social geografie*, 93:2 (2002), p. 129.

60  See Benedict Anderson, 'Long-distance nationalism' in his *The Spectre of Comparisons* (London: Verso, 1998) and Arjun Appadurai, *Modernity at Large: Cultural Dimensions of Globalization* (Minneapolis: University of Minnesota Press, 1996), pp. 10–40.

61  Ruba Salih, 'Shifting boundaries of self and other: Moroccan migrant women in Italy', *European Journal of Women's Studies* 7 (2002), pp. 321–35.

62  Caroline Bithell, 'On the playing fields of the world (and Corsica): politics, power, passion and polyphony', *British Journal of Ethnomusicology*, 12:1 (2003), pp. 67–95; and Sharif Gemie 'The politics of language: debates and identities in contemporary Brittany', *French Cultural Studies*, 13:2 (2002), pp. 145–64.

# Part I

---

# France's Geographic Borders

# Chapter one

# France as periphery? The challenge of change

*Alistair Cole*

### Editors' note

*This paper was written in the summer of 2002. It therefore does not evaluate the major changes that occurred in the France/USA relationship during the 2003 Gulf War.*

### Introduction

France is a European nation with a particular state tradition and historical legacy, which has been challenged by internal and external pressures since the 1970s. Arguably, it can no longer claim a leading role in the construction of European policies and in the continuing formation of the EU. This shift implies a move from a central to a more peripheral position. This paper suggests the political borders of the French Republic have correspondingly changed in nature. As a result, French politics and public policy-making have become far less introspective. There is much evidence of French resistance to unwelcome external ideas, such as 'neo-liberalism', and there are also deep obstacles to reform from entrenched domestic interests, as illustrated during the Jospin government by the difficulty in implementing policy reforms in the education or fiscal administrations. But, in many important respects, French political elites have dealt with external and internal challenges in ways that are consistent with overarching national traditions. The institutions, interests and ideas that together comprise the French model of politics and policy-making have proved remarkably resilient in the face of so many challenges. After identifying the traditional model of French politics and policy-making, and analysing the factors stimulating change, I will conclude that the French polity has indeed mutated under the combined impact of internal and external pressures for change.

## 1. A traditional French model of politics and policy-making

Notions of 'the French exception' – or, come to that, of the republican model – have a useful heuristic value, insofar as they describe an assortment of features (some of which are contradictory within their own terms of reference) commonly associated with a traditional model of French politics and policy.[1] They also elucidate a particular type of political discourse that remains deeply embedded within French discursive and ideological frames. The speeches of French politicians provide us with daily examples of positive exceptionalism: France is presented as a beacon for the rest of the world to imitate; it has exceptional status on account of being France. This is a form of *sui generis* exceptionalism. In the eyes of a leader such as de Gaulle, the superior claims of French civilization justified such a stance. French leaders still point to the status of the French Revolution, the idea of France as the country of the rights of man and citizen, the role of French culture, and so on, to justify this incipient leadership claim. This image of the paradoxical alchemy of exceptionalism and universality captures the perception that many French institutions and political actors have of their role.

This should not surprise us. Any country attempts to draw a positive reading from the lessons of its past and France is not alone in having leadership pretensions. One only has to think of Britain or the United States in this respect. In spite of this, the central argument in this chapter is that France became a country that was rather less different from its European neighbours in the year 2000 than it had been in 1970. While I would hesitate before adopting any naïve thesis of political or policy convergence, there are powerful forces pushing European countries in similar directions. There are external forces such as Europeanization and globalization; internal pressures, including drives to reform domestic welfare states and forms of macro-economic management; and the emergence of comparable post-modern political movements across European countries. On the other hand, countries faced with comparable pressures might adopt dissimilar responses consistent with their own political traditions. More importantly, external challenges are often interpreted by referential frames shaped according to dominant domestic discursive traditions. Change might in some respects reinforce national policy styles.

The French model of politics and policies consists of a combination of institutions, interests and ideas. It allocates a focal role to the French state and state-driven paradigms of public policy, stresses the importance of ideas and political discourse, assumes the inefficacy of social movements and political parties, and advocates the leading role of France in the world.

We can identify several key features of this traditional republican model of French politics and policies. The existence of a powerful central state was a legacy of the process of nation-building, whereby centralization and uniformity were imposed from above on rebellious provinces and local identities. This produced a model of Parisian centralization, and a homogeneous political and administrative elite rigorously selected through a system of elite schools and competitive examinations. A natural corollary was the tradition of state interventionism in the economic and industrial sphere *(dirigisme)*. The role of the state was to lead and to compensate for the lack of dynamism of domestic capitalism.

At the level of political representation, this traditional model expressed a distrust of intermediary institutions, such as parties, groups and regions, considering them as threatening the general will. Though powerful provincial counterweights survived, these only operated within the confines of Jacobin legality. Contemporary French politics repeatedly highlights the paradox of a rather weak bargaining culture and divided, unrepresentative interest groups, producing strong social counterweights imbued with an ethic of direct action. The farming lobby, for example, acts as a particularly powerful domestic constraint in the French case, which has no real equivalent elsewhere in Europe.

The Fifth Republic has generally had executive-dominated governments, relatively weak political and judicial counterweights to a powerful executive authority and a high territorial concentration of power. Even after the far-reaching decentralization laws of 1982–3, which created directly elected regional councils, there is still no equivalent of the powerful German *Länder* governments, and metaphors of multi-level governance have more resonance in the German case than the French. Parliamentary counterweights to executive authority have also generally been rather weak. The lower chamber, the National Assembly, enjoys limited constitutional sovereignty and exercises weak parliamentary scrutiny, though the institution has acquired more powers and prestige in recent years. The Second Chamber – the Senate – is an archaic and ineffective institution, which over-represents rural and small-town France at the expense of the urban population. By contrast, the rise of judicial and regulatory counterweights to executive authority has been a prominent feature of French politics in the 1990s.

This traditional model of French politics and policies is an ideal type – some might say a straw man. It has been subjected to intense pressures for change since the late 1970s. We can summarize the challenges to the traditional French model under four headings:

a.  reinventing the state
b.  Europeanization and globalization
c.  the challenge of 'La France d'en bas' [or grassroots France]
d.  the problem of political legitimacy

### a. Reinventing the state?

The history of France is to some extent the history of the French state, and today there is still a widespread positive connotation of the state as an instrument of public service, and a guarantee of equality between French citizens. The equality and neutrality of the state forms an important part of the French republican tradition. Challenges to the French state have come from several directions: in sum, the interventionist state has ceded ground under the combined pressures of fiscal austerity, European regulation, and policy fashion, in the form of the privatization programmes. In the domestic arena, the decentralization and reforms of the 1980s and 1990s have substantially altered the nature of centre-periphery relations, leading to a constraining impact upon the state going beyond that originally envisaged. Certain traditionally pre-eminent policy actors (those in the *grands corps* especially) have had to re-evaluate their positions and accept a diminished role. Though there remain close links between government and business, the French state no longer has the capacity to call the captains of industry to obey its orders.

This challenge to the State-centred model of the making of public policy has gone hand in hand with the development of a near-complete domestic consensus on many – though by no means all – of the most important issues of public policy. This is particularly the case in relation to economic policy. Debates between left and right – over issues of economic management at least – have become merely differences of degree. With a constrained convergence on issues of economic management, the battleground between the French Left and Right is increasingly fought in the area of security and civil liberties, and social and employment policies, as seen in the Jospin government and the 35-hour week. The range of economic options has narrowed, as it has in other European countries. We should recall that the Jospin government privatized more assiduously than any of its predecessors.

In recent decades, governments in all European countries have been weakened in their capacity to steer society, and have been forced to lower expectations of public policy action and to develop new policy instruments. In France, the United Kingdom and other EU states, the state can no longer assume alone the management of complexity, but has had to reformulate its role, particularly in the light of Europeanization and globalization.

### b. Europeanization and globalization

Both European integration and globalization have called into question many features of the traditional model of French politics and policies. The EU has appeared both as a powerful constraint on domestic public policy, and as a source of unrivalled opportunity for contemporary French governments to exercise influence on a wider world stage and to effect domestic change. French approaches to European integration have combined an astute mix of visionary discourse and instrumental policy position-taking that has proved very effective in defending French national interests over time. France also believed in a European finality, though there were many contradictions in the French vision of Europe. Though its political discourse has been visionary, supranational and integrationist, in practice France has embraced more overtly the realist presupposition of Europe as an extension of national influence than any other European country. French governments in the Fifth Republic long accepted the canons of classical Gaullism unquestioningly. The Gaullist paradigm that prevailed until the mid-1980s – and which still remains influential – might be summarized in terms of six principal features: a cultural attachment to European values and civilization, notably as embodied by France; a Europe prepared to protect its industry and agriculture; the promotion of common European policies where these do not endanger French interests; a marked anti-Americanism and advocacy of a more independent security and defence identity; a tight community based on a Franco-German directorate, rather than a looser more nebulous grouping of nations; and a preference for intergovernmental over supranational institutions. There were many contradictions in this (Gaullist) French vision of Europe. France wanted a strong Europe with weak institutions.[2] There was a supranational discourse that stressed the primacy of politics, but also a fear that a genuinely supranational entity might challenge the (self-appointed) role of French political leadership of the European integration project. In essence, France wanted to retain its role as a great power and to harness the resources of the community to this effect. The European Community (EC) was explicitly framed in national (and European) terms, as a means whereby France could escape dependency, recover sovereignty and export its policy models to the supranational institutional arena. The terms of the French debate have not altered that much, whether over European Monetary Union (EMU), the Common Foreign and Security Policy (CFSP), or the 2004 Convention.

There was an inherent tension between substantive and procedural views of Europe. In substantive terms, France has always wanted a strong Europe. A strong Europe signified a cultural attachment to European values, the advocacy of a Europe prepared to protect its industry and agriculture, to engage in ambitious common European policies and to recover international prestige under progressive French leadership. In procedural terms, there was a manifest gulf between the European policy ambition of French governments and the supranational institutional adaptation of the EC/EU called for by countries such as Germany. Though French governments have accepted – some would say instigated – major shifts in a more integrated European polity, the dominant representation of European integration in France has been largely synonymous with a state-centric notion of a strong Europe, with power channelled through national institutions and delegated where appropriate to weak European institutions. This elucidates the intellectual tradition of the Fifth Republic which, applied to Europe, has been based on the primacy of national sovereignty in opposition to doctrines of federalism. French politicians for long resisted any strengthening of the EU supranational institutions – the European Commission and the European Parliament – and there remains deep unease with the 'foreign' concept of federalism that runs against the grain of French republican traditions.

Though the legacy of Gaullism remains highly influential, the debate has moved on since the paradigmatic shift of the mid-1980s. By the end of the century, the mainstays of traditional French understandings in Europe have been challenged in many respects. The most important of these were: German unification and its aftermath, which altered the internal equilibrium within the Franco-German alliance; the widening of the EU and the corresponding challenge to French policies such as the Common Agricultural Policy (CAP); the activism of individual policy entrepreneurs in areas of sensitive domestic concern, such as competition policy and public services – an emerging referential paradigm that challenged many French conceptions about the role and nature of the EU.

France has had an even more complex and paradoxical relationship with *mondialisation*. There is a mainstream ideological reluctance to accept ascendancy of what is willingly described as neo-liberalism; that is, economic liberalism and unregulated international free markets. The poor score achieved by the free-market liberal, Alain Madelin, in the 2002 presidential election demonstrated that there is little support for explicit liberalism. Apart from the Madelin tendency, rightwing parties in France rarely openly espouse liberalism. Except for a brief period in the 1980s, Gaullism has eschewed any reference to economic liberalism, while the Centre-Right has at most advocated social-liberalism. Within the Left, there are only a handful of avowed social-liberals, most notably Laurent Fabius and Dominque Strauss-Kahn. One of the few social movements to have experienced real growth in the past few years is the anti-globalization movement, symbolized by the Association pour la taxation des transactions pour l'aide aux citoyens (ATTAC) and by Jose Bové, each interpreted as a defence of a particular vision of the French model.[3]

Globalization challenges the traditional French model in several ways. This uneasy relationship with globalization exists in part because of the obvious threat the global-American model poses to a French culture that has always proclaimed itself universalistic, quite apart from the threat posed to the French language by rampant American English. In the economic arena, global capitalism lessens the reliance of French business on the French state and increases the importance of international capital flows, cross-shareholdings and the international strategies of French groups. Inward investment decisions taken by foreign companies can have a major impact on French employment levels. Foreign companies, however, are not usually willing to channel their investment in accordance with French regional policy objectives. Globalization also threatens well-entrenched domestic interests, especially in two very influential areas: culture and agriculture. In short, globalization not only lessens the capacity of the state to act in a *dirigiste* manner, but also its ability to protect its key client groups.

In order to protect the French/European model, French governments have sought to build the EU as a space to re-regulate capitalism and – under the Left at least – to develop a European social model. On balance, however, France has not been particularly successful in orientating the EU towards its way of thinking, especially in the field of competition policy, social policy and employment policy. The EU remains a formidable melting pot, which challenges in different ways the traditions of each member state.

In their strongest definition, Europeanization and globalization both appear to challenge many traditional French public policy preferences. Rather than specific policies, however, Europeanization and globalization can both appear to go against the grain of *une certaine idée de la France*. The belief in the universal mission of French civilization is menaced by European integration *and* by globalization once European construction becomes a melting pot of European cultural influences, rather than a mirror to reflect French grandeur or a policy space to regulate world capitalism. We will consider below whether the loss of a sense of identity so dramatically expressed in the 2002 presidential election can be linked to Europeanization and/or to globalization as metaphors for the weakening of French national self-confidence.

### c. The challenge of 'La France d'en bas'

Equality is an important part of the French reference frame. A demand for equal treatment underpins the French republican model; the glue that binds the rich diversity of territories that together constitute contemporary France. We must not forget that the republican form of government itself was vigorously contested by powerful sections of French society for a century and a half after the French Revolution. The efforts of republicans to inculcate a universal model of French citizenship were broadly inspired by the ideals of the Enlightenment and the legacy of the French revolution. The question today is not whether the republican founding fathers acted in good faith, but rather whether the defence of the republic can continue to be used as a legitimate excuse to suppress any deviation from a centrally defined norm. The French model of republican citizenship has great difficulties in accepting diversity and hence in adapting to the reality of a multi-ethnic, regionally differentiated society.

This is nowhere more the case than in relation to France's regions, cities and localities. The deep penetration of the state into civil society is characteristic of the Napoleonic model of state-society relations that still impregnates central-local relations in France. In its positivist, Jacobin version, the French model of territorial administration is held up as a benchmark of civic virtue. The general interest is safeguarded by a benevolent state, which plans the development of the whole French territory in the public good. As only the state can embody this general will, it is therefore essential that it be organized systematically at all levels, down to the tax offices and sub-prefectures in small French towns. In this positive interpretation, the French republican model is held up as the paradigm for a modern public administration, guaranteeing neutrality, equal and fair treatment and good public services. French citizens have a right to equality and a duty to accept uniformity. In the interests of equity, all parts of the French territory must be treated exactly the same.

This obsession with territorial uniformity has been increasingly undermined and does not appear to fit well with the prevailing European ethos. In practice, the dogma of equality of treatment grinds away at regional identities and suffocates regional difference in the French cultural mosaic. Worse, equality is a misnomer,

since Paris prospers, while the provinces continue to form part of
the French desert. If this constitutes French 'exceptionalism',
then this is to France's great shame.

France can only temporarily resist the relentless pressures that
have produced varying degrees of asymmetrical regionalization in
its European neighbours, Germany, Spain, and now the UK and
Italy. The Raffarin government will make regionalization into its
own *grande affaire*. It is proposing to grant constitutional recognition
to French regions, alongside communes and *départements*, to deepen
the experimental transfer of new powers and to bestow certain
powers on regions to adapt regulations. We will have to wait and
see, but it seems probable that the regionalism on offer will still
be of the technocratic variety and will fall short of the asymmetrical
devolution witnessed in the UK.

As for the issue of regional languages: though the French lament
the encroaching of English in the name of linguistic pluralism,
the prominent French institutions of state – Council of State and
Constitutional Council – still appear very hostile to the expression
of linguistic pluralism within France itself. France's regional
languages are barely tolerated. Several examples illustrate the point,
such as France's refusal to ratify the European Charter of Lesser
Used Languages after a decision by the Council of State; the striking
down by the Constitutional Council of the dispositions on the
Corcisan language in 2001; or the decision by the Council of State
to halt the integration of the Breton-language Diwan school
network into the public education service in 2002.

### d. The problem of political legitimacy

The results of the 2002 electoral series pose the issue of political
legitimacy. Let us recall some stark facts: Chirac and Jospin, the
announced second-round contenders, obtained only just over
one-third of votes and one-quarter of registered electors between
them. France's historic political families were each challenged on
21 April 2002: Communists, Socialists, Gaullists, Liberals, Christian
Democrats, even Greens. None of these candidates performed as
well as they might have expected and many electors were dissatisfied
with all of them. The strong performance of the far Left and far
Right candidates; the high abstention rate of 28.30 per cent, a
record in any presidential election; and the general dispersion of

votes to candidates not generally considered to be genuine presidential contenders (such as St Josse, Chevènement and others) were all part of this trend. Once again, the election went against the incumbent government, as has every decisive election since 1978 with the exceptions of the elections of 1981, 1988 and 2002, when parliamentary elections have followed shortly after the presidential contest.

The exceptional nature of Chirac's second-round victory on 5 May, however, cannot conceal his poor first-round performance of 21 April. His final victory does not provide a sure basis for holding all the key offices of the republic. While clarifying institutional practice in a pro-presidential sense, the 2002 electoral series leaves many questions unanswered. The most important issue is whether France's new rulers will be able to build bridges with that sizeable proportion of the French electorate that appears alienated from political processes and takes refuge in support for extremes. The long-term future of the republic might depend upon this.

Le Pen's accession to the second round was *the* story of the election. As ever, Le Pen seemed to offer a real choice. Taken together, the two candidates of the far Right – Le Pen and Megret – polled 19.20 per cent, which, to put it in context, was more in mainland France than Jospin and Hue combined. By comparison to his past demagogic campaigns, in 2002 Le Pen adopted the mantle of elder statesman, confidently expecting that events and the security-focused campaigns fought by most of the other candidates would play into his hands. Le Pen's electorate embodied a popular France down on its luck. It was more masculine than feminine and older rather than younger. More than ever, the Le Pen electorate is over-representative of those suffering from the most acute sentiments of economic and physical insecurity. It is the least well-educated electorate of the three main candidates. Le Pen was the favourite of the lower middle classes (31.9 per cent) and of workers (26.1 per cent), far outdistancing both the Socialist Jospin and the Communist Hue in working class support. In terms of its geographical distribution, there were several layers to the 2002 electorate. The Le Pen heartlands were those areas lying to the north and east of a line from Le Havre to Perpignan.[4] The Front National (FN) continues to recruit principally in urban areas in the eastern half of France, but Le Pen did especially well this time in rural areas juxtaposing urban centres. Urban populations have spilled over from the suburbs to the countryside or, in the words of one expert: 'urban fears have been transferred to the countryside'.[5] Le Pen also addressed a specific message to France's rural populations worried by EU enlargement and the prospect of reduced farm subsidies. The effectiveness of this message could be observed in the Beaujolais wine-growing region and several other areas.

Fuller analysis of Le Pen's 21 April performance lies beyond this article.[6] The French electorate's vote on 21 April suggests an unresolved tension between French identity; the implicit promises of French citizenship, including the economic promises; and the uncertainty provoked by Europeanization, globalization and an unclear future.

## 2. The continuity of the French model

In the above pages, I have evaluated the challenges posed to the traditional French model by external and internal forces. Equally important, however, is the continuity of the French model as provided by an interconnecting set of institutions, interests and ideas that provide long-term cohesion and allow internal and external changes to be interpreted in manners that are comprehensible to the French. As for the permanent institutions, it suffices to say that the Fifth Republic is France's second-longest-lasting regime and that it has demonstrated a certain flexibility. The end result of the 2002 electoral series is that presidentialism was reaffirmed as the key organizing principle of the Fifth Republic, albeit by a circuitous route. The underlying legitimacy of the system is shaped by the choices made by all key actors in favour of the presidential election as the decisive election in the Fifth Republic. A president genuinely representing the French nation was invested by the electorate with a 'clear and consistent' majority, as he had requested. Better still, the electoral series was crowned by an overall majority in seats for the new-style presidential party, the best performance of a rightwing presidential rally since the heyday of Gaullism. Moreover, excepting unforeseen circumstances, the five-year parliament elected in 2002 will coincide with a five-year term in office for President Chirac. The converging of the presidential and parliamentary majorities and the subordinate relationship of the latter to the former would appear to signal a return to a suitably modernized but pre-eminently presidential practice.

The case for continuity is strengthened even more once we move from the formal institutional superstructure to regarding deeper institutions – those that are not dependent on any particular regime, but those that go to the heart of the state and which defend the French state tradition. These institutions are: the *fonction publique* and the interests to which this gives rise, the Council of State and the Constitutional Council. A recently published report by the Institut National de la Statistique et des Études Économiques (INSEE) emphasized the impossibility of controlling the *fonction publique*. The number of *fonctionnaires* has increased by 10 per cent over the last ten years, in spite of a permanent campaign to reduce their number and the creation of a division specifically designed to achieve this effect. The number of employees of the Education Ministry is now 1,200,000, a number inflated by the Jospin government's *emploi-jeunes* programmes and the decision to reward a number of these employees with permanent tenure. The same conclusion can be applied to the police, a predicable consequence of the concern of public opinion with security. These internally driven, path-dependent processes render more difficult the reform of the state to which all politicians are, in theory, committed. The other institutions mentioned – Council of State and Constitutional Council – act as real brakes on change, or least on the type of change that concerns this chapter. The problem lies not just with the institutions, but with the constitution they are sworn to uphold. The creation of new regulatory agencies in spheres such as telecommunications, is certainly important, but the overarching existence of a system of public law closely monitored by a rather conservative Council of State is probably more significant. These institutions appear as a real brake on any change that challenges a rather conservative republican uniformity.

Continuity is provided not just by institutions, but also by interests and ideas. Existing institutions are defended by sets of interests that occupy a precise position within the French state, and which rely on the state to promote their interests in Brussels and elsewhere. The role of the farm lobby is very well documented in shaping the position adopted by French governments of all persuasions in international arenas, including the EU and the World Trade Organization (WTO). President Chirac has already announced that France will take a tough line of reining in the agricultural budget in the ongoing enlargement negotiations. The farmers are an easy target, as is the teaching profession, routinely fingered as the culprit for preventing any profound reform of the education ministry. Equally remarkable has been the role of the medical profession, which is at the heart of the efficient functioning of the French social security system. In short, powerful interests within the state and civil society generally frustrate reform, as was repeatedly demonstrated during the Jospin government. Established positions are very difficult to challenge, hence reinforcing the model of routine authoritarianism and sporadic direct action much beloved of the classical commentators. Underpinning institutions and interests is a set of well-defined ideas: about the appropriate relationships between politics and economics, the role of the individual and the collectivity, and the need for equal treatment to which political discourse needs to appeal, and that consolidates existing preferences and practices. Ideas such as the general will, equal treatment, and solidarity support the network of interests and institutions that promote stability, to the extent that sectional groups seek to capture these ideas in order to defend their own causes.

## 3. Conclusion

The foregoing demonstrates the shifting nature of France's political borders over the past three decades. Not only has France seen its political position in Europe challenged, it has also witnessed a severe crisis in internal political legitimacy, leading in turn to the construction of new borders which are both invisible and internal. (The social consequences of which are examined in Chapter seven.)

Although the strains produced by external and internal policy change have altered ingrained national traditions, there remains a strong element of continuity in French public life. Recent French governments, especially that of Jospin, have attempted to recodify change in accordance with French reference frames. The really interesting question is not the balance between continuity and change, but whether change reinforces national contextual traditions, or goes against the grain of them. To some extent, this is sector-specific. In the case of economic policy, there is a strong argument that global economic change has forced a radical rethink of the French model of macro-economic management. In the case of education, on the other hand, there is a fairly strong argument that policy changes are path-dependent; that is, they are interpreted and managed in ways that are entirely consistent with national traditions.

However interpreted, the French polity has mutated under the combined impact of internal and external pressures for change. Long a country that exported its model to others – within and beyond Europe – France has had to integrate new ideas and practices into her patterns of domestic government. National context must not be confused with a static version of national purpose. Arguments based solely on national, institutional or cultural distinctiveness, such as that of the French exception, run against the overwhelming evidence of policy change. French responses to change are embedded in precise contexts, but they are not literally pre-shaped. As France moves into the twenty-first century, all we can safely predict is that the French polity will continue to adapt to processes of domestic and external change and slowly transform itself in the process.

## Notes

1   For a fuller discussion of the French model, see Alistair Cole, *French Politics and Society* (London: Longman, 1997).
2   Pierre Hassner and Anne-Marie Le Gloannec, 'L'Allemagne et la France: deux cultures politiques', *Esprit*, 5 (1996).
3   ATTAC: Association pour une taxation des transactions financières pour l'aide des citoyens: a group that campaigns for the implementation of the Tobin Tax and on other issues raised by globalization.
4   Le Pen came first in all the *départements* of Provence-Alpes-Cote d-Azar except one (Hautes-Alpes); in seven out of the eight *départements* in the Rhone-Alpes region; in all but two in Languedoc-Roussillon; in all *départements* in Franche-Comté, as well as in Alsace; in all but one in Lorraine, as well as in Ardennes, Aisne, Nord, Pas-de-Calais, Oise, Eure, Lot-et-Garonne et Tarn-et-Garonne. All in all the FN leader polled more than 20 per cent in forty *départements* – 50 per cent of the total – and more than 20 per cent in fifteen *départements*.
5   Pascal Perrineau, 'L'extrême droite'. Communication at the French Political Science Association one-day conference on 'L'élection présidentielle entre deux tours', Institute of Political Studies, Paris, 26 April 2002.
6   See Alistair Cole, 'A strange affair: the 2002 presidential and parliamentary elections in France', *Government and Opposition* 37:3 (2002), pp. 317–42.

# Chapter two

# The making of the eastern frontier: the French–German border, 1815–70

*François Roth (translated by Sharif Gemie)*

The Napoleonic Empire was defeated in 1814, and its collapse was confirmed in 1815. The treaties of 1815, which shaped Europe's territorial reconstruction, were the most significant diplomatic consequence of Napoleon's defeat. The French state was expelled from the German zone, and the area was remodelled, under the guidance of the Austrian Empire, to form the German Confederation. On this new confederation's western border lay, to the north, the new kingdom of the Netherlands and, to the south, the kingdom of France, ruled by the restored Bourbon monarchy. When compared with the border set by the great French Empire of 1810–11, this new border marked a considerable territorial loss for France.[1]

How was this new border formed? According to which criteria? To what extent was it a military border? An economic border? How was this border managed during its existence? Lastly, to what extent was this new border truly accepted by the French and by the Germans? The argument presented here will demonstrate that borders are not passive: they are active, in the sense that they consolidate power structures, strengthen governments and enhance individual political careers.

## 1. The line of the new border

The line of the border was established by diplomats, without any consultation with the people concerned. It was based on the 1790

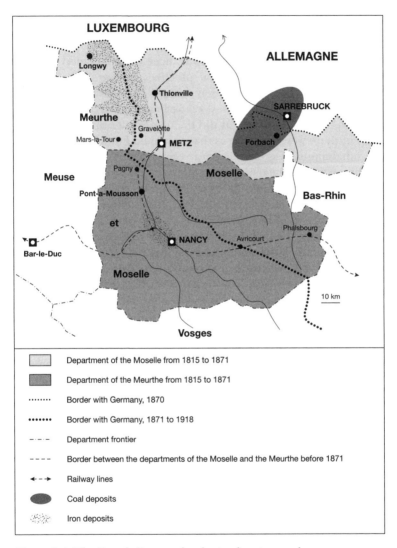

Figure 2.1 *The French-German border in the nineteenth century.*

border, but adopted a straighter course, as the German princes' small territories had disappeared once and for all. The three French departments of the Moselle, the Rhin and the Bas-Rhin reverted to their previous status as frontier-departments.[2]

The border was not formed by geographic features, with the exception of the frontier between the Grand Duchy of Baden and France. No natural landmarks distinguished those areas that became, once more, German, from those that remained French. The landscape and agricultural practices in the small German territory of the Palatinate closely resembled those of the French region of Alsace; the medium-sized Sarre valley crossed the border between the two nations. Nor did the new border mark a linguistic barrier: there were many areas that remained French, but in which the inhabitants' first language was German.

The second treaty of Paris (20 November 1815) was more punitive than the first (30 May 1814). It took the cantons of Sarrelouis, Saint-Jean, Sarrebrucken and Relling, consisting of about forty thousand people, from France to place them in Prussia. The Protestant, German-speaking notables of Sarrebrucken had been in contact with the Prussian government, and had acted during the Paris negotiations to request that they be placed under the Prussian king's rule. This amputation had two consequences. The first was military: France lost the Sarrelouis fortress, built in the reign of Louis XIV and which, alongside Landau fortress, had protected Alsace. The second was economic: the mines of Sarrebrucken, a vital source of energy for the industries in the department of Moselle, were transferred to the Prussian state.

In comparison with the *Ancien Régime*, however, the most significant change was not so much the newly straightened borderline as the creation by the Germans of new states on the left bank of the Rhine, in areas that had been French territory. The kingdom of Prussia had become the policeman for the great powers: in 1813–14 it had led the struggle against Napoleon and his systematic domination of Germany. In the decades that followed, Prussia exploited memories of these Wars of Liberation in order to strengthen a particular sense of German nationhood. French control of departments on the left bank of the Rhine during the Empire had only been superficial. After 1814 these areas, now once again German, were re-grouped in the Rhine Province. The main obstacle to their integration into the Prussian state was not their inhabitants' use of French, but their attachment to Catholicism. As for the Palatinate, it was re-attached to the kingdom of Bavaria, and henceforth governed from Munich. On the right bank of the Rhine, the Grand Duchy of Baden, with Karlsruhe as

its capital, faced French Alsace. Aside from some minor amend-
ments, dealt with through negotiation and settled by the 1828
Conventions, this part of the border remained unchanged until
1871.

One important change needs to be noted. In 1814 the old
department of Forêts became the personal property of Wilhelm
I, the Dutch king. It was not integrated into his kingdom, but
formed the Grand Duchy of Luxembourg, and joined the German
Confederation.[3] In order to monitor France, a Prussian garrison
was installed in Luxembourg. When Belgium won independence
in 1830, part of Luxembourg was added to the new state, and the
Grand Duchy was reduced to a collection of German-speaking rural
areas. In 1842 it entered the Zollverein, in which its interests were
represented by Prussia. It was placed by Prussia into the same
customs and commercial zone as the Rhine Province.

## 2. Social and economic aspects of the border

In the short term, the new border hardly affected travel and local
trade. There was, of course, the new requirement of a passport,
but inspection was only loosely enforced and those living alongside
the border were exempted. A Prussian could therefore work
in Moselle or Metz without hindrance, and a German citizen of
Baden could choose to live in French Alsace. The creation of
customs posts in Alsace and in Lorraine in 1816, and the imposition
of relatively high tariffs, contributed to a long-term commercial
depression.

A customs post at Brême d'Or, between Forbach (Moselle) and
Sarrebrucken, on the highway from Paris to Mayence in the Grand
Duchy of Hesse, did not create a barrier between the two regions,
but it did assist the commercial re-orientation of the zone around
the Sarre River and the Rhine valley. The French certainly continued to import coal from the Prussian state mines of the Sarre
and Nassau.[4] Some was transported by horse-drawn carriages and
the rest was taken by boat, along the Moselle river when its water
levels were sufficiently high. The main importers were the Wendel
saltworks in Dieuze (Meurthe) and the forges at Hayange and
Moyeuvre (Moselle).

The development of a railway network facilitated trade and
accelerated industrialization. It was also accompanied by the slow

relaxation of customs restraints. The opening of the Paris-Metz-Sarrebrucken line in 1852 was greeted by major festivals at which French and Prussian authorities celebrated the benefits of science, their good relations, and the peace that reigned between the two countries.

In order to escape from the commercial domination of the Prussian state mines, which fixed prices at a high level, Wendel built a coking plant near their mines on Prussian territory, at Hirschbach. This provided coal for the new rail and girder factory that opened in Stiring in 1853, near the French-German border. Looking for still greater independence, Théodore de Gargan and Charles de Wendel examined the Sarre basin, searching for a suitable site for a coal mine on French territory. They invested heavily in prospecting around Forbach, near Petite-Rosselle, after 1848.[5] Twelve years later, coal production began at Saint-Charles and Saint-Jacques: the discovery of a rich vein of coal, named the Henri vein, led to the sinking of the Wendel shaft in 1866–8.

Until 1861, the Paris-Metz-Strasbourg railway stopped on the left bank of the Rhine. The opening of the Kehl bridge allowed the river to be crossed by rail, and encouraged trade between Alsace and Baden, and between France and Germany. In 1865, a border station was opened at Wissembourg. The railway and the general lowering of customs barriers encouraged the sale of Sarre coal and coke in France during these years: in 1850, 198,000 tonnes were sold, and in 1869, 1,229,000. The main markets were metal-works in Lorraine and the Haut-Marne, the Eastern Company and gas-producing factories in Paris. In 1866, a canal for transporting coal was opened: it connected the Sarre river to Dieuze. This was a source of competition to the rail network, as it lowered transport charges. Furthermore, the Sarre forge masters were interested in the mineral resources of Lorraine, and were asking for concessions in France.

These new activities demanded a new workforce: miners, puddlers and forge workers. Some of them came from Germany.[6] Among their ranks were Prussians from the depressed region of Eifel, called to Hayange (Moselle) by Wendel. The new mines had to compete with the Prussian state mines for labour, and so the miners employed by Wendel were given the same social benefits as those who worked in Prussia. In other words, the labour market was at least partially a cross-border one.

Alongside the growth in trade, there were other economic cross-border initiatives. Several examples can be cited:

- The Adt family from Einsheim, in the Palatinate, started as manufacturers of wooden tobacco boxes. They turned to papier mâché work, which was used for many decorative objects, and opened a factory in France, at Forbach, which grew rapidly.[7]
- The French invested heavily in the Sarre valley, at Saint-Jean and in the forges at Dillingen.
- In the Moselle valley, there was considerable Prussian investment in coal production, ironworks and iron casting.
- Prussian coal merchants set up warehouses in Metz and Nancy.
- The firms of Karcher and Westermann, from Sarrebrucken in the Rhine Province, opened a mine and several forges at Ars-sur-Moselle.
- The Prussian Puricelli brothers opened a business at Novéant (Moselle).
- Burbach Forges opened a mine and several blast furnaces at Maxéville, near Nancy.
- Haldy and Roechling, industrialists from Sarrebrucken, bought forges in Pont-à-Mousson, north of Nancy, which specialized in smelting and in pipe manufacture. The firm's accounts were held in Saint-Jean, in the Rhine Province.[8]

The international trend towards lower customs duties encouraged discussions about a Franco-Prussian trade agreement.[9] When Bismarck came to power in August 1862, he found that a treaty had been accepted by the Prussian Landtag. He was able to overcome the reluctance of the South German states, all members of the Zollverein, to accept it, and the Franco-Prussian trade agreement was implemented in 1865. The agreement and wider economic trends encouraged the opening up of borders and co-operation between states.

## 3. Military aspects of the border

One must never imagine that mid-nineteenth century borders resembled the Maginot Line or the Iron Curtain. The new border, far from being a barrier, was completely open to any invading force to march on Paris, as had happened in 1814 and 1815. The provisions of the 1814 and 1815 treaties required that France lose its *Ancien Régime* fortresses at Landau and Sarrelouis. Its whole defence strategy had to be re-thought, starting with a re-evaluation of the concepts that had been dominant at the end of the eighteenth century. A study in 1818 described the border from Thionville to Biche as 'a weak border when we held Sarrelouis, far weaker now'. The author, however, added: 'It is not our intention to exaggerate the importance of the loss of Sarrelouis: in fact, this site was not the key to any significant line of communication; it did not protect either Thionville or Metz. Possession of Sarrelouis will not assist the enemy in advancing between these two sites.'[10]

All the military studies in the 1820s were concerned with the defence of the homeland and the means by which a new invasion, aimed at Paris, could be stopped. Two themes were central: first, the control of roads and other lines of communication; and second, the role of fortifications. Many military studies analysed the manner in which roads and other features could potentially aid enemy armies. Natural features of the landscape – forests, rivers, high points – were examined meticulously, and evaluated to see whether they could be occupied and used by French soldiers in order to stop the enemy. These studies concerned specific geographic zones and particular parts of the highways: the roads from Metz to Luxembourg, from Metz to Sarrebrucken, the 'passes of the Vosges', and so on. Very few authors considered wider issues, or attempted to integrate their specific studies into a strategic perspective. General Haxo's study, written in 1819, was quite exceptional in that it did present a broader picture.[11]

Another key theme in these military studies was the use and improvement of fortifications. There are countless studies of Biche, Thionville, Longwy and – above all – Metz, the centrepiece of French fortifications and the French military town *par excellence*. Nobody questioned the ability of these sites to resist any potential enemy; this was demonstrated by their undefeated record in 1814 and 1815. Had anyone ever taken Metz? This proud tradition, however, had not changed the final result of the conflicts in 1814 and 1815. In the mid-nineteenth century, French military studies were dominated by defensive questions: from 1815 until 1854, with the exceptions of the expedition to Spain in 1823 and the campaign to conquer Algeria, French armies remained stationed in France. Military experts considered the means by which a new enemy could be stopped, and how an invasion could be repulsed. Analyses inevitably returned to the most recent campaigns: 1792–3 and 1814–15.

The study by Lieutenant-Colonel de Ceynart, published in 1859, examined the north-east frontier, from the Vosges to the Meuse. He stressed the need for 'solid military positions' to stop a Confederal German army which, using the Coblenz-Mayence railways to produce an efficient concentration of troops, could be ready in four to six days. If they marched via Luxembourg, then the defensive forces would make use of the Anmetz plateau, and the Crusnes and Orne rivers. If they marched via Kaiserlautern, Forbach and along the Sarre, then the French defenders would make use of the Forbach and Saint-Avold hills and the Nied and Seille rivers. Metz was vital:

> *This great fortress occupies and dominates the course of the Moselle river. Eleven roads and three railway lines meet there. It is the pivot of the defence for the section of the border that we are examining. Its great buildings and its vast wall will provide refuge for an army that has suffered a setback. The importance of this site becomes more obvious when one considers that any siege of Metz would be very long and require a large army.*[12]

These notes are certainly far-sighted: to a large degree, they anticipate the actual events of 1870.

In Alsace, crossing the Rhine would cause immense problems for any army. Furthermore, Strasbourg possessed a fortress almost as well equipped as Metz. On the other hand, there were few such obstacles north of Strasbourg: the passes in the Vosges were neither closed nor fortified, and in the Col de Savenne, the little town of Phalsbourg had no means with which to stop an invading army, and could easily be bypassed.

In the German Confederation, the situation was more complex. The principal duty of the Confederal army, controlled by Austria, was to act as an internal police force. The troops in Baden (opposite Alsace) and those of Bavaria (at Landau, in the Palatinate) were considered to be second rate. The Prussian garrisons at Luxembourg and Sarrelouis were primarily reconnaissance and defensive forces. The bulk of the Prussian army was on the Rhine: it was grouped around the forts of Cologne, Coblenz and Mayence, and it was from this zone that an infantry offensive could be launched against France. In this eventuality, Prussia hoped that it would not be fighting alone: the Prussians expected the southern German states to follow them. This would only happen, however, if it were the French who declared war. Bismarck would do all he could to ensure this happened. The railway network changed none of these considerations: the plans for a western offensive drawn up after the battle of Sadowa in 1866 still forecast the concentration and formation of armies on the Rhine. But all these projects did not prevent social contacts: Prussian officers were invited to festivals and garrison dances in Thionville, Metz and Nancy.

## 4. Perceptions of the border

For the French, this was a border that they were forced to accept: it was imposed on them, following their military defeat. The restored Bourbons refused to question the treaty of 1815, and this stance contributed to their unpopularity. In order to be accepted by the European powers and, in particular, to please Britain, Louis Philippe's government declared that it would respect the territorial status quo. This was demonstrated in the Franco-British and international negotiations concerning Belgium's independence and neutrality. The peasants of rural France were willing to accept this situation: after all, if negotiations had failed, they would have been required to provide the bulk of the conscripts. Among the elites, the journalists, writers, high officials, officers and officers' families, there was a different attitude. Although the phrase 'the shameful treaties of 1815' was banned from official discourse, it was still used in unofficial contexts, suggesting the extent to which memories of 'La Grande Nation' still resonated. In eastern France, in Alsace and in Paris, a particular attitude was noted among officers who had fought in Germany or who had been stationed in Treves, Mayence or Coblenz. They were nostalgic for the Greater France, whose 'natural frontier' had been the Rhine, as the men of 1789 had proclaimed. Edgar Quinet reiterated this point several times. Many were sure that the lands that had formed French departments, situated on the left bank of the Rhine, would one day become French again as the people within them hated Prussia so much. These opinions were common among the Metz bourgeoisie, among military families and among those who had lived in Sarrelouis before it was 'Germanized' by becoming a Prussian fort. Were such attitudes based on illusions? The people on the left bank of the Rhine were increasingly coming to think of themselves as Germans. Anti-Prussian feeling was not clear proof that such people wished to recover their French identity. Sarrebruck had become a German town and, following inward migration, the mining and industrial areas of the Sarre were overwhelmingly German. The first use of the term *Saargebiet* (the Sarre region) can be dated to 1832.

Therefore, while cross-border relations between France and Prussia remained correct, there were those in France who considered that Prussia was repressing all that was French in its new territories, and that Prussia was increasingly attached to German national aspirations.

On the German side, one must distinguish between state politics and popular political culture. Among the German states, Prussia was the great beneficiary of the treaties of 1814 and 1815. The new border pushed France back into its place, from which it was not to be permitted to leave. This border was the guarantee of peace in Europe: it was to be monitored to ensure that it was not modified. Within the German Confederation, Prussia was subordinated to Austria, from where Chancellor Metternich directed international politics. Prussia's army, while important, was small. After 1834, Prussia succeeded in building links with several small states through a customs union, the Zollverein. The project proved successful, and subsequently grew.

In 1840 a now-forgotten international crisis concerning political developments in the Middle East broke out, in which France confronted other powers. Thiers acted aggressively, and demanded the left bank of the Rhine in compensation for French acceptance of the eventual settlement. Louis Philippe saw the potential danger, and promptly replaced Thiers with Guizot, a move which reassured the European powers. The revival of French nationalist agitation during this period provoked reactions in Germany: Nicolas Becker recalled the earlier patriotic poetry of Ernst Arndt, and cited his lines for 1813: 'They won't get the free German Rhine.' Alfred Musset replied to him: 'We had your German Rhine.' This exchange illustrates the main theme of the clash: German Rhine or French Rhine?[13] Another poet, Max Schenkenberger, wrote a more aggressive, militaristic text: *The Watch on the Rhine*. Was the

Rhine going to form the natural frontier between two peoples once more? To the Germans, it was clear that the Rhine was a 'German river', and that French claims had to be fought off.

While the Napoleonic Code had been preserved in the Rhine Province, this region's 'Germanization' was progressing. Its Prussian schools taught German culture and language. Its nobility and educated bourgeoisie continued to speak French, but a widespread sense of attachment to the German Confederation had developed. The Prussian state encouraged such attitudes. For example, Friedrich Wilhelm IV ordered the completion of Cologne cathedral, describing it as a 'national German monument'. None of its inhabitants suggested that the Rhine Province should return to its status as a French department. Even among industrialists and businessmen who spoke and wrote French, and who worked with French firms, the same tendency could be seen. Karl Roechling, the founder of the Konzern mining and metal firm based in Völklingen, in the Sarre, became a German patriot. The engineers and directors of the Sarre state mines, whose headquarters were in Sarrebrucken, showed the same attitude.

Two further points can be made about the 1840 crisis. Musset was not followed by all French writers. Lamartine described the Rhine as 'the Nile of Europe' and Hugo – who published travel writing concerning the Rhine – also saw the river as a symbol for Europe. But on the German side, the nationalist discourse of *The Watch on the Rhine* dominated public opinion for at least three generations. The poem reappeared in German textbooks until the 1930s.

The year 1848 marked another step in German evaluations of the Rhine as a border. The Frankfurt parliament debated Germany's borders. There were questions about Alsace. Was it a German land? The failure of the movements of 1848 has been exaggerated: some ideas that circulated in the Frankfurt parliament survived, and were heard once more in 1859 and again after 1866. Germans questioned the legitimacy of France's eastern border. Had not Alsace, and particularly Strasbourg, and a part of Lorraine been torn or stolen by France from the German nation? One day, these lands should be recovered. The speed with which the southern German states accepted an annexationist programme in 1870 shows the extent to which such ideas had been diffused. Too often it has been noted that the French sought to re-draw the

1815 borders in their favour: it should not be forgotten that similar impulses motivated some Germans as well. All that was needed was an event and a favourable context for such discourses to develop from brochures and vague aspirations to become political projects.

Finally, however, one must not exaggerate the severity of such fevers. The border remained peaceful and un-militarized; sustained cross-border exchanges continued.

## 5. The second empire and the north-east border

With the restoration of the empire in 1852 there was a pronounced shift in French foreign policy. Like the republicans, the bonapartists were nostalgic for 'Greater France'. In Napoleon III's thinking, the revision of the 'shameful treaties' of 1815 was a legitimate aspiration, on condition that the project was pursued discreetly, so as not to alarm the great powers, in particular Britain, which was needed as an ally against Russian ambitions. At the Congress of Paris in 1856, French diplomats showed the first signs of the revised French foreign policy.[14] At the same time, Napoleon III remained cautious. In 1857, as he returned from a journey in Germany, he stopped at the border to visit Wendel's businesses, then based in Metz. He refrained from making any public reference to the left bank of the Rhine. Nonetheless, German historians and writers would later refer to 'Napoleon III's hidden dream'.

In 1859, France supported Piedmont's struggle against the Austrian Empire; this military intervention caused a brief period of tension with the German Confederation.[15] It also allowed the return of Nice and Savoie to France: the first revision of the treaty of 1815. This easy success encouraged many French people to hope for a similar modification of the north-east border in France's favour.

At this point, few predicted Prussia's development into both a German and an international power. During the 1850s, Prussia had not been involved in either the Crimean or the Italian conflicts. Napoleon III even encouraged good relations with a state which, he hoped, would one day be useful to French interests. When the new king Wilhelm I proposed military reforms, his ideas aroused such opposition in the Landtag that he even considered abdicating. In order to overcome their opposition and to implement a

reinforcement of Prussia's military capacity, in September 1862
he appointed Otto von Bismarck, then ambassador in Paris, as
chancellor. Bismarck had understood the true nature of Napoleon
III's territorial ambitions, but rather than acting as an adversary,
Bismarck presented Prussia as a partner when negotiating with
the French. Formal agreements were not required: his aim was to
maintain good relations. However, Bismarck considered that
Napoleon III's regime was revisionist and revolutionary, in the
sense that it aimed to re-draft the map of Europe in its own interest,
and to re-establish French hegemony. Bismarck had no intention of allowing this, and he understood that soon Prussia would
be in a position to rival the French. In the early 1860s, however,
he was aware of Prussia's relative weakness, and 'pragmatic
collaboration' was his official policy.

The battles of 1866 reversed the power relationship between
Prussia and Austria. Bismarck had resolutely led the campaign
against Austria, aiming to push this rival out of the German zone,
and to create Prussian control over the movement for German
unification. Napoleon III favoured the construction of an anti-
Austrian alliance between Prussia and Italy, considering that this
would drag the two states into a long, uncertain war with Austria,
during which he would be able to intervene through a French
military initiative on the Rhine. His mediation would have a price:
territory. His speech at Auxerre, on 6 May 1866, hinted at this.
Bismarck plunged in, and spoke of territorial concessions to
France. But the definitive victory of Prussia over Austria at Sadowa,
and its consolidation through Bismarck's negotiations with the
Austrian government at Nikolsbourg in July 1866 and the Prague
peace treaty in August 1866, made a French intervention unnecessary. Napoleon III's hopes were dashed. When, at the end of
July 1866, the French ambassador Benedetti presented the
French proposals concerning a return to the 1814 borders, he was
too late, and Bismarck refused his claims. What was at stake was
not so much a question of surface area or number of citizens,
but the German identity of these people. At the same time, the
liberal press in Sarrebruck, particularly the *Saarbrucher Zeitung*,
regularly voiced its anger about French claims based on 'so-called
natural frontiers', and stressed the populations' refusal to return
to France. Such journalists insisted that the priority was peace on
the border.

On the French side, in Moselle, for a few weeks there was a belief that war was imminent. Anti-Prussian sentiments were common. This episode crystallized the French identity of those living in the Moselle, now clearly different from the Prussians on the other side of the border. Tempers quickly cooled, but something had changed. Henceforth, there was a clear enemy: it was Prussia that had destroyed the old German Confederation, which had annexed Frankfurt, pushed Austria out of Germany, and under whose authority the North German Confederation had been constructed. For Bismarck, this was one more step towards unification. French borders had not changed as a result of this internal re-shaping of the German zone, but the French felt threatened by this new military power. For this reason, the construction of new forts near Metz and Belfort began in 1867.

If Napoleon III had acted quickly during the 1866 crisis, he could probably have wrenched some territorial compensations in the Rhineland from Bismarck. At the beginning of 1867, he attempted to annex the Grand Duchy of Luxembourg, in which French railway companies were already established, but it was too late.[16] The Dutch king was willing to assist him, but had to step back as Bismarck, flushed with his success, kept Napoleon III waiting. In the parliament of the new North German Confederation, Napoleon III's proposal provoked a response from the National Liberal leader Rudolf von Bennigsen. He discussed Prussia's historic rights, and then asserted that an old German country like Luxembourg could not be separated from the German fatherland. His speech was applauded by all the deputies, and it was followed by many speeches and articles across the whole of Germany. Some even considered that such an annexation could lead to war with France. Bismarck had no desire for a conflict; instead, he exploited the wave of emotion as a means of pressure to arrange an international conference in London. On 11 May 1867 it concluded that the Grand Duchy was neutral, and was recognized by all the great powers. Bismarck's one concession was to accept the removal of the Prussian garrison from Luxembourg, which had been based there since 1816.

Napoleon III returned to the issue: he asked Benedetti, his ambassador in Berlin, to discuss with the Prussian government whether France could obtain compensation in Belgium and on the left bank of the Rhine.[17] But the territories along the Rhine

had been Prussian since 1815, and an increasingly strong sense
of German identity had developed among their inhabitants.
None of them were asking for their return to French rule: there
was no 'French Party'. Prussian officials' reports confirm this point:
they found that in Sarrebrucken, industrialists and the Chamber
of Commerce were hostile to France. Bismarck constantly refused
all negotiations on compensation for France, and would not allow
the 1815 border to be modified. In July 1870, following revelations
in the British press, Bismarck made public Napoleon III's proposals,
in order to demonstrate who was the real war-monger.[18] During
the Franco-Prussian war, conscripts from the Rhine Province were
mobilized within the Prussian army, and fought in France as
German soldiers alongside Poles, Saxons and Bavarians.

## 6. The legacy of the 1814 and 1815 borders

The French defeat in 1871 wiped out this border. The Treaty of
Frankfurt (10 May 1871) authorized the annexation of Alsace-
Lorraine by the German Empire, and the new French-German
border was drawn far to the west of the previous one.[19] The Rhine,
from Bâle to Emmerich, was completely German. This new border,
which the French recognized without truly accepting, remained
the legal border between the two countries until November 1918.

During the First World War, the two sides both considered
changes to the border. The Germans, during their initial advances,
planned to annex all the areas rich in iron ore, principally the
arrondissement of Briey.[20] The French discussed a return to the
1814 border and the eventual annexation of the Sarre. Some
politicians, authors and intellectuals were sympathetic.[21] On 15
February 1916, a speaker declared at the prestigious Société de
Géographie, which counted academics, officers, explorers and
colonialists among its members: 'There is no question about Alsace-
Lorraine. Our lost provinces must be returned, in full: the legal
border is that of 1814.' The issue of the annexation of the Saar
coal basin, Prussian since 1815, was debated in several meetings.
To consider this question, Aristide Briand, the Cabinet secretary,
created a Committee of Study for the Ministry of Foreign Affairs,
with Ernest Lavisse, the historian, as president and Paul Vidal
de la Blache, the geographer, as vice-president.[22] In their 1917
meetings they considered France's future border. Several speakers

spoke in favour of a return to the 1814 border. Others took the 1814 line as the territorial border, but argued for a separate economic border, and for the use of the Rhine as a military border. In a second report on the Sarre, Lavisse rejected the idea of annexation. His committee stopped meeting in 1919, and their work had little influence on the debates at Versailles. It is known that Clemenceau considered re-taking Sarrelouis and Landau, but gave in to American and British pressure, and renounced the 1814 border.

The Versailles Treaty was based on the 1815 border. If Sarrelouis and Landau did not return to France, Clemenceau did win the creation of the Sarreland, separated from Germany for fifteen years, with French control of its mines.[23] From 1920 to 1935 a whole strand of politicized history re-considered Napoleon III's Rhineland policies from a German nationalist perspective.[24] Until the 1955 plebiscite, which authorized the return of the Sarreland to Germany, relations between France and the new federal republic remained tense. This peaceful solution was accepted by the two countries, and the debate concerning the line of the border seemed to be over.

## Notes

1  *Relations internationales*, 62–3 (1990) is a special issue concerning the border. It contains theoretical perspectives and case studies that have helped shape this text. See also Ilja Mieck, 'Deutschlands Westgrenze', in Alexander Demant (ed.), *Deutschlands Grenze in der Geschichte* (München,1993) and the still useful study by Roger Dion, *Les frontières de la France* (Paris, 1947, re-published in 1979).

2  The *thèse de doctorat* by Henry Contamine, 'Metz et la Moselle de 1814 à 1870' (Nancy, 1932) remains the essential reference work on this issue. See also Raymond Poidevin and Heinz Otto Sieburg (eds), *Aspects des relations franco-allemandes, 1830–48* (Metz, 1977).

3  Gilbert Trausch, *Histoire du Luxembourg* (Paris, 1992).

4  Robert Capot-Rey, *Le développement économique des pays sarrois sous la Révolution et l'Empire (1791–1815)* (Paris, 1928). In the last twenty years, the history of the Saar region has been thoroughly revised: an essential contribution to its economic history is the two-volume work by Ralf Banken, *Die Industrialisierung des Saarregion, 1815–1914* (Stuttgart, 2000).

5  Marcel Gangloff, 'Les débuts du puits Wendel', *Cahiers Lorrains*, 2002, pp. 159–86.

6  Gilberte Muller, 'Les relations entre la Lorraine et l'Allemagne: relations entre populations voisines (1851–66)' in *Aspects des relations*

*franco-allemandes à l'époque du Second Empire, 1851–66* (Metz, 1982); François Roth, 'Sarrebruck – Metz: Deux siècles de relations urbaines', *Zeitschrift für die Geschichte der Saargegend*, 48 (2000).

7 Henri Vilmin, 'Les Adt et leurs industries', Annales de l'Est (1963), and his *Histoire de Forbach*. Henri Hiegel, *Sarreguemines: principale ville de l'Est Mosellan* (Sarreguemines, 1972).

8 François Roth, 'Les Prussiens à Pont-à-Mousson: histoire d'une interprétation d'intérêt', *Annales de l'Est*, 3 (1989).

9 Raymond Poidevin, 'Les relations économiques entre la France et le Zollverein (1851–66)' in *Aspects des relations franco-allemands*; Dagmar Soleymani, *Les échanges commerciaux entre la France et les Etats allemands, 1834–69* (Bouvier Verlag Bonn, 1996).

10 Service historique de l'armée de Terre (SHAT), 1M 1178; reconnaissance, plans et projets.

11 SHAT, 1M 1178; similar points arose at the conference and accompanying exhibition, *Un digne successeur de Vauban: François Nicholas Benoît Haxo (1774–1838)*, Musée d'art et histoire (Belfort: 2001).

12 SHAT, 1M 1178.

13 The Rhine has been the subject of many historical and polemical studies by both French and German authors. One of the best examples of French writing is Lucien Febvre, *Le Rhin: histoire, mythes et réalité* (Perrin, 1997, originally published 1935). The recent edited collection by Pierre Ayçoberry and Marc Ferro, *Une histoire du Rhin* (Paris, 1981), is also interesting. Two of its studies are particularly relevant to this paper: Pierre Ayçoberry, 'Les Prussiens sur le Rhin', pp. 206–24; and Klaus Wenger, 'Le Rhin, enjeu du siècle', pp. 255–86. Among German writing, of particular interest is the collection of essays *Der Rhein: Mythos und Realität eines europäischen Stromes* (Düsseldorf, 1988).

14 Yves Bruley, 'Le concert européen à l'époque du Second Empire', *Relations internationales*, 97 (1997).

15 Lothar Gall, 'Preussen und Frankreich in der Zeit des Second Empire', in *Aspects des relations franco-allemands*.

16 Josef Becker, 'Zur Resonanz der Luxemburger Krise 1867 in der deutschen Öffentlichkeit', in Raymond Poidevin and Gilbert Trausch (eds), *Les relations luxembourgeoises de Louis XIV à Robert Schumann* (Metz, 1978).

17 Christophe Verneuil, 'La Belgique et l'ordre européen au XIXe siècle', *Relations internationales*, 97 (1997).

18 François Roth, *La Guerre de 1870* (Paris, 1990).

19 François Roth, 'La frontière franco-allemande, 1871–1918', in *Les frontières en Europe occidentale* (Sarrebruck, 1994).

20 Fritz Fischer, *Griff nach des Weltmacht: die Kriegszielpolitik des kaiserichen Deutschland, 1914/1918* (Düsseldorf, 1971).

21 Jacques Bariéty, 'La Grande Guerre et les géographes français', *Relations internationales* 109 (2002).

22  *Travaux du Comité d'Etudes, tome I: l'Alsace-Lorraine et la frontière du Nord-Est* (Paris: Imprimerie Nationale, 1918). See also Jacques Bariéty, 'Le "Comité d'études" du Quai d'Orsay et la frontière rhénane (1917–19)', in *L'établissement des frontières en Europe après les deux guerres mondiales* (Bern, Berlin, 1996).

23  Alphonse Aulard, 'Landau et Sarrelouis: villes françaises', *Revue de Paris* (1919).

24  Good examples of this school of history are: Hermann Oncken, *Der Rheinpolitik Napoleons III von 1863 bis 1870 und der Ursprung des Kreiges von 1870–1* (Stuttgart, Berlin, Leipzig, 1926); and his disciple Fritz Hellwig, *Der Kampf an die Saar, 1860–70: Beiträge zur Rheinpolitik Napoléon III* (Leipzig, 1934).

# Chapter three

# Algeria and the Mediterranean frontier: a hostile horizon?

*Marianne Durand*

This chapter explores the political symbolism of Algeria's territorial frontiers from pre-colonial times to the present day. It compares 'official' depictions of geopolitical borders with more intangible notions of national space and identity; sets out how Algeria's territorial borders have been manipulated and politicized by different groups; and demonstrates that its geopolitical structures have been shaped and re-shaped by demographic, social, cultural, economic, political and religious forces.[1]

These different territorial patterns invite us to re-evaluate and question Algeria's connections with the European north, the Islamic and Arab east, and the African south. It will be argued that geographical, historical and political factors have made Algeria into a crossroads of peoples, civilizations and religions, and that the country should not be seen as a hostile horizon by Europe or as a defensive barrier by the Maghreb, but rather as a threshold or meeting place between north and south.

## 1. The mercurial boundaries of the Ottoman Maghreb, 1525–1830

A map is a symbolic, pictorial representation of a complex, three-dimensional territorial reality. The cartographer filters, sacrifices and omits information in order to produce a final creation, which is at the interface of reality and representation.[2] As such, the tracing of borders on a piece of paper invites a simplistic understanding of the complex geo-historical relations between people and territory. We look to maps to enable us to grasp instantly the organization and occupation of a territory; but paper depictions of borders are deceptive. Their lines should invite us to question rather than to conclude.

Algeria's physical boundaries as outlined on today's maps can be traced back to Ottoman rule. They were designed to establish an administrative system that guaranteed the maximum tax revenue and were to a large extent dictated by and reflective of the existing complex and genuinely organic socio-political structures of the tribes in the rural Maghreb. The Ottoman administrative unit was characterized by a decentralized 'triangular' hierarchy existing on two synchronized levels: state and local. This meant that political power and decision-making were focused locally. At the top of the system was a governor, or *dey*, chosen by a state council whose influence outside of the capital of Algiers was minimal. The *dey* chose independent rulers called *beys*, who each governed a *beylik* (province). The country was divided into four *beyliks:* Constantine, Titrii, Wihran, and the capital *beylik* of Algiers, which was under the dominion of the *dey* (*dâr al-sultân*). Constantine, Titrii and Wihran were divided into different districts, usually containing several tribes, and administered by the district official, the *agha*, who was aided by *qaʿids* and the *shaikhs*. The *qaʿids* were appointed by the *bey* and came from among the Turks. The *shaikhs* were typically members of the most important tribe. The *bey* policed his *beylik* using a strategically stationed military garrison. He also employed the Makhzan tribes, created in 1563, who in return for fiscal immunity ensured that subjects paid their taxes. This highly hierarchical yet decentralized military and bureaucratic apparatus enabled the Ottomans to remain in power for more than three centuries.[3]

Throughout the Ottoman period there were also socio-political units, which were connected to the geopolitical organization of the Ottoman authority through commercial and religious networks, but remained independent or semi-independent. There were, for example, independent principalities, dissident in character, which frequently challenged and sometimes attacked the authority of the Turks. By the end of the eighteenth century, various other groups besides these (semi) independent units, such as the Kaybyles; the Derqawa brotherhood; and the marabout, Bin Sharif,

made it difficult for the Turks to control their territories in the
middle Maghreb. At the same time, however, Algiers began to
lose its economic prosperity, which meant that the authorities
could no longer afford to control disturbances, and rebellions
broke out in the late eighteenth and early nineteenth centuries.
The socio-political and physical frontiers of Turkish rule arguably
followed, in part, the natural decision-making process of the
Maghreb tribes. Nevertheless, the Turkish rule was that of a foreign
state and its physical boundaries did not match the fluidity of
natural territorial boundaries. One could say that the Ottoman
geopolitical organization constituted a 'false territory', which was
continually pressurized by more organic patterns.

## 2. The illusionary boundaries of *Algérie Française*, 1830–1954

The French invaded the territory in 1830 and annexed Algeria
to France as three departments, building on the geopolitical
boundaries of Ottoman Imperial rule. It is important to note that
Algeria was annexed to metropolitan France not as a colony, but
as an integral part of France. The message that the newly created
'Algeria' was as much part of France as the Pays de la Loire or
Provence was disseminated through maps of the French Empire.

> *Like my father and grandfather and great-grandfather before me, I was*
> *taught at school that Algeria was a part of France, that it was a province*
> *like the others, and that it was made up of three French departments each*
> *with its* chef-lieu *and* sous-préfecture, *whose names – after those of all*
> *the others – we had to recite by heart.*[4]

However, this representation of a 'false territory' was not simply
cartographic. Algeria became a *colonie de peuplement*; that is, an
economically, legally and culturally assimilated extension of France.
Colonialists argued that the Mediterranean Sea flowed between
the metropolitan society and *Algérie Française* as the Seine flowed
through Paris. 'In the same way as Ireland was for a long time
simply a province of the United Kingdom in the British national
consciousness, children at school and college learned that Algeria
was simply an extension of the Metropole.'[5] The construction of
the false territory of *Algérie Française* was predicated on the

destruction of pre-colonial Algerian society. To prepare the way for the French and European settlers, Algeria was promoted as a land of limitless possibilities, a place where new lives could be built under the warm Mediterranean sun.

French colonization started with the military invasion and subjugation of, firstly, the urban centres along the Mediterranean coast and their immediate hinterlands (1830–9) and, secondly, the agricultural lands of northern Algeria (1840–7). In a later stage of colonization (1848–73), the French colonial army concentrated its efforts on crushing the stubborn resistance of the rural populations, using the most barbaric military strategies. Settlers quickly followed the army; many, however, died from disease and thousands returned home.

From 1860 onwards, a more systematic method of colonization was adopted. Using the smokescreens of European law and the Napoleonic Code, the French colonialists dislocated and destroyed Algeria's tribal organization. As Captain Charles Richard noted: 'The main thing is to locate this people who are everywhere and nowhere: we need to be able to reach them. When that happens, then we can do things that are still unachievable today and this, maybe, will help us capture its spirit after seizing its body.'[6]

Between 1863 and 1870, the first *Sénatus Consulte* brought about the geographical enclosure of tribal property, an enormous departure from the pre-colonial period. The *Sénatus Consulte* created property boundaries and stipulated that communal property could be transferred through sale. As a result, tribes in the agricultural areas of northern Algerian were broken up into smaller groups and allocated parts of the demarcated property. The *Sénatus Consulte* was the first of several legal methods of land colonization, which caused a significant increase in settler land appropriation. The Warnier Law of 1873 and the second *Sénatus Consulte* of 1887 allowed individual tribal members to sell their share of tribal territory and thus, as one French civil servant had foreseen in 1864, private ownership and its consequent inequality undermined the strength and value of communal possession.

*In Arab society as we have found it . . . everyone had his share of annual ploughing on collective property . . . At the bottom of that chaos was some guarantee of work and a certain feeling of equality; with the beginning of individualisation it will no longer be the same. Once the land is definitely acquired privately, inequality begins; on one side the owners, on the other side the proletarians.*[7]

The European minority benefited greatly from the pseudo-legal appropriation of tribal land in the late nineteenth century. European settlers obtained the most fertile agricultural lands and forests, whilst most Algerians became small peasant landowners or sharecroppers (*khammès*) who worked tiny areas of land.[8] The *khammès* could not survive with their allotted share of the crop and were gradually forced to join the mass of property-less labourers, whose survival depended on low-paid work for European property owners and companies. A great many of these labourers found themselves under-employed and facing the most terrible poverty.

As mentioned, colonial propaganda emphasized the message that the vast territory of Algeria, stretching from the Mediterranean to the Sahara, was an integral part of France. The artificial frontiers of this *Algérie Française* were constructed by destroying the intangible but authentic and organic frontiers of Algerian society. The lines and colours on a map represented this Algerian territory as 'France', but in reality the country was a complex, racially polarized society of one million European settlers and approximately nine million Algerians.

### 3. The colonial fantasy: new frontiers

Algerian Islam differed from that practised in the Arab east and sub-Saharan Africa. It was a rural Islam, characterized by the activities of Sufi orders and maraboutism, and permeated with ancient Berber beliefs and pre-Islamic customs.[9] In spite of their differences in religious beliefs and practices, the Algerian population sustained relations with Muslims in sub-Saharan Africa and the Arab east, whose language and culture were similar to theirs. At times, this 'macro-national' sentiment could pose a severe challenge for the French colonial administration. For example, the revivalist *Salafiyya* movement began in Egypt in the nineteenth century and arrived in Algeria, through the visit of the Egyptian reformer Sheikh Mohammed Abduh, in 1903. The movement played a major role in the establishment of the 'Ulama Association', which advocated reform and questioned European cultural domination. It suggested, for instance, the return to the pure, original religious practice of the 'pious ancestors' as means to contain Islam's moral and civilizational decline. In May 1931 Sheikh Abdelhamid Ben Badis formed the Association of Muslim Ulama of Algeria (AUMA). Its anti-colonial stance can most clearly be deduced from its slogan 'Islam is my religion, Arabic my language, Algeria my fatherland'. Not surprisingly, the activities of this organization were met with increasing colonial repression, which contributed to its eventual participation in the struggle for Algerian independence.

Although French colonial officials tried hard to destroy them, various old territorial patterns continued to exist. In the south there were Beduin tribes who had been forced by the *Sénatus Consulte* and other legal practices to give up their nomadic customs for a sedentary existence but who successfully averted many other attempts to change their socio-political framework because they were so distant from colonial pressure.[10] In particular, regions that failed to attract settlers were able to sustain their traditional social structures: such as Kabylia, a region in the east of the country, which lacked arable land and had a harsh mountain climate. One of the customs that the Kabyles managed to keep up was that of seasonal labour migration. Over time, however, this custom underwent changes. By the late nineteenth century many Kabyles migrated to work for French settlers, and in the course of the twentieth century, many migrated to France to work in the factories.[11]

The Kabyles were not the only ones whose 'labour migration' became 'settlement migration'.[12] Numerous Algerian men followed the pattern of migration described by Adelmalek Sayad. In the first stage, an individual wage-seeking man would travel to France during periods of low employment in Algeria to earn money, which he would send back to his family. The next stage was settlement: the man no longer returned to Algeria, but brought his family to France.[13] While individual labour migration weakened the social, cultural and moral codes of the sending community, family migration led to the break-up of traditional ties between the migrants and the homeland community, damaging them at their roots. Algerians who moved on their own or as part of family no longer felt at home in their homeland community, or as one retired Algerian labourer describes:

*France, I'm gonna tell you, is a low-life woman, like a whore. Without you knowing it, she encircles you, she takes to seducing you until you've fallen for her and then she sucks your blood, she makes you wait on her hand and foot . . . She is a sorceress. She has taken so many men with her . . . she has a way of keeping you a prisoner. Yes, she is a prison, a prison from which you cannot get out, a prison for life. This is a curse . . . Now I have no more reason to return [to my home village in Algeria]. I have nothing left to do there. It no longer interests me. Everything has changed. Things no longer have the same meaning. You no longer know why you are here in France, of what use you are. There is no more order.*[14]

French manufacturers, desperate for manpower, considered Algerians as a workforce they could readily use 'in occupations deserted by the European workers . . . in the hardest, the dirtiest and most dangerous tasks'. In other words, 'the "native" status follow[ed] the Algerian worker even when he crosse[d] the Mediterranean Sea'.[15] Migration resulted then not only in the erosion of old frontiers between groups but also in the creation of new frontiers.

Many Algerian migrants became active in the French Communist Party (PCF). One of these was Abdelkader Hadj-Ali who founded in 1924 the North African Star (ENA). Marxist in organization, the ENA promoted pan-Arabism and pan-Islamic values as factors uniting anti-colonial Algerian nationalists. In 1935, the ENA moved into the hands of Hadj-Ali's second-in-command, Messali Hadj, and the party separated from the PCF. From then onwards, the ENA:

*retained the character of a tribune party: while vigorously proclaiming the separatist objective of Algerian independence, it canvassed this cause within the framework of the one and indivisible French Republic of which colonial Algeria was constitutionally a part, and its modus operandi presupposed the framework of the French state.*[16]

The ENA was especially successful amongst the Maghrebian workers in Paris because it demanded independence for Algeria, Morocco and Tunisia and challenged the political, religious and linguistic marginalization of the Maghrebians by the French colonial system.

The patterns of traditional Algerian society and Franco-Algerian interaction produced both a strengthening and erosion of traditional frontiers between groups, in addition to creating new cross-border patterns of territoriality. The dislocation of tribal society meant that some traditional patterns of territory became confused, and encouraged Algerians to bond as a common people with a new source of identity. A central element of this self-identity was the recognition of the common colonial enemy. As the French lumped all Algerians under the banner of 'indigènes' or 'musulmans', one could feel equally 'Algerian' whether living in Paris or in Biskra. Algerian identity, in other words, was not one simply of 'musulmans' that could be contained inside the phoney colonial geopolitical frontiers of *Algérie Française.*

## 4. The FLN: the inconsistency of borders, 1954–62

The event that instigated the Algerian revolution was a proc-lamation issued by the Front de Libération Nationale (FLN) on 1 November 1954, calling for Algerian independence through armed struggle. The proclamation outlined the FLN's main aim and strategy: 'North African unity in its natural Arabo-Islamic context'.[17] The proclamation was followed by some seventy attacks on French property throughout Algeria. Violence, then, was another strategy adopted by the FLN to achieve its goal of unity. Building on the concept of France as the colonial enemy of all Muslim Algerians, wherever they lived, the FLN sought to unite Algeria politically and socially in a victorious violent struggle for independence.

The FLN wanted a political organization for an independent and united Algeria that would be entirely Algerian and not predis-posed to the French political model. Since it launched the war for independence from the mountains and countryside of the Aurès and Kabylia, only moving into the cities as a deliberate strategy after 1956, the political structure of traditional Algerian society became the framework for the FLN's political organization.

The FLN was not the only modern Algerian political party at the time. There were also the Algerian Communist Party (PCA) and the Movement for the Triumph of Democratic Liberties (MTLD) of Messali Hadj whose military arm – the Algerian Nationalist Movement (MNA) – became a rival to the FLN's military wing, the National Liberation Army (ALN). For the FLN, the PCA was too ready to follow the Moscow party line and the French Communist Party, which meant that the majority of PCA members were not inclined to support Algerian nationalism or Algerian workers. The MTLD, which formed the MNA in December 1954, was a political party operating within the political model of the French state. Coloured by its past communist association, it was convinced that the Algerian problem could be resolved by a common struggle of the Algerian and French working classes. Many other Algerians besides members of the PCA and MTLD/MNA refused to follow the FLN. For example, at least a quarter of a million Algerians fought as auxiliary troops on the side of the French against the FLN. Their name, *harki*, has become synonymous for traitor.

The FLN sought to contain Algeria's diversity by creating an authentic *Algerian state*, which would destroy the artificial, forced frontiers of the Ottoman Maghreb and *Algérie Française*. To achieve this melting-pot ideal, the nationalists presented the Algerian Revolution as the re-birth of the Algerian nation, and a break with the past through violence. It would allow Algerians to free themselves of French repression and become 'new': 'Our revolution is becoming a melting pot in which men of all walks of life and conditions, peasants, artisans, workers, intellectual, rich or poor are undergoing a process of intermixing, which will lead to the birth of a new type of man.'[18]

The re-birth through revolutionary violence was considered to be the moral duty of every Algerian and part of his struggle towards becoming a better human being. This notion is arguably an echo of the Muslim's spiritual struggle towards perfect faith, *jihad*. Any Algerian who did not join the revolution was considered a traitor and an enemy. No neutral zone existed for the FLN between the imagined frontiers of *Algérie Française* and those of the new Algerian state. Through a mixture of negotiation and violence, the FLN gradually overcame the PCA's and MNA's opposition. In the summer of 1962, after Algeria was declared independent, thousands of *harkis* were killed by nationalists or joined the masses of Europeans leaving Algeria. Most *harkis* went to France, where they were made unwelcome and remained non-integrated.

In its ambition to create the frontiers of a *new* independent Algeria, the FLN was constantly plagued by Algerians' links to the past. One FLN goal was to deepen the political divide between Europeans and Algerians. This was hard to achieve, however, as FLN activity and propaganda also appealed to a small minority of *pied-noir* Europeans. Notable among them was the doctor Pierre

Chaulet, who joined the FLN and treated ALN wounded. Members of European-instigated political parties, such as the PCA, also eventually supported the FLN. Other non-Muslims who provided the FLN with invaluable help during the war of liberation include Henri Alleg, a journalist of Anglo-Jewish origin who was arrested and tortured by French paratroopers in 1957; the French intellectual Jean-Paul Sartre who attacked French colonialism in his writing; and Frantz Fanon, a psychiatrist from Martinique whose work contributed to the FLN's concept of the 'new man'.[19]

Thus, the FLN organized itself politically by taking into consideration the natural political traditions of rural Algeria. Its aim was to make Algeria into a new society, the antithesis of France. The FLN promoted an Arab-Islamic identity that appeared to echo the proto-national characteristics of Algerian popular nationalism. Rather than celebrating heterogeneity, this approach led to the *exclusion* of regional and local diversity. Hugh Roberts explains:

> *Neither the Arabic language nor the Islamic faith is in any way particular to Algeria. The Arabo-Muslim identity could be Tunisian or Kuwaiti, etc., as easily as Algerian. There is nothing specifically Algerian about it whatever. This insistence on an abstract and nationally unspecific conception of identity is explained by the fact that the other, specific, aspects of Algerian culture – whether, for example, architecture or cuisine or dress – tend to be regionally specific; that is, characteristic of and so identified with a particular region of the country (the Constantinois, Kabylia, the Algérois, the Oranie, the South, etc.). They are therefore regarded as divisive of the nation by implication or tendency, and cannot be allowed to figure in a definition of the nation's identity for this reason.[20]*

In utilizing Islam to gain social cohesion and thus political hold over the Algerian people, the FLN neglected the heterogeneous character of religious practice in the middle Maghreb. In doing so, it also did away with the linguistic diversity of the region. In the 1950s, Algeria was a pluri-lingual society, reflecting the regions and peoples within the geopolitical boundaries of *Algérie Française* (Kabyles, Chouia, Mozabite, Tuareg, Shawiyya, French, etc.). The FLN actively promoted Arabic and excluded various languages, in particular the Berber language of *Thamazighth*. Thus, by attempting to ensure an Algerian identity that was completely distinct from that of the French, the FLN endorsed an Arab-Islamic monoculture.

## 5. Post-independence: the Islamist assault

When Algeria finally achieved independence in 1962, all the political objectives outlined in the proclamation of November 1954 had been achieved, and the FLN had developed into an organization comprising an extensive number of groups. On 3 July 1962 it was recognized internationally as the organization embodying the sovereign state of Algeria. The task facing the FLN from then onwards was to preserve the unity of the first Algerian nation-state.

One of the main threats to unity has been the Islamic movement, which strongly opposes the notion that Algeria constitutes a *nation*-state. The Islamic theory of the *umma*, the universal community of believers, by definition transcends regional allegiances and opposes national loyalties. It has also found fault with the proclamation of 1 November 1954, which stated the FLN's intention to restore 'the sovereign democratic and social Algerian State in the framework of Islamic principles'. The Islamists want a state in which Islamic Law, *Shar'ia*, and religion take precedence over politics. They therefore refuse to recognize the 'Islamic' character of the state created by the FLN's struggle.

The shared history of the AUMA and the FLN explains much of this complex relation between notions of Islamic state and FLN state.[21] In 1956, the AUMA sacrificed its autonomy for the collective political mission of an independent Algerian nation-state by dissolving into the FLN. From then onwards this mission contained contradictory projects. On the one hand, it proposed the building of a state founded on 'the framework of Islamic principles'. Critics from the Middle East in particular demanded that the FLN give up the idea that Algeria was re-born as a society founded on the 'new man' concept on 1 November 1954, and that it should dissolve the nation-state's borders within the wider Islamic *umma*. On the other hand, the FLN also proposed the rooting of modern Islam in Algeria in the uniqueness of Algerian nationalism. The interplay between the pressures of *umma*, the community of believers, and *watan*, the homeland, has led to the re-defining of Algerian national identity.

The radical Islamic movement that began in the 1970s has been the most serious threat to the new Algeria. In particular, one must note the influence of the Islamic Salvation Front (FIS, *Al-Jebha al-Islamiyya li'l-Inqâdh*), which became a legal political party in

September 1989. The party expressed great admiration for the Islamic states of the eastern Arab world, especially for their promotion of the concept of the *umma* and their Islamic state model based on *Shar'ia*. It furthermore advocated the idea that they were the true 'Sons of the FLN', the disappointed inheritors of the 1954–62 FLN. Thus the FIS represented an attack on the FLN state model in its entirety. The FIS became the most influential Islamic party in Algeria in 1990. In June that year, it already held power in the majority of Algeria's provinces, communes and important cities. It also posed a major threat to the nation-state because it operated *within* the framework of the 1989 constitution. In the January 1992 elections, the FIS managed to obtain 25 per cent of the vote. However, because of Algeria's 'first-past-the-post' voting system, it was heading for an all-out victory in the National Assembly elections. For many Algerians, this relatively small range of support did not fully legitimize the creation of an Islamic state.[22] On 11 January 1992, the Algerian army forced President Chadli, who had a mere 12 per cent of the vote, to resign. This event stopped the electoral process and the FLN salvaged the leftovers of the state structure, and re-trenched religion within the state's limits.

The various challenges to the post-1962 Algerian state were challenges to the state model in its entirety, rather than challenges to particular aspects of the state: this is perhaps, paradoxically, a sign of the FLN's earlier success in integrating different factions of Algerian society into its revolutionary counter-state model between 1954–62. The most significant post-1962 challenges pose the key question that underpins post-independence Algerian politics: how can the nebulous frontiers and alliances of Islamic religious belief be contained within the undeniable historical frontiers of Algerian nationalism?

## 6. Algeria and the Mediterranean: a shared border crossing

We have seen that all the states imposed upon the Algerians have not been organic but 'false' geopolitical systems. Whether the forced homogeneity of the FLN state or the *Shar'ia* state advocated by the radical Islamist movement, it is evident that – to date – no political model representative of all the nuances of Algerian identity

has been created. This absence is closely linked to Algeria's geographical position. Algeria is central to the Maghreb and bordered
by Africa to the south and the Mediterranean Sea to the north.
Algeria, I would argue, has an in-built tendency to 'look outwards'.
In the west, it faces the Muslim countries of Morocco, Mauritania
and Mali; while in the east, it looks towards the Arab-Muslim states
and the older centres of Islam in the Middle East.[23]

Algeria's western and eastern boundaries face the challenges of
pan-Arabism and Islamization. The country faces a rather different
challenge in the south: the Sahara. For centuries, peoples have
intermingled, and languages, religions, cultures and nomadic and
sedentary lifestyles have become latticed in this vast sea of sand
so that the identity of the zone is as mercurial as the shifting
sands, but nevertheless notably 'Saharan'.[24] Algeria's northern
border is equally fluid: the Mediterranean Sea. It sees its economic
future closely linked to those European nations bordering this
sea, in particular France and Spain: Algeria already exports some
of her minerals to these countries. Its state oil and gas company,
SONATRACH,[25] for example, exports liquefied gas to Spain and
Italy through two sub-Mediterranean pipelines. The countries
north of the Mediterrean Sea have over the years tried to exercise
some influence over Algeria's economy. France, for instance, has
promoted economic liberalization and the development of a full-
market economy, and has supported any political strategy that it
considers to be 'democratic'.[26]

The economic pressures towards Europe arguably force Algeria
to recognize the flexibility of her national borders. Another important factor that has made the northern border more permeable
in recent years is migration. The Mediterranean Sea provides a
permanent link between the economic migrant Algerians living
on French soil and the Algerians of the homeland. One could
argue, then, that this sea is France's southern border and Algeria's
northern limit. In colonial times this image of a 'unity' was
exploited so as to convince the French people of the greatness of
their empire. Today, the shared Franco-Algerian demarcation is
both a border and a shared frontier that challenges not only
exclusive Algerian notions of national identity but also the supposed
links between national identity and national territory.

There are then three 'extra-territorial' zones in Algeria – the
east, the south and the north/Mediterranean – which transcend

the country's physical 'official' borders.[27] I would argue the Mediterranean zone will play a more prominent role than the other two in the Algerian people's evolution towards a future representative and congruous political system. As the historians Fernand Braudel and Henri Pirenne and others have shown, the idea of the Mediterranean as a unique and separate region has been around since Roman times.[28] Interest in this idea has risen since the demise of the Cold War, as local and regional factors have grown more prominent than the ideological confrontation between two superpowers. Since the fall of the Berlin Wall, the EU has made substantial efforts to promote democratic systems of government in the Mediterranean region, hoping that a commitment to democratic principles and respect for human rights and the rule of law would bring forth political and economic stability, peace and prosperity. One of the most recent and far-reaching efforts is the Euro-Mediterranean Partnership that emerged from the Conference of EU and Mediterranean Foreign Ministers held in Barcelona on 27 and 28 November 1995. The participants included the fifteen EU member-states and twelve non-member Mediterranean countries: Algeria, Cyprus, Egypt, Israel, Jordan, Lebanon, Malta, Morocco, Syria, Tunisia, Turkey and the Palestinian Authority.

The Barcelona Declaration announced the twenty-seven partners' three major goals:

> *to establish a comprehensive partnership among the participants . . . through strengthened political dialogue on a regular basis, the development of economic and financial co-operation and greater emphasis on the social, cultural and human dimension.*[29]

Whether the Barcelona Declaration and its complementary agreements have been successful so far must be the topic for another discussion. The point to stress here is that European initiatives such as this have recognized that for a level of practical co-operation in the Mediterranean, it is essential to 'dispel misconceptions'.[30] Algeria's unique political history equips it to make a distinctive contribution to the resolution of tensions in the Mediterranean zone. To give an example, the Barcelona Declaration was launched in the wake of the Middle East Peace

Process and has generally been regarded as an attempt by the EU to help the Peace Process. It stated most clearly that peace in the Middle East was vital for Mediterranean peace and prosperity.[31] Many Arab countries had regarded previous EU attempts to persuade them to accept Israel as nothing but a colonial strategy of 'divide and rule', as it would further divide the Arab world. Outside the Maghreb, then, the Euro-Mediterranean Partnership was viewed with suspicion. Algerian diplomacy, with its legacy of looking outwards to the east and the north, however, helped to bridge the divide between the political ambitions of north and south.

The diversity of Algerian society and its territorial patterns reflect the transformations and new shapes emerging within the Mediterranean region: this allows Algeria to act as a facilitator of greater co-operation between the countries bordering the sea and Europe. The Mediterranean region is like Algeria, a geographical unit marked by deep-rooted political, cultural and socio-economic diversity that eludes a coherent, all-encompassing definition. Rooted in a past of colonialism, nationalism and regionalism, this diversity has caused suspicion, resentment and even violence. One only has to think of the incidents of racist violence towards Moroccan immigrants that took place in El Ejido in February 2000 in Spain. Or of the ship containing 1,000 Kurdish refugees, the *Monica,* that arrived in Sicily in March 2002, and was towed into the port of Catania only when some of the migrants threatened to throw their children into the sea. This caused a state of emergency to be declared in Italy and a rightwing backlash over illegal immigrants. The diversity that can give rise to such tensions, however, coexists with a degree of unity brought about by geographical proximity, economic interdependency and shared historical experiences. This sense of unity could form the basis of increased cross-regional co-operation.

Algeria is a country that for years has been forced to face and deal with opposing trends, including traditional versus modern, regionalism versus nationalism, and past versus future. It has become the doorway between conflicting civilizations – European and Islamic – and a threshold of change. Algeria is therefore in a unique position to understand the problems facing the Mediterranean zone and contribute to the resolution of them.

## Conclusion

In his article 'Colonial/Postcolonial Intersections, *Lieux de mémoire* in Algiers',[32] Zeynep Çelik traces the history of the central 'plaza' in Algiers. This history illustrates most clearly the shaping and re-shaping of Algeria's geopolitical structures. In Ottoman times, the plaza was called *Al-Qaisariya* and was a busy commercial area dominated by the *al-Djadid* mosque and the palace of the *dey*, with the *al-Sayyid* mosque in front of it. Under French rule it was renamed first 'Place d'Armes' and then 'Place du Gouvernment', thus underlining the transfer from military to civilian rule in the colony. Finally, the FLN gave the plaza the name 'Place des Martyres' in memory of those who died in the Algerian war of liberation. The FLN administration not only renamed the plaza but also imposed on it its own set of marks. For example, in 1845 'an imposing five-metres high equestrian statue of the Duke of Orléans, the prince to the throne who had fought and was wounded in Algeria in 1836, was erected on the site'.[33] The statue, which was strategically positioned with its back to the al-Djadid mosque and overlooking the Casbah, became symbolic of colonial power in Algeria.

> *Elevated on a high base and contrasting with the serene mass of the white mosque in its blackness and dynamic shape, and with its back to the mosque, it conveyed a straightforward message about the power structure in Algeria. The Duke of Orléans' gaze turned away from the plaza to face the Casbah, underlined the statement about French control over the Algerian people.*[34]

In 1962 this statue was taken down and an abstract memorial to honour the dead of the Algerian War was erected. Although the focus of the plaza has moved since 1962, namely from the Casbah to the *al-Djadid* mosque, its actual boundaries have remained those created under French rule. Throughout the country one can find many similar examples, which suggest that the traces of colonization have not been removed. In fact, these traces, along with those of Ottoman rule and the FLN struggle for independence, have been woven into the very earth of the country.

Algeria is a border country, marking the gateway not only between north and south but also between east and west. It is often seen as a hostile horizon, because of its past of struggles between tradition and modernity and between regionalism and nationalism. The lessons that this country has learned from its negative past, however, give it the potential to play a major role in bringing about a new, forward-looking and peaceful Mediterranean region.

## Notes

1   Achille Mbembe, 'Les frontières mouvantes du continent africain', *Le Monde diplomatique* (Novembre 1999), pp. 22–3.

2   Phillippe Rekacewicz, 'Regards politiques sur les territoires', *Le Monde diplomatique* (May 2000).

3   Mahfoud Bennoune, *The Making of Contemporary Algeria 1830–1987* (Cambridge: Cambridge University Press, 1988), p. 17.

4   Robert Davies, 'Le Temps de la justice', quoted in Martin Evans, *Memory of the Algerian War* (Oxford: Berg, 1997), p. 102.

5   Pierre Vidal-Naquet, *La Torture dans la Republique* (Paris: Minuit, 1972), p. 23.

6   Capitaine Charles Richard, 'Etude sur l'insurrection du Dahra (1845–6)' quoted in Pierre Bourdieu and A. Sayad, *Le Déracinement* (Paris: Minuit, 1964).

7   Quoted in Bennoune, *The Making*, p. 45.

8   Neil Macmaster, *Colonial Migrants and Racism, Algerians in France 1900–62* (London: Macmillan, 1997), p. 31.

9   Hugh Roberts, *The Battlefield Algeria 1988–2002* (London: Verso, 2003), pp. xxiii–xxiv.

10  Roberts, *The Battlefield Algeria*, p. xxi.

11  Macmaster, *Colonial Migrants*, p. 41.

12  Abdelmalek Sayad's theories of anthropology of immigration are discussed in Pierre Bourdieu and Loïc Wacquant, 'The organic ethnologist of Algerian migration', *Ethnography*, vol 1:2, pp. 173–82.

13  See the film *Vivre au paradis*, by Bourlem Guerdjou, 105 min., France/Belgium, 1998.

14  Abdelmalek Sayad, *L'immigration ou les paradoxes de l'altérité*, quoted in Bourdieu and Wacquant, 'The organic ethnologist', 176.

15  André Michel, 'Les Travailleurs coloniaux en France', quoted in Bennoune, *The Making*, pp. 77–8.

16  Roberts, *The Battlefield Algeria*, p. 39.

17  'Proclamation du Front de Libération Nationale' reproduced in Mohammed Harbi (ed.), *Les Archives de la revolution algérienne* (Paris: Jeune Afrique, 1981), pp. 101–3.

18  Krim Belkacem in *El Moudjahid*, 1 November 1958, quoted by Margaret A. Majumdar in, 'The New Man at the dawn of the 21st century: challenges and shifts in Algerian identity', in Mohammed Saad and Margaret Majumdar (eds), *Transition and Development: Patterns, Challenges and Implications of Change in Algeria* (Bristol: Intellect, 2004).

19  See Jean-Paul Sartre's preface to Frantz Fanon, *Les Damnés de la terre* (Paris: Maspero, 1961).
20  Roberts, *The Battlefield Algeria*, p. 142.
21  Roberts, *The Battlefield Algeria*, p. 8.
22  Roberts, *The Battlefield Algeria*, p. 121.
23  For more information on the social and regional identities of the Maghreb touched by pan-Arabism and Islamization, including Berber organizations and women's movements, see Mohamed Benrabah, *Langue et pouvoir en Algérie* (Paris: Séguier, 1999); and Monique Gadant, *Le Nationalisme Algérien et les Femmes* (Paris: L'Harmattan, 1995).
24  Mbembe, 'Les frontières mouvantes'.
25  Société Nationale pour la Recherche, la Production, le Transport, la Transformation et la Commercialisation des Hydrocarbures.
26  Roberts, *The Battlefield Algeria*, p. 229.
27  Rekacewicz, 'Regards politiques sur les territoires'.
28  See Peregrin Hordern and Nicholas Purcell, *The Corrupting Sea: A Study of Mediterranean History* (Oxford: Blackwell, 2000).
29  'European Commission External Relations, Barcelona Declaration adopted at the Euro-Mediterranean Conference 27–8/11/95', retrieved 05/11/03 from *http://europa.eu.int/comm/external_relations/euromed/bd.htm*
30  'NATO Issues: Upgrading the Mediterranean Dialogue', retrieved 05/11/03 from *http://www.nato.int/med-dial/upgrading.htm*
31  'Common Strategy of The European Council of 19 June 2000 on the Mediterranean region' in *Official Journal of the European Communities* 22.7.2000, retrieved 05.11.03 from *http://europa.eu.int/comm/external_relations/euromed/common_strategy_med_en.pdf*
32  Zeynep Çelik, 'Colonial/postcolonial intersections, *Lieux de mémoire* in Algiers', *Third Text* 49 (1999–2000), pp. 63–72.
33  Çelik, 'Colonial/Postcolonial Intersections', p. 65.
34  Çelik, 'Colonial/Postcolonial Intersections', p. 66.

# Part II

---

# Between the Centre and the Margin: the French Regions

# Chapter four

# From the other side of the mirror: the French–German border in landscape and memory: Lorraine, 1871–1914

*Didier Francfort (translated by Sharif Gemie)*

What happens to old political borders? This question is growing more pertinent as France is integrated into the 'Schengen zone'. The last 'real' continental border surviving today, separating France from one of its neighbours, is the Franco-Swiss border. It lies in the Jura region, along the line of the Paris-Lausanne TGV, where forest roads lead to unexpected dead ends. Elsewhere, in theory, the free circulation of goods, people and services is guaranteed. The old borders are dead.

After the Franco-Prussian war of 1870–1, France was forced to accept a new eastern border, imposed by the 1871 Treaty of Frankfurt. Studying its traces, which still run through the landscape and survive in memories, we can understand what happens to an old border. This paper presents an inventory of the 1871 border's traces, evaluating what remains of the line, now barely perceptible and devoid of any political significance. (See the map in Chapter two.)

The Treaty of Frankfurt cut the Alsace region and a part of the region of Lorraine from France. It was perceived by the French as a dreadful injustice, a violation of all international norms. The speed with which the phrase 'the blue line of the Vosges' became popular is a clear indication of the depth of this trauma.[1] We will not, however, be studying the watershed of these mountains. The ramblers who follow mountain tracks can still see the boundary stones that marked the old border. Its line did not correspond to the cultural and linguistic border: many French-speaking villages of the Alsatian *pays velche* (a term derived from an old German term for Latin) were located on the German side of the border. A sense of a separate Alsatian identity, however, had remained strong within the borders of mid nineteenth-century France, and this was exploited by the German victors. It was cited as a reason for the forcible integration of Alsatians into the new Reich, a nation defined by its common culture. Renan and Mommsen, in their famous debate on the nature of nationhood, returned to this issue.

It is not the 'blue line' that we will study, but rather the line that separates the departments of the Meurthe-et-Moselle and the Moselle in today's Lorraine region. This is a more arbitrarily constructed line, reflecting above all a power relationship: it does not correspond to any pattern in the landscape, it does not follow any river, it is not based on any linguistic frontier. The published research of François Roth provides a fine introduction to the 1871 negotiations that led to the construction of this border.[2] To summarize: the department of the Meurthe lost its easterly section, the *pays* of Saulnois (including the communes of Château-Salins, Marsal and Dieuze), and the town of Sarrebourg. It gained, however, the arrondissement of Briey, taken from the now-annexed department of the Moselle. The French authorities then changed the department's name from the Meurthe to Meurthe-et-Moselle in order to recall the lost territory.

## 1. The formation of the fault line

The 1871 border was never an iron curtain, bristling with bunkers, observation posts and barbed wire. After 1873, it could easily be crossed: many photographs record this, showing French and German soldiers side by side, often with Italian miners, standing by a border post. The only sign that one was crossing from one country to another was a series of posts. Those on the French side bore the prosaic sign 'frontière'. On the German side, the border posts were marked with the phrase 'Deutsches Reich', topped with an eagle, the symbol of the Empire.[3] There was only a minor military presence on the 1871 border in Lorraine. The French forts designed by Raymond Séré de Rivières (1815–95) were not placed immediately on the border, but 12 miles further back, near the towns of Toul and Verdun. They faced the newly German Metz, the most modern fortress in Europe. In general, after 1873, people could circulate freely across the border, except during the crisis that began with the Schnaebelé Affair in 1887 and ended in 1891.

In practice, the 1871 border cut the territory of the Lorraine region into quite different geographic, historic and economic zones. Each of the sections of this new border was marked by some distinguishing feature. To the north was the ironworking region, marked by mines and factories, with its most northerly tip running alongside the Grand Duchy of Luxembourg. This 'triple border', between France, Germany and Luxembourg, was a true frontier region in every sense of the word. The industrial towns of Villerupt (Meurthe-et-Moselle) merged with that of Audun-le-Tiche (which became Deutsch-Oth after its 1871 annexation), and the conurbation spread into Esch-sur-Alzette, in Luxembourg. Nearby, Rédange was in the middle of what appeared to be a no-man's-land: an enclave, surrounded by wasteland and slag-heaps; a startling contrast with Luxembourg's economic dynamism and prosperity. To the south, the border cut through the hills and valleys of the iron mines.

In some cases, links were established between settlements on either side of the border; for example, in the Orne valley, Joeuf, Homécourt and Auboué on the French side were linked with the now-German Moyeuvre, Rosselange, Clouange and Rombas. For such ironworking towns, the border meant instability, even a certain marginalization. Between the two lands, often, the line of the border ran along slopes, which were sometimes pronounced and steep in this hilly region. This was the 'kingdom of the cliffs' evoked in Pierre Fritsch's novel.[4] Further to the south, the iron region ended, and one entered the battlefields of 1870: Gravelotte and Mars-la-Tour. The border cut communications routes between the old rivals, Metz and Nancy. It cut through the railway line, on the Pagny-sur-Moselle to Novéant route, and it crossed the river, the canal and the highway. Pont-à-Mousson, in Meurthe-et-Moselle, was an industrial town close to the border. To the east of the Moselle valley, the border crossed a predominantly rural district, with the exception of the Bata factories, near Avricourt. The border then followed the Seille, a charming little river that now became a symbol, and a tourist attraction.[5] The borderland villages on the east bank of the Seille, in German territory, were seen as so 'typically French', that they were cited as a type of comic refutation of the 'Deutsches Reich' posts that cut them off from France.[6]

If one consults detailed local maps of the region today, one can still spot the near-intangible trace of the old border in the landscape. Here, one finds the edge of a forest, there a track stops, further along a road twists to follow the line of the border. Such indications mark the limits of the two departments of the Meurthe-et-Moselle and the Moselle.

The Moselle was part of Alsace-Lorraine, and placed in the German Reich until the First World War. Following its reintegration into France, despite many discussions, the departmental limits between it and the Meurthe-et-Moselle were not revised. Henceforth, the limits of the two departments preserved the memory of the old international border, rather in the manner that the shape of Africa can be seen in South America: a point that stimulated Wegener's theory concerning continental drift and tectonic plates. The Meurthe-et-Moselle's length, and the distance and difficulty of communications between Nancy, its administrative centre, and Longwy, its second town, were all the results of the 1871 fault line. The department's unusual shape is often conceptualized as a strange joining of two distinct territories. To the north of the department, from Briey to Longwy, lies what is called 'the high land'. This is an industrial area of ironworking, mining and factories. To the south, the presence of Nancy dominated, overshadowing mining and industrial areas like Pompey, and giving the impression that there was no heavy industry in this territory. This representation of the contrast between the two sections is little more than a caricature. But, even today, in the University of Nancy, one hears students and colleagues from 'the high land' speaking more and more proudly of their distinct identity. Such stereotypes suggest that all who live in the department's northern section are working-class descendants from immigrant families, while the southerners, those with their roots in Lorraine, are all peasants or bourgeois. (Thankfully, as the department is proud of its reputation as a 'melting pot', such concepts of 'roots' have never grown popular.[7])

The shape created by the department's new limits was very distinctive. Children playing with jigsaw games of the French departments always recognize its profile, which is sometimes represented as a goose. This distinctive shape has in itself become a symbol: it was used by the newly decentralized authorities of the 1980s, but it was also paraded at the demonstrations and protest meetings caused by the crisis of the ironworks and their subsequent decline.

Meurthe-et-Moselle's particular administrative history is therefore clearly represented by maps, but the Moselle's experience is quite different. In the east of this department a German dialect is spoken, but the 1871 border did not correspond to this linguistic frontier. Across the whole of the Moselle, however, there are specific laws that are quite different from legislation anywhere else in France (with the exception of Alsace), concerning religion, schools and social security. The secular legislation of the Third Republic, adopted between 1871 and 1914, is not applied. In the Moselle, the 1801 Concordat between the French head of state and the Pope is still in force. Religious instruction remains compulsory in schools, and the churches are subsidized. The 1901 law on associations is not applied. The left-leaning coalition government of 1924–8, the Cartel des Gauches, tried in vain to make the Moselle respect the Republic's secular legislation. The project aroused such opposition that it was dropped, and it has not been proposed again. Even those who invoke the centralizing tradition of the Republic in order to oppose a special status for Corsica or to prevent the recognition of regional languages, do not propose to impose secular legislation on Moselle or Alsace.

## 2. The border and the world wars

The metaphor of the border as a geological fault line seems all the more appropriate when one considers the repeated 'tremors' that have shaken it. The Moselle went through 'de-annexation' after the First World War, but passed once more into German control in 1940. No legislation was passed to formalize this move, and its re-annexation was not mentioned in the text of the June 1940 armistice but, *de facto*, it became German and Nazi. The Meurthe-et-Moselle was in the northern, occupied, half of France. It was given a special status as part of the 'forbidden zone', stretching from the Somme to the Vosges, in which particularly strict regulations were applied by the German authorities.

In Nancy, resistance networks worked to help escaped prisoners cross the reconstituted border. Conflicts and traumas from this period of the border's history remain in popular memory: their traces can still be seen on the landscape. Each war memorial can be examined in turn to see if it records the battles of 1870–1, those of 1914–18, or the battles of the Second World War, the deportation of civilians and the extermination of the Jews. Many memorials draw together all these intense, traumatic memories in a manner reminiscent of de Gaulle's concept of a Franco-German Hundred Years War. The memory of 1870–1 is also preserved by those memorials that commemorate the German war dead, which are scattered along the 1871 border, often built in the characteristic yellow stone of Metz. Mars-la-Tour was the only battlefield in the 1870–1 conflict that remained in French territory after 1871. For that part of Lorraine that remained French, this border commune became the centre for the commemoration of the 1870–1 war, and for the expression of the grief caused by the loss of Moselle to Germany. Full-scale pilgrimages were organized to it by Abbé Faller, and the speeches of Monseigneur Turinaz, the Bishop of Nancy, voiced a culture that was at once Catholic and republican.

The region's monuments for the First World War dead, in general, do not appear distinctively different from those found in the rest of France. Some aspects of them, however, are particular. In the Moselle it was difficult to claim that the soldiers who had lost their lives had died for France. Yet, in some cases, precisely this case was made. The military cemeteries, such as that in Lagarde, show the scale to which the region suffered, and how quickly the battles took place. Most of the war memorials either take the form of *pietà*, or show a soldier standing, crowned with glory.[8] In the square outside the Pagny-sur-Moselle town hall, the war memorial is in the form of a sentry for this border town; under the statue the names of deported civilians and executed hostages have been added.

Serge Bonnet's works have investigated the intertwining of traumas, myths and legends in these borderlands.[9] Rumours circulated about the blind reprisals that were carried out by the Germans during the First World War following actions by French irregular forces. French businessmen were accused of collaboration with the enemy, and the fact that their factories were not hit by German bombs was cited as proof. It is true that French industry did contribute to the Reich's war machine. Even though these memories, drawn from two world wars, are telescoped together, they are not simply myths. John Horne's research on the war in Lorraine and the German atrocities in Belgium during the First World War show that the war, before being reconstructed in popular memory, really did contain some episodes of extreme violence.[10] Memories of this long, violent period and the associated commemorations have often ignored whole areas of history. For example, one can note that monuments to the French Resistance, which insist that these martyrs 'died for France', and that they were French patriots, thereby forget that many resistors came from immigrant families, including Italian anti-fascists and veterans from the Spanish International Brigades. Their anti-Nazi struggle was not limited to a defence of the French nation, but involved a wider form of universal anti-fascist commitment. The reconstitution of the 1871 border in 1940 woke up old memories once more. Returning to our geological metaphor of a fault line, one could say that although the 1940 line was far more visible than the line of 1871, it was still seen as a mere continuation of the previous line.

What remains of the restructured borderline of 1940? There are a few bunkers or *blockhaus*. The most poignant signs, however, are the ruins of the Nazi Terror. By Thil, near the vast no-man's-land that stretches into Luxembourg, there is a necropolis that commemorates a concentration camp, the only one on French territory, which had a gas oven to incinerate the dead, and was sometimes used on the near dead. Hundreds of deportees, Russians, resistors and Hungarian Jews were slave labourers here in 1944. The Tiercelet mine was transformed into a vast underground factory for the construction of V1 rockets, after the Peenemünde site was put out of action by Allied bombing in August 1943. The site near Thil was chosen by the Germans because of its mines and because it was close to the German railway network, which ran to Audun-le-Tiche (renamed, once more, Deutsch-Oth), just over the border from Thil.[11] The necropolis, whose crypt was inaugurated in Novemver 1946, is a desolate site that attracts few visitors. The mine has been walled up, and the concentration camp barracks have been destroyed.

### 3. Mines as markers

Different forms of mines lie either side of the old border. In the Moselle, hillside galleries were constructed. There were, however, some shafts and tracks for horses. Those at Aumetz have become emblematic of a mining and industrial past: there is now an eco-museum at their base. The post-war negotiations in 1871 raised the question of the Moyeuvre mines, which were split by the new border. Bismarck is said to have declared that customs officers and policemen would have to be stationed underground in the mines.

Once abandoned, the mines were flooded: often this caused massive subsidence. The most spectacular example of this process concerned the company towns of Moyeuvre-Grande and Auboué, right next to the old border. Many of these properties had been owned by the firm of Wendel, which practised an innovative and far-reaching form of industrial paternalism. When the mining companies pulled out, from the 1960s to the 1990s, they sold the houses to the workers and miners who had previously rented them. These buildings were then destroyed by a massive wave of subsidence. The town council of Auboué (Meurthe-et-Moselle) tried to repair the damaged areas.

As in so many other places, the line of the old border runs through abandoned, forgotten and enclosed areas. Around Auboué a quite separate zone has been formed, cut off from all urban centres and commercial activity. In Moyeuvre-Grand, the subsidence caused most damage in an area cut off from the town centre by the railway line to Joeuf. Photos of its Cité Curel and its Rue Heurteaux look as if they had been taken in a town that has been bombed or hit by an earthquake. People in the mining company towns to the north grew worried: the town hall at Aumetz was prominent in voicing concerns.

De-industrialization and the end of mining was often seen as another form of foreign occupation, a demonstration of the power of multinational companies and unpatriotic capitalism. Debates concerning the crisis and final collapse of Lorraine mining suggest the continuing vitality of a form of 'frontier consciousness'. Gérard Noiriel cites texts from the French Communist Party (PCF) in the Longwy basin that repeatedly call on 'patriotic feelings' in a way that indicates a specific type of border identity.[12] The mining crisis was blamed on the economic and political policies of

'German Europe'. Auboué town council forbade the transport of imported iron through the commune in 1979, just as it had forbidden German soldiers to travel through the commune in 1960.[13] Even the Confédération française démocratique du travail (CFDT), the Socialist-linked trade union confederation, was affected by the end of mining in a similar manner: it made use of the same patriotic discourse in its campaigns to defend the miners. Serge Bonnet cites a letter from a CFDT militant, René Boudot, to the managing director of Usinor: 'This is as bad as the worst periods of the German invasions: you're replacing them with your mad destruction.'[14]

These sad images often hide a quite different reality: the old borderlands have prospered, in part because of the wealth that was accumulated by the mining industries, but also because of their geographic location, a point of contact between France and Germany. In a thought-provoking little book, *La nuit de Moyeuvre*, Gilles Ortlieb presents poetic descriptions of the mining villages alongside snippets of conversation 'which echo in the silence of the industrial wastelands'.

> *In the days of the mines, it was like Texas here. Now, it's like the Californian desert. There were twenty thousand people here in Moyeuvre. Now, there's hardly six thousand . . .*
>
> *Miner's wife, master's wife. You shouldn't believe everything people tell you: they earnt a lot. I've known miners who bought new cars more often than their bosses. Not like the iron-workers, who ride bikes and mopeds. In the evenings, as the factories closed, you had to watch out to make sure that you weren't knocked down by a cyclist, they were everywhere, like in China. There were bars and cafés at each street corner. In Joeuf, after the procession for Sainte-Barbe, they'd do them all, one after another, all twenty down the high street.*[15]

The communes along the old border often try, in a touching way, to save and to validate the architectural heritage left by the mines and factories. In the streets of Montois-la-Montagne (Moselle), near Joeuf, there are plaques explaining to passers-by the previous functions of some of the oldest properties. One can walk by buildings that were workers' cafés, meeting halls or engineers' casinos. Hayange and Joeuf still lie in the shadow of the Wendel château.

## 4. Stations and housing

The Third Republic was unwilling to mark out this unjust border
with signs to note the limits of its sovereignty: there were no posts
like those put up by the Germans. On the German side, buildings
designed in a monumental and prestigious architectural style were
paraded along the borders of the new, united Germany. The most
striking example of this desire to mark the territory was the design
of the new German border stations, which celebrated economic
prosperity and German culture.[16] One step away from the border
was also Metz station, opened in 1908. This was the boldest of
these new monuments, and it was ironically described by French
patriots as *kolossal.*

The design for Novéant station borrowed from the classical-
paladian tradition, suggesting links between the newly German
Moselle and imperial Roman culture. It is still a working station,
on the Metz-Nancy line. Chambrey station, however, has been
closed, as has the Nancy-Sarreguemine line. Today, tourists are
told that it was an 'imperial station'. It has become a leisure
centre, and can be hired for marriages or meetings. Avricourt is
a special case: the frontier runs along the railway line, and the
1871 negotiations split the village in two. The surprising result is
that, today, there are two neighbouring communes with the same
name: Avricourt (Moselle) and Avricourt (Meurthe-et-Moselle). It
would have been appropriate if, at this point, I had been able
to include a photo of a road sign showing that one was leaving
Avricourt in order to enter Avricourt. Regrettably, the local
authorities have not commissioned such a memorable sign.

Comparing the two Avricourt stations, one notes the originality
of the historical styles of architecture commissioned in imperial
Germany. The station in German Avricourt looks like a Florentine
palace, as if the Renaissance reached Germany in 1871 and created
this cultural trophy, to be used to decorate the luxurious villas of
Blasewitz, the residential suburb of Dresden. Avricourt (Moselle)
station was about a hundred yards long, and contained three
waiting rooms and two cafés. To French observers, it epitomized
a disgraceful German culture. 'The German station at Avricourt
is one of the most lugubrious buildings in the world. It is a morgue,
an ambitious, turreted morgue. During the endless waits, the
travellers collapse on its benches, as if they were dead, or slink
about its halls like ghosts.'[17]

A few hundred yards from this abandoned station, on the other side of the tracks and the other side of the old border, is the quite modest French station of Igney-Avricourt. All the French stations are the same: Pagny, destroyed during the Second World War, was no grander. For the French, giving the border buildings any sense of solemnity would have implied an acceptance of this arbitrary treaty, imposed by force.

Station architecture is not the only indication of the contrast between cultural traditions at the old border. The new suburbs for officials, customs officers and railway workers built in German Moselle also made use of historic forms of architecture. A whole new quarter was built near Avricourt: a utopian administrative town. This is now Nouvel Avricourt, once Deutsch-Avricourt. It included villas for the highest officials, and a square street plan around a Lutheran church, a vision of an ideal Germany. None of this is properly maintained today, and many of the buildings have been abandoned.

In a more modest manner, here and there, a house or a building gives the landscape of the border a French or a German touch. Nancy was the regional centre for an important form of Art Nouveau style, which influenced designs in the Briey arrondissement. Elsewhere in the Moselle there are houses like those in the new quarter around Metz station.

This cultural border can be traced through the landscape and its buildings, but it no longer corresponds to any political or linguistic border. German is no longer commonly spoken, not even in the houses built in the Moselle during the German era, nor in the miners' and ironworkers' quarters, built for migrants from the rest of Germany. The Moselle, particularly the western parts of the department, tends to forget its German past and, in a way, also forgets its old mono-industrial role. It presents itself as 'the department of lakes'. The old commune of Stahlheim, now Annéville, was created to house German migrants. It was one of the first communist town councils in France. Now it is run by a very right-wing mayor, and has become a holiday resort with a thermal centre, a zoo and a casino. It is possible that the make-over of the department as a tourist site, similar to the process in the neighbouring Alsace, will make the trauma of the annexation grow more serious: it remains a history that people have neither forgotten nor come to terms with.

## 5. Political identity at the border

This borderlands trauma has led to identity problems for some people. There are still issues concerning the Moselle's religious and educational legislation: a well-rooted Mosellean peculiarity. But we have a more reliable test to detect the presence of troubled minds and confused identities in France: the votes for Jean-Marie Le Pen and Bruno Mégret in the first round of the presidential elections in April 2002. More people in the Moselle voted for the extreme right than in the Meurthe-et-Moselle. Le Pen won 18.1 per cent in the Meurthe-et-Moselle and 23.7 per cent in the Moselle; Mégret won 2.8 per cent in the Meurthe-et-Moselle and 3.4 per cent in the Moselle. This tendency is strongest in the old German-speaking, coal-mining east of the Moselle, closest to the Saar and Germany. But the extreme Right wins support along the whole of the old border. In some of the smallest communes their score can be noticeably high: a point that sometimes needs qualification. In Atilloncourtt (Moselle), Le Pen got 30 per cent of the vote, or eighteen votes. The overall tendency, however, is clear. In Gorze, Le Pen's 25 per cent meant 135 voters, to which Mégret's eighteen voters could be added. In Gravelotte, Le Pen won more than 25 per cent, and almost as many in Chambrey.

This is a complex issue, however, and cannot be reduced to a simple opposition between an extremist Moselle and a republican, loyalist Meurthe-et-Moselle. There are some small rural communes, with no ghettos or 'difficult areas', that voted in significant numbers for Le Pen or Mégret. Sometimes the extreme Right won one-third of the vote in such places, in both the Moselle and the Meurthe-et-Moselle. Fear explains much of this vote: but fear of what? In these small rural communes there is no problem of deindustrialization, and very few immigrants. But rumours circulate, and the rural people easily grow terrified about conditions in the nearest big towns, Nancy and Metz, particularly as they hear so much about 'insecurity' on their televisions. Are they affected by the nearby presence of the old border? Perhaps it does play some role in suggesting mythical forms of identification, such as the defence of 'French-ness': a role in which this part of the Lorraine has frequently been the vanguard.

On the other hand, in the northern 'high land', the old industrial heartlands, communes that have now been almost annihilated by deindustrialization remain clearly leftwing. Old communist communes are now turning to the protest vote represented by the candidates of the extreme Left. Villerupt (Meurthe-et-Moselle) is still a leftwing and extreme leftwing town. Here 23 per cent were for Jospin, 16 per cent for Hue and 15 per cent for the three Trotskyists. Audun-le-Tiche put Jospin ahead of Le Pen, and Hue almost won 12 per cent, despite the 15 per cent for the Trotskyists Laguiller and Besancenot. But the mining and ironworking zone was not immune to Le Pen's influence: he took almost a quarter of the votes in Moyeuvre-Grande (Meurthe-et-Moselle), which is normally considered a leftwing commune. There was a clear difference between Le Pen's score here, and that which he obtained in Joeuf (Meurthe-et-Moselle), which, giving Le Pen less than 20 per cent, remained rooted in the Left. The Le Pen vote was never simply a Mosellean particularity but, often, the line of the old border seems to reinforce other political oppositions.

## 6. Host communities and migrants

The identity issues raised in these old borderlands are not limited to reenactments of French-German clashes. The region was also at the centre of a vast influx of immigrants from Belgium, Luxembourg, Poland, Slovenia and, above all, from Italy. On both sides of the 1871 border, mining and ironworking towns contained 'little Italies'. Adrien Printz, a worker and historian of the Fentsch-d'Henaye valley, notes that the Wendel firm appealed for Italians, so as to avoid employing Germans and thus contribute to the Germanization of the Moselle,[18] though this argument has been challenged. Today, it is clear that in the years before the First World War, the region was marked by violence, instability and marginality. The borderlands would have been a Wild West. One observer noted that near Homécourt, he met Italians whom he had first seen in Chicago. The border provided an escape route from the police, and social instability was exacerbated by management policies, attempting to attract workers with better salaries. The turnover of workers grew more rapid. Piero Gallero, however, has argued that beneath this job instability, these shifts from one firm to another, there was a deeper process of integration.[19]

The borderlands were a particularly attractive region for the first, pioneering migrants. The Rue de Franchepré in Joeuf was nicknamed the Boulevard des Italiens. German legislation was less permissive than the French laws, so migrants' cafés spread fastest in the Meurthe-et-Moselle. The memory of this marginalized but lively community is still alive, a distinctive feature of the old borderlands.[20]

At the outbreak of war in 1914, Italy was seen to be an ally of the Germans, and many Italians were expelled. The 1915 Franco-Italian alliance changed the situation: Italians were now more likely to be accepted by local notables. Following the First World War, the idea of an anti-German, Latin fraternity opposed to Germany was spread by the French and Italian authorities throughout Lorraine: it then assisted the spread of fascism.[21] The French police tolerated the activities of Italian consular agents: they were allowed to recruit migrants, and to attempt to discipline the migrant community through a reign of terror. Across the region as a whole, however, there was a strong anti-fascist movement. The Confédération générale du travail unitaire (CGTU), the Communist trade union confederation formed in 1921, and the Italian-language sections of the PCF, formed an important framework for the migrants' sociability and integration. The PCF also formed the Union Populaire Italienne, a mass organization working to integrate migrants, but also to affirm their identity.[22] During the 1930s, many Italians resisted the pressure of the Consulate, the Catholic missons and the Fascist groups, and chose to acquire French nationality. In 1939, however, there were still more than 37,000 foreigners in Briey arrondissement.[23]

The prominence of foreign communists in the anti-Nazi resistance demonstrates the success of a process of integration which began during the Popular Front. For many communist militants, their resistance activities began with their participation in the International Brigades in Spain. An important group from Auboué volunteered. Some later left the party, but others became leading resistance activists, both in Lorraine and farther afield in the Isère and the Gironde. A group of *passeurs* based in the Orne valley included many migrants, such as Torquato Baraldi or Ermidore Martinelli, both from Joeuf. In August 1944, the Germans arrested many trade-union and communist militants in Villerupt; among them was Camille Salvi, who later died at Sachsenhausen. Gérard Noiriel has demonstrated how important these heroes and martyrs have become in the memory of the northern 'high land', the industrial north of the Meurthe-et-Moselle.[24] In many cases, this process of integration culminated in the election of communist town councils.

Part of the same process, however, was the internalization of a certain xenophobia. A saying sums up this point: the last one in closes the door. Northern Italians were hostile to immigrants from south Italy or north Africa. PCF propaganda against German re-armament took up a particular patriotic form in these old borderlands. On this issue – opposition to the European Defence Community – Gaullists and communists were as one in their rejection of German re-armament. Lorraine-based communists were, however, particularly virulent in their hostility to the threat of 'Bonn's revenge'. This could be seen in their efforts to build links with the 'other Germany'. Moyeuvre-Grande, while it had a communist council, tried to find a twin town in East Germany. Lorraine's communists also spoke of the defence of communist 'Latinity' against a 'German-reactionary' culture. Militant German workers had been systematically expelled from the de-annexed areas in 1918; their absence may help explain why Lorraine's communists were so quick to equate German culture with reactionary values. But even this observation must be qualified: even in the Moselle there were communist workers who preserved elements of German culture, such as using *Francique*, a German dialect to be found in the east of the Moselle, around Forbach and Merlebach.

## Conclusion

For the moment, integration is a fact. A recent conference sponsored by the Université de Nancy 2 and the Lorraine Regional Council, described the region as 'a land of hospitality and a melting-pot of peoples'. At Montois, the Italian flag flies next to the French tricolour. One old border, that which isolated the Italian community from the rest of the population, has faded away. Each year, Villerupt organizes an Italian film festival. One could almost argue that the fact that the old Franco-German border is remembered proves how integrated Italian and Polish migrants have become.

The tension between Moselleans and the 'mainland French' is re-enacted at a local level in the contrasts between the Italo-Lorrain population of Moyeuvre and the people of Joeuf. On Sundays, the shops are open in Joeuf, but not in Moyeuvre. In Joeuf, they talk of the strict discipline and the lack of humour of those who live in Moyeuvre. These contrasts are even present in the two departments' respective PCF sections. The militants in Moselle are seen as loyalists, while those in the Meurthe-et-Moselle, during the 1970s and 1980s, tended to be more critical of the party leadership. Points such as these suggest the extent to which the border has a greater presence in people's memories and in their minds than it does within the landscape.

Following the iron and steel crisis and the feeling that the new border with Germany has grown blurred, these vague memories of a now apolitical borderline have remained alive. It seems unlikely that this border will be reactivated, but it is still there, secret and hidden, unwithered in people's memories. This type of cultural persistence may provide a model for the future of inland borders in the new Europe formed by the Schengen zone.

## Notes

1   See Pierre Barral *L'Esprit Lorrain. Cet accent singulier du patriotisme français* (Nancy: PUN, 1989).
2   See François Roth, 'La frontière franco-allemande 1871–1918' in Wolfgang Haubrichs and Reinhard Schneider (eds), *Grenzen und Grenzregionen; Frontières et régions frontalières; Borders and Border Regions; Veröffentlichungen der Kommission für Saarländische Landesgeschichte und Volksforschung*, 22 (Sarrebruck, Saarbrücken, 1994), pp. 131–45. François Roth, *La guerre de 70*, (Paris: Fayard, 1990).
3   *Metz-Nancy, Nancy-Metz, une histoire de frontière* (Metz: Catalogue de l'exposition des musées de la cour d'or, décembre 1999–mars 2000).
4   Pierre Fritsch, *Le royaume de la côte* (Paris: Grasset, 1967).
5   My colleague, François Roth, records that when Louis Madelin, a student at Nancy, was waiting for his viva, he was taken to this river at Brin-sur-Seille by his professor Christian Pfister, a medievalist from Alsace. Pfister told the student: 'You should always come back to this provisional border, which twists the knife in your heart.'
6   *L'Est Républicain*, 18 février 1913; quoted in Pierre Barral, *L'Esprit Lorrain* (Nancy: PUN, 1989), p. 99.
7   See François Roth (ed.), *Lorraine: terre de bressage et d'accueil des populations* (Longwy/Longlaville: Presses Universitaires de Nancy, 2001).
8   Antoine Prost, 'Les monuments aux morts. Culte républicain? Culte civique? Culte patriotique?', in Pierre Nora (ed.), *Les lieux de mémoire I: La République* (Paris: Gallimard, 1984), pp. 195–225.

9   Serge Bonnet, *L'homme du fer* n°4.
10  John Horne, 'Corps, lieux, nation: la France et l'invasion de 1914', *AHSS*, 2000 (1), pp. 73–109. See also his *Guerre et cultures, 1914–18* (Paris: Armand Colin, 1994).
11  *http://www.outoftime.de/thil/textes/nom.html*
12  Gérard Noiriel, *Vivre et lutter à Longwy* (Paris: François Maspero 1980), pp. 136–40.
13  Serge Bonnet, *L'homme du fer: Mineurs et sidérurgistes lorrains* (Nancy: PUN, Éditions Serpenoise, 1985), pp. 257–9.
14  *L'homme du fer*, pp. 249–50.
15  Gilles Ortlieb, *La nuit de Moyeuvre* (Nancy: Editions Le temps qu'il fait, 2000), pp. 106–8.
16  Jean-Pierre Bureau, 'Les gares frontières françaises issues du Traité de Francfort' (Université de Nancy: Maîtrise, Faculté des Lettres et Sciences humaines, novembre 1970). See also André Schontz, *Le chemin de fer et la gare de Metz* (Metz: Éditions Serpenoise, 1990) and, the more collaborative recent work by André Schontz, Arsène Felten, Marcel Gourlot, *Le chemin de fer en Lorraine* (Metz: Éditions Serpenoise, 1999).
17  E. Hinzelin, *En Alsace-Lorraine* (1904), p. 7.
18  Adrien Printz, *La vallée usinière: histoire d'un ruisseau: la Fentsch* (Sérémange, 1966).
19  Piero-D. Galloro, *La main d'œuvre des usines sidérurgiques de Lorraine; 1880–1939; Etude des flux; Analyse des Forges de Joeuf* (Metz: Thèse de doctorat, 1996) and, in particular, his 'La frontière à l'épreuve de la mobilité ouvrière en Lorraine (1880–1914)', in Jeanne-Marie Demarolle (ed.), *Frontières en Europe occidentale et médiane de l'Antiquité à l'An 2000* (Metz: Colloque de l'Association interuniversitaire de l'Est 9–10 décembre 1999, 2001), pp. 409–30.
20  Didier Francfort, 'Peut-on parler d'une sociabilité des frontières?', in Demarolle, *Frontières*, pp. 545–51.
21  Didier Francfort, 'Être mussolinien en Lorraine: les fascistes italiens face aux associations (1921–39)', *Revue d'Histoire Moderne et Contemporaine*, juin 1991, pp. 313–36.
22  Eric Vial, 'Affirmation de l'*italianità* et intégration: l'Union Populaire Italienne, une organisation de masse du PCI, entre Front Populaire et "Drôle de guerre"', in F. Roth (ed.), *Lorraine, terre d'accueil et de brassage des populations: Colloque Longlaville-Longwy, octobre 2000* (Nancy: PUN, 2001), pp. 102–13.
23  Archives départementales de Meurthe-et-Moselle, VC 4054.
24  Gérard Noirel, 'Le rôle de la résistance dans l'intégration des immigrés: l'exemple lorrain', in P. Joutard and F. Marcot (eds), *Les étrangers dans la Résistance en France* (Besançon: Colloque de Besançon, 1992), pp. 152–4.

# Chapter five

# Between borders: the remembrance practices of Spanish exiles in the south west of France[1]

*Scott Soo*

## Introduction

The history of the Spanish exiles in France is replete with borders of all kinds. The first and perhaps the most obvious that they experienced was the geopolitical border separating southwest France from the Iberian Peninsula. This is not to say that borders are without material form or physical consequences. The oral and written narratives of the refugees reveal that the journey across the Pyrenean border in 1939 proved to be a traumatic experience due to an amalgam of the mountainous terrain, the weather, the lack of provisions and transport, the attacks from Nationalist planes, and last but not least, the reticence of the French authorities in allowing the refugees to enter French territory. The exiles' narratives further indicate that the crossing of this border did not alleviate the trauma hitherto endured. Once inside France, the exiles negotiated a plethora of other borders, a series of boundaries that related less to national territory than to the metaphorical and cultural delineation of French national identity.[2] Less visible to the naked eye, these boundaries nonetheless exercised a tangible influence on the lives of Spanish refugees.

The broad focus of this chapter concerns the historical, political, and cultural boundaries both confronted and constructed by the refugees in France. It begins with a critique of Pierre Nora's conceptualization of memory in relation to the absence of refugees from French historical memory. A brief account of the memorial activities of the Spanish refugees in the concentration camps of the French Third Republic is subsequently provided, and is followed by a discussion of the origins, development, and characteristics of a number of associations that currently commemorate this episode of history. The latter section of the chapter shifts to the microanalysis of memory and everyday actions within the home of one Spanish couple. Within the symbolic space of the home, it can be seen that the creation of the commemorative associations has not altered the significance of memory within the lived environment of some refugees. The aim of this chapter is twofold: in the first place, to demonstrate that the nexus of boundaries that once excluded Spanish refugees from various aspects of French society has been superseded by a commemorative culture that potentially transcends the sectoral identities associated with the current era of commemoration; and secondly, to suggest that the exclusion of the exiles' histories and memories from dominant post-war narratives has at once intensified the importance of memory within the home and produced a personal ambivalence towards integration in France.

## 1. Realms of memory

'There are realms of memory because there are no more memory-environments', states Pierre Nora in his introduction to the impressive seven-volume work, *Les Lieux de Mémoire*.[3] In pre-modern society, memory used to be an integral facet of everyday actions, but it has since become externalized and substituted by the phenomenon of the '*lieu de mémoire*'. Although this process may be relevant to the memory dynamics of a nation-state such as France, it is not necessarily true of migrant groups within France. In respect of the Spanish refugees, it appears that the combination of exile and the problematic development of a public memorial culture generated new meanings in relation to everyday actions, prompting what we may consider as a return of the 'memory-environment'.[4] The emergence of an organized commemorative culture across the southwest of France has finally begun to address some of the forgotten aspects of this history. An interesting characteristic of this unfolding memorial fabric lies in its relationship to national boundaries. Unlike realms of memory as understood in the usual sense of the term, the mechanics of these refugee realms of memory are not at work within a national context. They can be characterized as neither French nor Spanish, but rather as existing in an indeterminate space between the borders of these two body politics.

Before addressing the empirical aspects of this study, it may be helpful to review some of the most salient aspects of Pierre Nora's project in relation to the subject of this chapter. *Les Lieux de Mémoire* is a collection of a hundred and thirty essays by a team of eminent researchers under the direction of Pierre Nora that provides an inventory and analysis of the historical memory of the nodal points constituting contemporary French national identity. The term '*lieux de mémoire*' has been translated variously as 'place of memory' or 'site of memory', but in the following will be referred to as 'realm of memory'. Though the difference may appear to be slight, the third term tends to place less stress upon topography than 'site' or 'place'. In this way the vast scope of the concept, which stretches from the most concrete of objects (such as war memorials) to the most abstract of subjects (such as coffee), is given greater emphasis.

In Nora's definition, a realm of memory relates to a material or abstract object possessing a material, symbolic, and functional framework, of an enduring presence either through the human will to remember or through the effects of time.[5] It is not so much the content of the realm that is of interest as the framework within which memory is at work, together with its function within the overall memorial fabric from which contemporary French society draws its repertoire of symbolic meanings.[6] The seven volumes were published over a span of nine years, with the titles *La République* (1984), *La Nation* (1986), and *Les France* (1992). The first volume on 'The Republic' investigates an array of symbols, monuments, pedagogical devices, commemorations, and counter-memories that have constitutively located the nation within the ideal of the Republic. The next three volumes cover 'The Nation', exploring the construction of the 'memory nation' across a number of realms that are organized under the headings of the immaterial, the material, and the ideal. The last three volumes are grouped under the title *Les France*. As the use of the definite article in the plural suggests, this tome stresses a pluralistic vision of memory that signals the decline of the 'memory nation' and the corresponding creation of the 'era of commemoration'.

The era of commemoration is both the title of the concluding chapter and the label used to designate the state of memory within contemporary France.[7] A number of concerns are raised about the current fascination with memory. Amongst the most relevant to his particular study are Pierre Nora's deliberations concerning the concept of the realm of memory, and the rise of a patrimonial culture. The observation is made that the tool initially conceived to critique memory had become part of the commemorative process itself. There had been a proliferation, dilution and misrepresentation of 'realm of memory' within contemporary commemorative discourse to the extent that it had become part of the project of national identification. Throughout the chapter, Nora consequently draws the reader's attention back to the original definition and purpose of the concept.

An additional characteristic of the current fascination with commemoration relates to the existence of a patrimonial culture. This is not regarded as representing a collective ensemble but rather as a means through which sectoral identities can be enacted, which raises the unsavoury prospect of an emotional ambivalence towards strangers. While this latter concern should not be taken lightly – the relationship between patrimonial culture and the development of sectoral identities is a clearly a worrying phenomenon – it will be demonstrated that essentialism and exclusivity are not the only outcome of a commemorative process that has begun to function from the bottom upwards. On the contrary, there exists the potential to both create and reinforce networks of solidarity that may in fact transcend sectoral identities, whether at the local or indeed the national level. This may particularly be the case for realms of memory involving the participation of immigrant groups. There is thus a convincing argument for the identification and analysis of those realms of memory that encourage transnational forms of collective memory and solidarity.

In this respect, the article by Pierre Birnbaum entitled, 'Grégoire, Dreyfus, Drancy et Copernic', in the volume of 'Les France: Conflits et partages', is at once promising and disappointing.[8] The delineation of the wider discourses surrounding the relationship between France and its Jewish population charts the mostly successful but twisted and bumpy road leading to the recognition of the significance of this religious minority within the French Republic. A surprising feature of the article resides in the epistemological presentation of some of the obscured or perhaps repressed realms of memory: the French concentration camps. It is unfortunate that while underlining the absence of Jewish realms of memory the author, albeit inadvertently, is simultaneously contributing to the obfuscation of the memory of the Spanish refugees and International Brigaders. Following a reference to the transit camp at Drancy, the article states: 'The same applies to other camps where, from 1939, so many foreign and then French Jews endured atrocious conditions before in the majority of cases being deported. For example, Argelès and Saint-Cyprien . . .'[9]

It is curious that no contextual basis surrounding the camps is provided. Argelès and Saint-Cyprien were originally constructed in order to contain the exodus of February 1939. Perhaps some would argue that this forms a small detail and that its omission is understandable given the context of the overall chapter. The camps mentioned in the article were certainly a prominent part of the French state's machinery of deportation. Moreover, the Holocaust clearly represents a form of brutality that far exceeds the dynamics involved in the internment of the refugees from the Iberian Peninsula. Nevertheless, the lack of any acknowledgement of the origin of the camps runs the risk of privileging a particular version of history to the exclusion of all others.[10] To some degree, this focus constitutes a lost opportunity, insofar as it fails to accommodate an interpretation of the camps as a realm of memory that is not restricted to a single nation or ethnic group. Perhaps an overall emphasis on the larger narratives of the nation explains the neglect of such detail. The article does indicate that realms evoking a Jewish memory in France are as rare as they are difficult to find.[11] At this point, though, it would have been interesting to question how memory functions when it is obscured from the public eye. When prominent realms of memory are repressed, what strategies are adopted to ensure the continual transmission of the memory in question?[12]

In another chapter charting the historical memory of the relationship between France and foreigners, Gérard Noiriel acknowledges the absence of immigrants from the national memory and partly addresses the above point.[13] The correlation between the absence of public remembrance and the importance of memory within the home is hinted at when Noiriel affirms that: 'Due to the fact that immigration has not been a legitimate object of the national memory until relatively recently, an entire parcel of the collective history of the French has remained confined within the framework of memories of their private life.'[14]

When the article was published in 1986, Noiriel observed a growing concern amongst immigrants to render their history public. In particular, the proliferation of associations founded by descendants of Spanish refugees in the southwest of France is described as fulfilling the need to maintain a culture of origin. Despite the existence of these associations, however, the essential traces of refugee history are, according to Noiriel, to be found more modestly in the form of personal archives, furniture, and photographs.

Within the three tomes of *Les lieux de mémoire*, the two aforementioned chapters raise interesting questions about the mechanics of memory within two diasporic groups. Both acknowledge the difficulties involved in finding realms of memory that exist beyond the narratives of the nation-state. If the presence of memory is revealed as manifesting itself in significant ways in both the home and the public space, there is no discussion of the relationship between the two. For the refugees, the trials and tribulations of exile in conjunction with the restriction on memorial activity in the public space have heightened the presence and importance of memory within the home. Before turning to the dynamics of this 'memory environment', the origins, development, and characteristics of the commemorative culture of Spanish exiles will be discussed.

## 2. Exile and internment

'*La Retirada*', literally 'the retreat', is the name given to the largest exodus ever experienced in France.[15] Between 28 January and 9 February 1939, close to half a million people traversed the Franco-Pyrenean border following the collapse of the Catalonian front to the advancing armies commanded by General Franco. Many people had no option but to cross the border on foot, undertaking an exhausting journey that was compounded by a lack of provisions, the weather, the mountainous terrain, and notably the attacks from Nationalist planes. Within written and oral narratives the physical and psychological demands of this experience take the form of a trauma that, far from dissipating, actually intensifies as they enter French territory. Although they were greeted with many acts of solidarity and kindness, the government of the French Third Republic was far from enthusiastic about the reception of the refugees and their treatment on the whole left a great deal to be desired.[16]

The crisis of French national identity and concomitant xenophobia underlay the motivations of the Daladier government when it passed a series of decrees, between May and November of 1938, aimed at the control, surveillance and suppression of foreign residents.[17] These measures effectively provided the legal framework for the internment of the refugees in various camps and reception centres throughout metropolitan France and in French-controlled North Africa. On crossing the border, the processes normally associated with the refugee experience, that of marginality and liminality, were amplified by the xenophobia afflicting French society. Although territorially within the French border, the refugees were excluded by a boundary delineating French culture in the most extreme form; that of the *Univers concentrationnaire* or concentration camp universe.[18]

The label of 'concentration camp' to describe the places in which the Spanish refugees were interned continues to provoke controversy, and a caveat is certainly needed. The use of the term derives from a number of sources. In the initial period, conditions in the camps were often inhumane and numerous examples of brutality committed by the camp guardians can be found in refugee narratives. Moreover, French national and departmental archives reveal that the administration interchangeably referred to the camps as concentration camps, internment camps and reception centres. On the part of the refugees, 'concentration camp' was, and continues to be, the most frequently evoked term. Given the aforementioned, it is valid to maintain the designation of concentration camp but essential to stress that the camps of the French Third Republic bore no direct relation to the systematic dehumanization and elimination of internees within the concentration camps of the Third Reich.

The first camps were hastily constructed on the beaches of the Département of the Pyrénnées-Orientales at Argelès-sur-Mer, Saint-Cyprien and Barcarès. The lack of political will, and the concomitant improvisation of the relevant local authorities led to the internment of at least 180,000 refugees in these three camps alone in the most appalling conditions. Despite the miserable environment and lack of resources, a plethora of rich cultural activities quickly flourished.[19] One facet of this creative drive was the creation of a '*presse de sables*', which informed the internees of all of the cultural activities taking place within the camps. The activities, which varied from lessons in French and general literacy to poetry recitals and sports events, embodied a number of meanings. At the most general level they were entwined with the re-creation of an 'imagined community' in exile, representing a continuation of the cultural work undertaken during the Second Spanish Republic (1931–9). More specifically, they espoused an ideal of Spain that varied according to the specific stance of the paper: Basque, Catalan, communist, libertarian, republican, socialist, Trotskyist, etc. In a pragmatic sense, these activities gave the refugees a sense of purpose by breaking the monotony of daily camp life and by teaching certain skills that would be required upon their reintegration into society.[20]

A crystallization of the various discourses contained within the press occurred during celebrations within the camps. The commemoration of the third anniversary of the defeat of the military coup by the Spanish Republic in the camp of Barcarès on 19 July 1939 is one such example. One former internee described an exhibition of sculptures made out of sand and stone, and the performance of a Spanish orchestra composed of internees.[21] Symbolically, this event incorporated several meanings: the continuation of the values upon which the Second Spanish Republic had been founded under the label of the 'Real Spain'; the day of popular activism during which 'the Spanish people, united and powerful, took up arms to repel the criminal military rebellion';[22] the corresponding importance of democracy in an increasingly anti-democratic Europe; and lastly a critique of French republican values. Behind the barbed enclosure of the camps, such manifestations helped to allay the negative effects of the state of liminality in which the refugees found themselves. It constructed a sense of time and space, within an otherwise harsh environment, that provided the illusion of continuity with a more stable past. The monotony of time in the concentration camps was broken not only by the event itself, but also through its preparation.

Celebrations such as that of 19 July could not be enacted with the full fervour desired, since any form of political activity was strictly forbidden by the camp authorities; hence the extensive use

made of cultural allegory. Censorship was additionally exercised
by the internees due to the acrimonious divisions emanating from
the defeat of the republic in Spain. From the very beginning,
therefore, it is possible to perceive a certain compromise in
both the production and corresponding transmission of this
memory. If the political was once the subject of suppression, it
now appears to have been replaced by that of the cultural. In June
2002, the first commemoration of the *Association des amis pour la*
*mémoire de l'odyssée des réfugiés républicains Espagnols de Lot et Garonne*
(AMORE47) devoted a great deal of time to the arrival and
treatment of the refugees to the neglect of the aforementioned
cultural work.[23] In the various debates, discussion remained focused
upon issues of maltreatment, which tended to depict the refugees
as primarily victims and hence without any form of collective
agency. The fixation with this aspect undoubtedly testifies to the
sense of injustice arising from the lived experience of the camps,
together with the subsequent suppression of the associated memory.

A series of interrelated injustices has structured the collective
memory.[24] Political differences aside, a general resentment is
expressed towards the Western democracies concerning the
nonintervention treaty; one of the determining factors for the
Francoist victory and the Spanish exile. Secondly, there follows
the ambivalent treatment of the exiles by the French authorities.
This is compounded by the significant participation of Spanish
refugees in the Resistance in France and the subsequent exclusion
of this history from the Gaullist and communist myths of the post-
war years. In addition, the rapprochement between the Spanish
dictatorship and the French government influenced the latter
in limiting the political expression and activities of the exiles. In
part, this explains the absence within the exilic press of any serious
criticism of the French authorities in respect of the concentration
camps.[25] Lastly, the tendency of the French state to regard Vichy
as an anomaly within republican history is complicated by the fact
that the concentration camps were constructed by a republican
government; the embarrassment of the authorities has also played
a role in the suppression of this memory.

## 3. The advent of a memorial culture

Against this prevailing amnesia some of the former internees
immediately undertook the task of informing the wider public

through the publication of their memoirs. Reference to the camps in some of the earliest titles is an early indication of the development of the camps as a signifier for the maltreatment of the refugees by the authorities in France.[26] The Spanish press in exile also called for the history of the refugees' arrival, work, and resistance in France to be written, but without reproach to France.[27] Despite this effort, there was no substantial form of collective expression, nor any sustained historical investigation until thirty years after the events of 1939. In the late 1960s, historians began to publish research on this aspect of refugee history; the main corpus of historical analysis, however, did not occur until the late 1980s and early 1990s.[28]

The beginning of an organized memorial culture and the development of the camps as a *lieu de mémoire* can be traced back to the mid-1970s. The actual content of the memory was and still is ambivalent, evidence of which can be seen in the epitaphs of certain monuments. The monument erected on the beach of Barcarès in the mid-1970s evokes the memory of the Spanish who fought in the ranks of the French army rather than those who were interned in the camp of the same place. Further northeast, in the department of the Pyrénées-Atlantiques, the concentration camp of Gurs was initially built to contain the Basque refugees, who were soon joined by pilots of the republican airforce and members of the International Brigades. The camp later became infamous, as it was from here that 3,907 Jews were deported between 1940 and 1943.[29] To mark the fortieth anniversary of the camp, a wooden placard was produced in 1979, but the inscription was soon desecrated and the reference to the concentration camp erased.[30] Returning southwards to the department of the Pyrénées-Orientales, the inauguration of a memorial on the site of the former entrance to the camp at Argelès-sur-mer in the summer of 1999 provoked tension between representatives of the government and the local association *Fils et Filles de Républicains Espagnols et Enfants de l'Exode* (FFREEE). At the ceremony, the presence of the minister for transport and the minister for *anciens combattants* was dependent on the exact wording of the inscription of the memorial. Consequently, the words *camp d'Argelès* instead of the intended '*camp de concentration*' now figure on the epitaph.[31] During the commemoration in February of 2003, the end of the official speeches was marked by an intervention from a Spanish refugee who called for the inscription to be rewritten to include the reference 'concentration camp'. A combination of the pain, repression and ambivalence of this memory over the long duration explains why the conditions and treatment in the camps continue to form the central trope in narratives of arrival amongst the exiles.

The exact mechanisms involved in the process of forgetting are complex and can only be discovered through a detailed study of the various localities. If the state as well as people in the locality have contributed to the process of forgetting, the initiative of local inhabitants and the support of local authorities have been equally instrumental in the receding amnesia surrounding the camps. The prime driving force behind the creation of the memorial culture has been the creation of local commemorative associations.

The reunion leading to the creation of the *'Amicale du Camp de Gurs'* attracted former internees from all over Europe.[32] It was, in fact, the climax of a process of remembrance stretching back to at least 1945, when a visitor's book was placed in a farm opposite the cemetery of the camp at Gurs. The list of entries indicates that while there has been a constant flow of visitors from all over the world, there has been a comparative absence of French visitors. Up until the 1990s, the ceremonies remembering the deportations from Gurs were essentially attended by Germans and Spaniards, with hardly any French participants aside from the local notability.[33] The work of the *Amicale* has effectively contributed to the rediscovery of the camp within the locality and to the consolidation of inter-ethnic forms of solidarity. It maintains a permanent exhibition in Pau, publishes a bulletin, and organizes frequent school trips to the site of the camp. These activities reveal the potential for commemorative practices to overcome the preoccupation expressed by Pierre Nora regarding the correspondence between commemoration and sectoral interests. In short, the *Amicale du Camp de Gurs* and its activities may well be of relevance to the formulation of new memory-politics.

A similar observation applies to the activities of the association FFREEE, based in Argelès-sur-mer. Although primarily dedicated to re-grouping the children of the Spanish refugees, its membership is open to anyone interested in the history of the exodus and the camp. Indeed, one of the committee members, Michel Guisset, is not of Spanish descent but is rather a local autochthon. As in the association of the Camp de Gurs, FFREEE has the potential to create inter-ethnic forms of solidarity. The choice of acronym is particularly revealing about the motivations underlying the group's activities. The gathering at the monument every year is a reminder of the lack of freedom experienced by the refugees as they were herded into the camp on the beach. The will to remember, however, underlies an agenda firmly rooted, or perhaps 'route-d' in present and future realities.[34] The founding aims of the association include a commitment to 'bring aid and support to victims of forced displacement'. The extent to which the association has been able to implement this is difficult to gauge given the short period of its existence, although the results so far do appear positive. Hitherto, the association's activities have included the inauguration of the monument at Argelès, an annual commemoration of the Retirada in February of each year, the publication of a bulletin, and the participation in congresses devoted to the Spanish exodus. The gathering over three days from 21–3 February 2003 reminded adherents of the association's original aims by including a conference on the 'Palestinian exodus'. Lastly, FFREEE, for the second year running, organized the commemoration of a realm of memory that is radically different from the existing meaning of the term: the border crossing.

The *marche-symbole*, a symbolic hike across the border, was 'inaugurated' in 2002. The ritual begins with a speech at the monument dedicated to the exodus in the Catalonian village of Las Illas, and is followed by a trek across the border to the monolith in the French village of La Vajol. Another ceremony occurs before the more ardent participants return on foot to Las Illas via a different route that traverses the Coll de Manrella and passes in front of a monument dedicated to Lluis Companys.[35] The outward journey recalls one of the many paths taken by the Spanish refugees during the Retirada, while the second half of the walk symbolizes the return journey of those refugees determined to continue the struggle against the Francoist regime and the route taken by those wishing to join the Free French Forces.[36]

An in-depth analysis contextualizing this form of remembrance within the historical memory of the border crossing over a longer period would constitute a fascinating topic of study. A project of this kind could begin with the creation of the modern state and the concomitant consolidation of its borders, both of which created the conditions for smuggling objects and people across the Pyrenees. Crossing the border takes on significantly new meanings from the start of the Civil War: the unofficial attempts by men and women from all over the world to traverse the Pyrenees in order to defend the fledgling Spanish Republic; the exodus following the fall of the Basque country; the *Retirada*; the *passeurs* of the Resistance; the anti-Francoist resistance; the clandestine arrival of Spanish refugees in the post-war years. In all of these examples, memory and experience merged together as individuals tapped into local knowledge of ancient footpaths that had been passed from generation to generation. What were their common motivations, fears, and expectations? Just as the communities of the Pyrenean valleys have a tradition of autonomy from France and Spain, this particular historical memory exists within the interstice between nations and thus marks a departure from the notion of realm of memory as it is currently understood.[37]

## 4. The memory-environment

An analysis of the experiences of the Retirada depicted in Spanish refugees' writing has been carried out by Sharif Gemie. Although questioning the concept of a genre of refugee writing, he identifies a unifying strand of themes related to the shared historical experience of the Retirada and consequent reception in France.[38] The repetition of these tropes in the various texts suggests that refugee literature can be conceived as one of the conduits, or 'vectors of memory' through which knowledge of this past is transmitted.[39] A resurgence in the publication of memoirs, together with the rise in of a commemorative culture, has undoubtedly increased public awareness of the Spanish exile. The marginalization of this history from the dominant histories of France and Spain over such a long period of time, though, has aggravated the metaphysical boundaries distinguishing refugees from French culture. In the absence of a public memorial culture, everyday actions and material culture have been the agents through which memory is transmitted.

Within the life cycle of the refugees, it appears that the idea of a definitive return to the Iberian Peninsula exercises most influence at two stages in particular: on arrival in France, and during retirement. At each juncture, it is possible to discern a revival in the importance of memory in relation to everyday activities. Initially, the determining influences arise from the nature of exile itself, and also from the additional trauma of the disappointment concerning the reception in France. In the second phase, a combination of elements – retirement, the approaching end of the life cycle, and the rancour arising from the sentiment of having been one of the '*olvidados*' (those forgotten by history) – coalesce and reinforce the trauma of the initial experience. This is certainly the case within the life story data obtained from a series of interviews with Antonio and Pura Arías in the agglomeration of Bordeaux during the summer of 2002.[40] While acknowledging the limitations of a single case study, an informed but tentative insight can nevertheless be gleaned from their oral narratives.

In exile, the everyday actions of individuals become highly charged with emotional significance. In order to assuage the destabilising effects of the liminality of exile, a retrospective gaze to a seemingly stable and ordered reality often provides an illusion of continuity and hence stability. During this liminal process the individual is confronted with a number of intertwining possibilities: the reinvention of him/herself according to a new set of cultural codes; the re-creation and withdrawal into the former cultural codes in the context of the new country; or the production of a third culture out of a syncretic mixture of the old and the new.

It should be noted that the exilic discourse engages with a wide range of factors: social, political, gender, generational, etc. For the purposes of this investigation, the relationship between life cycle and exile is particularly relevant. Within the narratives of children and adolescents, the prior expectation and actual moment of entering French territory occurs within an overall mood of optimism. For this younger generation, France represented a haven from the terrifying bombing and strafing of the Nationalist, German and Italian planes, and the excitement of travelling to a different country. In the narratives of Antonio and Pura, the constant fear of attacks by planes is a dominant characteristic of their journey to the border. If France offered a respite from the terror of war, any other expectations on the part of Antonio and Pura were crushed through the segregation of families by the French authorities. The memory of the period in which they were interned in '*centres d'accueil*' as their fathers languished behind the barbed enclosures of the camps in the Languedoc-Roussillon is particularly painful.[41] Instability arising out of the absence of their fathers was aggravated by the uncertainty concerning what the future held for them. Under these circumstances, any everyday activity that provoked memories of pre-exilic family life was loaded with significance. Antonio, for example, described the reunion with his father and the family's fruitless attempt to recreate a Spanish dish of bread, olive oil, and sugar on New Year's Eve in 1939. The use of vegetable oil was far from pleasant and epitomized not only the daily struggle to eat, but to do so in a familiar and hence meaningful manner.[42]

Although the sense of injustice tends to be directed at the French state, the actual experience, together with the lack of remorse shown by the state, seems to have had a correlative effect on this couple's attitude to acculturation. While they are keen to express their internationalism, the sense of disappointment concerning their first years in France, together with the occlusion of their histories, has generally led to a rejection of daily practices deemed to be French. The degree of rejection has obviously varied through time. The daily demands of life and work in France are regarded as having forced them into adopting certain French customs, such as eating according to French mealtimes, and/or being overly respectful of neighbours in respect of the level of noise within the home. Indeed, the oral interviews conducted for the overall study from which this chapter originates have revealed that the level of noise is a prime signifier of difference in the construction of French and Spanish boundaries in the public and private domains. The birth of children may have provoked thoughts about returning to Spain, thereby providing a catalyst for the review of cultural practices in France. However, it is the arrival of retirement from paid work that has been most significant in the reappearance of a memory environment. The overarching difference between the post-retirement memory environment as opposed to that of the arrival in France is the recognition of the impossibility of returning and the concomitant spatial and temporal preoccupation with the there and then.

Retirement has enabled Antonio and Pura to revert to eating at Spanish mealtimes. Although there appears to be a relative continuity in the food itself and its preparation, the ability to eat later than is the norm in France lends a symbolic element to the food consumed. In addition to mealtimes, the possibility of staying up later and the ability to watch Spanish television with the aid of a satellite dish brings another possibility of recreating Spain within the home, as opposed to the previous intention of recreating the home in Spain. Despite these strategies, a feeling of being in a foreign country still prevails and is reflected in the material culture of the home.

The question of noise remains a significant signifier of difference, in relation to the volume of the television. Pura and her husband demonstrated how at night they plug headphones into the television set in order to watch their favourite programmes into the late night/early morning without disturbing their neighbours. Aside from the significance of the television set, the domain of human-object relations is also revealing in relation to the decoration of the front room. In more than one home, overt representations of Spain (such as photographs) tend to be placed opposite the main focal point of the room. In the case of Antonio and Pura, the main focus of the room is a collection of photos of their children and grandchildren that either hang from the wall or are perched on a cabinet next to the television. In another home, photos of children were situated opposite the only two objects that reminded the occupants of Spain and their family.[43] In a third home, various representations of Spain were again opposite the focal point of the room, which was decorated with a couple of pictures of Bordeaux, and a neighbouring town.[44] It is worth juxtaposing this form of decoration with a general tendency for most individuals to finish off an interview by talking about the achievements and lives of their children. I would argue that the presence and representation of children born in France embodies a form of ambiguity within the homes of Spanish refugees. As much as children remind parents of their inability to return to Spain, they also allay the discomfort this causes, through a mixture of familial support and parental pride concerning the achievements of their children in France.

The issues discussed in relation to memory environments require further empirical substantiation. Nevertheless, there does seem a convincing basis for the contention that memory environments appear within migrant groups at two significant junctures. For Spanish exiles, the arrival in exile resulted in individuals creating a symbolic emphasis to their everyday actions as a means of coping with trauma. The resurgence of the importance of memory

following retirement incorporates a considerable feeling of resentment which, as Nancy Wood underlines, is a common symptom
amongst communities whose traumatic experiences have not been
dealt with publicly.[45] The memories evoked this time around serve
to mediate between the knowledge that there will never be a
permanent return to Spain and the resentment arising from the
exclusion of a traumatic past from dominant historical narratives.
As much as the memory activities provide some respite from the
traumas of exile, they also engender emotional discomfort by
reminding the individuals of that which is absent.

## Conclusion

In contemporary Bordeaux, traces of a Spanish presence can be
most frequently seen in the form of street names, tapas bars or
shops specializing in Iberian products; they are mostly empty of
historical and political significance. Not all representations of the
Spanish influence in French life are completely vacuous, though
it takes a little determination in order find them: the archive of
the local federation of the Spanish Libertarian Movement in exile
tucked away in an inconspicuous home in Bègles; or the small
plaque on the Quai Richelieu dedicated to the memory of Pablo
Sanchez, a Spanish refugee killed by the German forces less than
twenty-four hours before Bordeaux experienced the Liberation.[46]
The memorial was created not by the French authorities, but by
a Spanish organization. A museum exhibition on the Resistance
in Bordeaux's *Centre national Jean Moulin* appears to perpetuate
the traditional narratives of the Resistance through the absence
of any reference to the contribution by the Spanish or any other
immigrant group. Given this relative obscurity, it is perhaps
unsurprising that amongst the Spanish exiles of Bordeaux, there
is a general sentiment that they personify an unknown history
buried beneath the interests of the French state. The combination
of their actual experience of the first months in France, together
with the suppression of this memory, has had adverse effects in
the way some of the individuals have approached matters of
acculturation. A striking moment in the film/documentary *No
pasarán, album souvenir* occurs during an interview with Casimir
Carbo in relation to his internment in the camp at Argelès.

'I won't talk about it,' he states, before adding, 'I'll never adopt the French nationality.'[47]

The pedagogical work of the various commemorative associations is central to the reconstitution of the local histories of the Spanish and other migrant groups. In some cases, the accompanying commemorations embody elements of a 'timeless Spain' by organizing 'traditional' Spanish cultural activities.[48] In the example of FFREEE, however, nostalgia is being mobilized in an innovative manner that is firmly rooted in the here and now. Activities of this kind contain the possibility for the creation and consolidation of inter-national forms of solidarity, and the concomitant development of realms of memory that, in the case of the *marche-symbole*, intersect the limits of French and Spanish national sovereignty; they should therefore be of interest to those concerned with formulating a new memory-politics. It is not inconceivable that a project of this kind, by incorporating a greater commitment to inter-ethnic memories, may go some of the way to alleviating the need of some refugees to shelter behind the bounded reality of the memory environment.

## Notes

1  I would like to thank Rod Kedward for his insights on a draft of this paper, as well as Sharif Gemie and Henrice Altink for their comments following the presentation of the study at the Association of Modern and Contemporary France conference in August 2002. I also wish to thank the AHRB for the financial support of the doctoral work from which this chapter originates. Finally, I would like to express my gratitude to the informants of this study.

2  The terms 'border' and 'boundary' have often been used interchangeably. In the interests of clarity, 'border' will be used solely in reference to the geopolitical line dividing southwestern France from the Iberian Peninsula.

3  Pierre Nora, 'Entre mémoire et histoire: La problématique des lieux,' in Pierre Nora (ed.), *Les lieux de mémoire*, vol. 1, (Paris: Éditions Gallimard, 1997), p. 23.

4  The characteristics of this environment will be discussed in the last section of the chapter.

5  Pierre Nora, 'Entre mémoire et histoire', pp. 23–43.

6  For a more detailed and complex review see Nancy Wood's, 'Memory's remains: *Les lieux de mémoire*', *History and Memory*, 6(1) (1994).

7  Pierre Nora, 'L'ére de la commémoration', in Pierre Nora (ed.), *Les lieux de mémoire*, vol. 3, (Paris: Éditions Gallimard, 1997), pp. 4687–719.

8   Pierre Birnbaum, 'Grégoire, Dreyfus, Drancy et Copernic', in Pierre Nora (ed.), *Les Lieux de mémoire*, vol. 2 (Paris: Éditions Gallimard, 1997), pp. 2679–718.

9   Pierre Nora, 'L'ére de la commémoration', 2680. All translations are mine unless otherwise stated.

10  See Henri Rousso's caveat about the risk of myth making and the exclusion of other important aspects of Vichy history by solely focusing upon the Jewish experience. Julian Jackson, *France, The Dark Years 1940–4* (Oxford, 2001), p. 618.

11  Julian Jackson, *France, The Dark Years*, p. 2680.

12  The last section of the paper will deal with this question more specifically through the discussion on memory-environments.

13  Gérard Noiriel, 'Français et étrangers' in Pierre Nora (ed.), *Les lieux de mémoire*, vol. 2, (Paris: Éditions Gallimard, 1997).

14  Gérard Noiriel, 'Français et étrangers', p. 2447.

15  Given the nature of the event, the exact number of refugees involved is unknown and official figures by the French authorities tend to vary. Nevertheless, consensus amongst historians indicates that close to half a million people were involved.

16  An account of the arrival, internment, and initial experiences of two refugees in France can be found in Neil MacMaster, *Spanish Fighters: An Oral History of Civil War and Exile* (Basingstoke: Macmillan, 1990).

17  Geneviève Dreyfus-Armand, *L'Exil des Républicains Espagnols en France: De la Guerre Civile à la Mort de Franco* (Paris: Albin Michel, 1999), p. 58. A detailed account of the xenophobia as well as the attempts to counter racism can be found in Vicki Caron, *Uneasy Asylum: France and the Jewish Refugee Crisis, 1933–42* (Stanford: Stanford University Press, 1999).

18  For an elaboration of this concept see Scott Soo, 'Identity, exile, and internment: reconstructing the "univers concentrationnaire" of Spanish Civil War exiles in the Pyrénées-Orientales' (MA dissertation, University of Sussex, 2000).

19  For details of these cultural activities see J. C. Villegas (ed.), *Plages d'exil. Les camps de réfugiés espagnols en France, 1939* (Dijon, 1989).

20  An analysis of this press containing illustrated examples can be found in J. C. Villegas (ed.), *Plages d'exil. Les camps de réfugiés espagnols en France, 1939* (Nanterre-Dijon: BDIC-Hispanistica XX, 1989). (A collection of essays published on the fiftieth anniversary of La Retirada.)

21  Eulalio Ferrer, *Derrière les Barbelés: Journal des Camps de Concentration en France (1939)*, French ed. (Limonest, 1993).

22  *Hoja de los Estudiantes*, 2, 27 July 1939.

23  The conference was revealingly entitled *'Le Lot et Garonne se souvient . . . La Retirada, Le Camp: Colloque à la mémoire des 500 000 Républicains espagnols exilés en Février 1939'*, and took place from 19–30 June 2002.

24  The lack of consensus regarding the notion of 'collective memory' has not stopped authors from using the term. In this chapter, the term is used to signify an ensemble of commonly remembered tropes within a specific group of people.

25 Geneviève Dreyfus-Armand, 'L'Emigration politique Espagnole en France au travers de sa presse 1939–75' (Thèse de Doctorat: Institut d'Etudes Politiques de Paris, 1994).

26 Manuel Andujar, *St Cyprien Plage: campo de concentración* (Cuadernos del Destierro: Mexico, 1942); Jaime Espinar, *Argelès-sur-Mer (Campo de concentración para Españoles)* (editorial Elite: Caracas, 1940); Manuel García Gerpé, *Alambradas. Mis nueve meses por los campos de concentración de Francia* (editorial Costa: Buenos Aires, 1941).

27 An article by Simone Martin in *L'Espagne républicaine*, No. 56, 20 July 1946, together with several articles in the *Suplemento literario de Solidaridad obrera* in 1954. Geneviève Dreyfus-Armand and Émile Temime, *Les Camps sur la Plage, un exil espagnol* (Editions Autrement: Paris, 1995), p. 120.

28 For a historiography of the Spanish exile in France see the introduction to Geneviève Dreyfus-Armand, *L'Exil des Républicains Espagnols en France: De la Guerre Civile à la Mort de Franco* (Paris: Albin Michel, 1999).

29 Claude Laharie, *Le Camp de Gurs, 1939–45: Un aspect méconnu de l'histoire du Béarn* (Biarritz: Société Atlantique d'Impression à Biarritz, 1993), p. 219.

30 Claude Laharie, *Le Camp de Gurs*, 359. Research into the manner in which local populations have remembered the concentration camps has yet to be conducted. In the meantime, we can only surmise that the veil of silence that smothered the history of the camps for so long was even greater where the deportation of Jews was implicated.

31 Conversation with Michel Guisset, local historian and member of FFREEE, on 20 June 2002 at Villeneuve sur Lot. Interview with Sonia Marzo, one of the founding members of the aforementioned association, 23 November 2002, Argelès-sur-Mer.

32 Claude Laharie, *Le Camp de Gurs*, p. 361.

33 Claude Laharie, *Le Camp de Gurs*, p. 360.

34 Gilroy, Paul, *The Black Atlantic: Modernity and Double Consciousness* (London: Verso: 1993), p. 19.

35 Lluis Companys y Jover, the Catalonian President extradited from France and executed by the Francoist dictatorship on 15 October 1940.

36 Description in the brochure detailing the events of 12–23 February 2003 entitled in French and Spanish: *Paths of the Retirada: commemoration of the Republican exile.*

37 Jay Winter has explored realms of memory in an international context in the study of monuments of the Great War in Europe in *Sites of Memory, Sites of Mourning: The Great War in European Memory* (Cambridge: Cambridge University Press, 1995).

38 Sharif Gemie, 'The ballad of Bourg-Madame: Spanish refugee writing and the Pyrenean border, 1939'. *International Review of Social History*, 51 (2006), pp. 1–40.

39 The notion of 'vector' in relation to memory was first used by Henri Rousso in his classic study, *The Vichy Syndrome: History and Memory in France since 1945* (London: Harvard University Press, 1991) and forms

the title of Nancy Wood's, *Vectors of Memory: Legacies of Trauma in Postwar Europe* (Oxford and New York: Berg, 1999).

40 I interviewed the couple at their home on three separate occasions during the month of July. The average length of each interview was four hours. Antonio and Pura were part of the exodus of February 1939. At the age of seventeen, Antonio became involved in the Spanish communist resistance during the Occupation, and was an active militant in the Juventudes Socialistas Unificadas (JSU) in the post-war years. Pura's political engagement took the form of participating in cultural productions of the JSU.

41 Pura was in a centre in Tulle in the Corrèze, and Antonio in a centre near to Blois in the Loir et Cher.

42 Interview on 4 July 2002, Lormont.

43 Interview with Ramon Falomir, 22 May 2002, Floirac.

44 Interviews with Agustin and Ignacia Juan Diez, 19 June 2002, 20 June 2002 and 25 September 2002 in Bordeaux.

45 Nancy Wood, *Vectors of Memory*, p. 199.

46 The plaque was inaugurated by the Junta Española de Liberación during a small ceremony attended by about twenty people on 28 August 1947.

47 Henri-François Imbert, *No pasarán, album souvenir* (France: Libre Cours/Shellac Distribution, 2003).

48 The commemoration in Villeneuve-sur-Lot in February 2003 began with an annual general meeting of AMORE and a ceremony at the monument dedicated to the Retirada. This was followed by a 'giant paella', a poetry reading, and a performance of Flamenco dancers.

# Chapter six

# Otherness, invisible borders and representations of identity in the Midi, 1920s

*Laure Teulières (translated by Sharif Gemie)*

Studies of borders and their nature should not ignore those borders defined *from within*, by specific social groups through their collective cultures. In practice, 'The boundary is differentiation: it always produces distinctions, whose disappearance leads to crisis.'[1] This chapter examines the invisible borders that defined 'otherness' in those parts of the Midi around the city of Toulouse, in the 1920s. It will consider the dividing lines and the various collective representations that governed relations with 'the other'; that is, foreigners and migrants. It will also analyse how 'otherness' was understood and judged in this period when immigration was so important and so widely debated, both at a national level and in the southwest region.

Debates and discussions in this period were clearly marked by a hierarchic sense of ethnic barriers, drawn from widely circulating forms of colonial and – often – racist thinking. But, alongside these, there were also some less offensive cultural divisions. These were the starting point for representations of the contrasting concepts of the north and the Midi (or 'south'), of the meridional character of the southerners and of the idea of Latinity (which included many diverse ideological themes), leading to a consideration of the Occitan dimension of regional identity. It seems that the idea of 'otherness' was largely created according to norms and guidelines that also determined those qualities that were to be rejected.

The Toulouse region was a profoundly rural society, transfixed by the de-population of the countryside and the social transformations that accompanied this process. Here, the distinction between 'self' and 'other' was operated by the play of contrasts between the rootless and the rooted, the itinerant and the settled, the forest dweller and the villager, the proletarian and the peasant, and so on.

## 1. The roots of national identity

The first issue to consider concerns the foundations of national identity. We will begin by briefly surveying some of the intellectual systems that shaped the manner in which this identity was understood. With the creation of the Third Republic in 1870, the national cause was more than ever equated with the triumph of unity over centrifugal forces. From this initial proposition, there grew the myth of an eternal France, fixed in a geographic setting and framed within 'natural' frontiers. This concept was further refined into the stereotype of the 'hexagon', which grew from the genealogical heritage of Charlemagne and the medieval dynasties to the nation-state. Territorial unification was conflated with the progress of civilization. One should also note the fiction of a centuries-long 'French' culture, linked to an analogous myth of a homogeneous people. These concepts were then explicitly invoked in the phrase 'nos ancêtres les gaulois', a formula recited on the school benches. The same ideas evoked the happy fusion of the great original peoples – the Celts, Latins and Franks – in the assimilatory model celebrated by republicans and radicals.

By its very nature, immigration posed questions about collective identity, the spread of population and its balance, and the real and symbolic barriers and openings that defined the nation's inhabitants. Debates about the arrival of outsiders reinforced ideas of the superior social harmony of 'the French people' and their civilization, while causing alarm about the effects of the entry of a heterogeneous element into the French community. The defence of national unity and social homogeneity inflamed an entire ideological tradition. According to one republican concept, the nation formed a unitary body. Its priority, above all, was to preserve its historical heritage. Differences were acceptable only if they remained mere individual traits. If differences were expressed collectively, and in particular if they became popular, they were then seen as threats to the nation's integrity. Any particularity, linguistic or cultural, was quickly denounced as a 'pocket' or an 'ethnic enclave', for it represented the beginning of a border *within* the national territory and within French society. Such forms of thinking were extremely common in the Toulouse region, particularly among powerfully established centrist groups, such as the Radical Party. For these observers, only the much-heralded process of 'assimilation' could prevent the 'communitarian enclosure' of the immigrant population.

These varied responses made reference to the dominant sociopolitical models. France was marked by a strongly centralized state, and a distinctive Jacobin tradition. Its central political model – the Republic – only recognized French individuals, not communities within France. This political philosophy upheld a unifying cultural model that tended to eliminate differences, favouring the creation of common reference points, beginning with the standardization of languages and regional cultures.[2] As for access to French nationality, this tradition, which combined the principles of *jus soli* and *jus sanguini,* had the clear aim of making foreigners become 'French'. It is widely recognized that the 1889 nationality law, based on the rights acquired by residence, was an expression of an 'assimilationist nationalism', grounded in a 'republican faith in assimilation'. Such processes worked in parallel with the growing homogenization of the nation, as republican institutions (the army, the school, etc.) aimed to create identical, or at least common, cultures from different populations and individuals.[3]

In this context, religious difference was seen as an insurmountable obstacle. The assimilation and integration of non-Christian foreigners was never considered – and indeed appeared inconceivable, becoming a type of taboo topic. However, even among Catholic peoples, 'practices could divide more than dogmas'.[4] This point applied to even the largely de-Christianized southwest during the inter-war years; as is illustrated, for instance, by the failure of an attempt to encourage the mass emigration of Breton peasants into the area, largely due to their strong religious faith. One could also cite the disquiet caused by the sight of Polish immigrants, supervised by their own priests. The same point was illustrated, once more, by the surprise that local people felt when they saw the outgoing, public faith of peasants from Venice and nearby Frioul, who closely integrated religion into their daily lives, following ostentatious collective rituals and particular forms of devotion connected to saints venerated in their homelands. In other words, there were distinctions made between different types of Christians, and even different types of Catholics, that contributed to a sense of 'otherness'.

In the 1920s, France's demographic decline provoked a general debate based on the poorly constructed notions of race and ethnicity, which then structured all anthropological debate. One could even suggest that the issues of demography and immigration created a racist barrier, to the extent that outsiders who were considered 'too exotic' suffered from an absolute form of ostracism. One typical journalist thought it was appropriate to refuse entry automatically to 'the Blacks', 'the Yellow', and to any 'Senegalese who may have slipped in between the sacks of peanuts'.[5] Such statements suggest the existence of accumulated sub-strata of prejudice and mental reflexes that structured the representation of 'the Other in Western society'.[6] They can be traced back to ancient fantasies about 'the barbarians', through to the modern obsession with 'purity of blood' mobilized against Jews or Arabs. The contribution made by philosophers to such thinking should not be ignored. It forms a troubling dimension to eighteenth-century thought and 'the French debate on human diversity'.[7] Despite its claims to universalism and humanism, the Enlightenment's silence concerning the slave trade clearly demonstrates the blind spot in this intellectual tradition.

There was a crystallization in colonial culture during the nineteenth century. Historians have shown the significance of the colonial images of 'the Other' and their role in 'the construction of the foreigner'.[8] From these images, the point clearly emerged that western civilization was superior, whether this was due, according to the right, to Christianity and God's decision about man's fate or, according to the left, to progress, the French Revolution and republican ideals. This claim became an absolute barrier, which severely curtailed all subsequent debates concerning immigration and assimilation. This distance between the observer and the other was understood in terms of the other's progress towards civilization, a measure based on an idea of the linear progression of humanity. At the summit was the West's modern scientific culture: below this, the cultures that were seen as overcome and stuck in their own decadence (the Arabs, Persians and Asians), and then, at the bottom, the savage peoples (the Blacks, Indians, aborigines, Polynesians, and so on). At the time, such thinking was summed up in common phrases such as 'the West's civilizing mission' and 'the white man's burden', so dear to Kipling. French political culture was dominated by a vision that was at once paternalistic and authoritarian: the world had to be illuminated by the West's genius, its ideals, its socio-economic models and its institutions. In brief, dominate to educate, and educate to dominate. This was a culture that repudiated, unthinkingly, everything that was not part of the European universe.

Recent historical works have examined the fantastic visions that were presented of 'exotic' people. Colonial expositions included stands of 'negro huts', 'moorish caravans', and 'Indo-Chinese pagodas'. This fashion for human zoos had begun in the Belle Epoque.[9] Crowds flocked to these attractions, which featured hired and contracted 'ethnic specimens'. In the zoological gardens in the Bois de Boulogne, successive exhibitions beginning in the 1880s showed Nubians, Ashantis and Dahomeans. The mass press popularized their images, and even the science of anthropology was implicated. Its original purpose was to study 'the primitive',[10] or the 'infant peoples', who were seen as remnants of an ancient culture, dating from the dawn of humanity. For these reasons, the 'primitives' were presented as the mirror opposites of the bourgeois values of the epoch. Their customs and cultures, that is, their food, scars and tattoos, and masks and totems, seemed barbaric, disgusting and naive. They were accused of diverse forms of immorality: superstition, credulity, obscurantism, laziness and improvidence, violence, anarchy, uncontrolled instincts, unbridled sexuality, etc. These clichés formed cultural themes that ran through editorials and shaped structures of thought.

In the same era, France was worried about demographic decline: a process that assumed particular gravity in the Toulouse region.[11] The most terrifying press reports suggested that the French people were on the verge of extinction. Such reflections provoked a nationalist backlash, often xenophobic in character. Pierre-André Taguieff provides a careful analysis of the diverse implications of this fear. He notes that 'on the question of immigration, nationalism synthesized three political-ideological projects: racism, eugenics and natalism'.[12] The recognized experts on demographic questions were often doctors, whose thinking was dominated by hygienist concepts. Their analyses led to the overwhelming acceptance of the concept of degeneration. They spoke of the danger of inherited human characteristics being corrupted, allowing the spread of the sick and the weak. These arguments led the public to support calls for the creation of unassailable sanitary and biological borders. It was suggested, for instance, that immigrants should be selected and would only be allowed entry if they would improve, or at least preserve, the French stock. Racists warned of an 'ethnic' danger, of the risk of a 'melting pot' and the mixing of races. They demanded a strict sexual segregation of the races: the border had to function as a biological barrier. Such ideas circulated widely in the daily regional press, whether radical, such as the prestigious *La Dépêche du Midi*; conservative, such as *L'Express du Midi*; or Catholic, in *Le Croix du Midi*. To cite a few examples: 'mixing [métissage] between different ethnic groups leads to the bastardization of the race';[13] the mixing of peoples was like 'cross-breeding incompatible species' in the animal world.[14] These phrases show the influence of pseudo-scientific representations. The concept of a hierarchy of human groups, divided into unequal races, was extremely common. Reading between the lines, one notes the influence of Darwinistic theories of evolution (the survival of the fittest), and of Gobineau's *Essai sur l'inégalité des races humaines* (1855), which asserted the superiority of the 'blond dolicho-cephaleus' type, found in western Europe, over all others.

## 2. A north/south split: Latinity and meridonial character

To return to the Midi: what was the dominant perception of meridonial character in this period? And how did this concept influence the way in which foreigners were seen? Sociologists have studied the link between the formation of particular French identities and the internal migrations of the nineteenth century. They suggest that such movements stimulated an awareness of regional identities, and led to their development into fixed forms.[15]

The idea that the people of the Midi have a specific character is very old. Much eighteenth-century literature refers to the opposition between the north and the south. Starting with Montesquieu's theory of climates, a strand within Enlightenment thinking elaborated on the theme of the contrasts between different countries according to their proper 'type' or 'temperament', traits that were conflated with the nature of the inhabitants.[16] More generally, a series of stereotypes circulated widely, opposing the north, which was linked to qualities such as coldness, strength, courage, the control of the instincts, self-control, rationality and innovation, to the south, which stood for the qualities of warmth, relaxation, weakness, sensitivity, hedonism or debauchery, imagination and permanence.

These points merit further consideration. In the 1920s, the ideological concept of a Latin union was extremely influential. 'Latinity' became a notion used by the learned. It was a scholarly invention which, nonetheless, circulated and became, to some extent, a common turn of phrase. It was linked to a geopolitical project, namely the community of 'Latin interests', and to an appeal for the alliance of 'sister nations', faced with common enemies: namely Protestant, commercial Great Britain and 'Prussian', militaristic Germany.[17] The union of the Latin races, it was argued, would create a new *Pax Romana*, opposing a 'Latin bloc' against the 'German expansionism' that threatened Europe. This cause attracted diverse individuals, such as diplomats and members of chambers of commerce, who were organized in lobbies and associations, and linked by the comités d'union latine. One such committee was formed in Toulouse in 1919, uniting many of the city's notables. Its vice presidents included, among others, a leading conservative member of the department's conseil général, and the honorary consuls of Italy and Romania. *Action Latine*, its weekly paper, served as the committee's mouthpiece in Toulouse. The committee's influence spread from the city's notables to many other groups and associations.

As a result, the concept of Latinity became a privileged reference point in the construction of identity. It implied the idea of a border between civilizations. Its political values were legitimated by a discourse that stressed the proximity of 'sister civilizations', 'Latin cousins', and the 'ancient ancestry of Latin civilizations'.[18] Their common sources, it was argued, were the classical world, Roman civilization, the similarity of their languages, their common customs and their 'race' and culture, as well as the universal values represented by the 'Latin spirit', symbolized by the Catholic faith, with Rome as its centre. Articles published in the leading regional daily, *La Dépêche*, returned frequently to the contribution made by classical culture, by its art and music, its literary tradition, and by the teaching of its great authors, such as Cicero and Virgil. Together, these formed the common sources of civilization. As one editor put it, this sense of close cultural proximity was inculcated in each person in school: 'When we were children, we learnt Roman history at the same time as we learnt our own, and we all know of the links that join us to Latinity.'[19] An entire historiographical tradition highlighted southwest France's Latin roots and stressed the significance of the very early Roman presence around Narbonne and in Acquitaine. This point clashed with some of the conceptual distinctions made by the idea of nationhood. A report on immigration rehearsed these arguments: 'From an ethnographic perspective, I consider that the Italians, who are Latin, are closer to us, the descendants of the Gallo-Romans, than the Bretons, who are of Celtic origins.'[20] Another regional writer observed that 'between Latins, there are more points of contact than between the French of the North and the French of the South.'[21]

Occitan regionalism experienced a limited revival during the 1920s: its themes and ideals also contributed to the assimilation debate.[22] From the Félibrege movement, grouped around Mistral in the nineteenth century, Occitanism developed a scholarly wing, centred on the Société d'Etudes Occitanes in Toulouse. One lecture in 1918 gives a clear example of Occitanist ideas on immigration. It was given by Bernard Sarrieu, a professor and general secretary of l'Escolo deras Pireneas, one of the leading Occitanist societies, in the 'Journées Régionalistes' at the Academy of Montauban.[23] His work formed the basis for debates among the region's learned circles. In the lecture, Sarrieu welcomed immigration both as a source of manual labour, and as a means to guarantee 'ethnographic reconstitution' following the butchery of the war. His key point, however, was to call for migrants from the nearest borderlands, that is those areas inhabited by people who were 'most closely related' to their host communities. Thus Italians were needed for Corsica and the southeast, Piedmontais for Provence and Valdotans for Savoy; Spaniards were best for Languedoc and the southwest; Aranais for Luchon, Aragonese for Gascony and Catalans for Languedoc. Sarrieu outlined a distinctive policy of 'regional assimilation': migration that was adapted to the proper needs of each specific zone. The elements that were best suited to the population of each zone should be naturalized. Their common classical tradition should be developed through education and the use of indigenous Occitan dialects should be reinforced to make their assimilation easier. This programme was inspired by some obvious political considerations: immigration was seen as a means to strengthen Occitania, as well as to preserve a meridonial identity against the influences of the north and against the state's programme of standardization. The frontier dweller – the foreigner at the border – became a neighbour, an ally in the resistance of the periphery against centralization and the northerners' seizure of power. In this programme, a French national conception of 'foreigners' was supplanted by a vision of the cross-border vocation of Occitan culture.

> *Occitania must survive and must remain true to herself. The pull of the capital and the great towns is eradicating her, and Parisian influences are threatening to change her character. It would be no bad thing if some Latin elements arrived to keep the balance, so to speak, and if they thrived here, they would contribute to maintaining the region's originality . . . How can Occitania assimilate elements from the south, from over the mountains, if she herself is losing her original identity, if she has become too nordic?*[24]

Ethnic stereotypes were central to this type of thinking. They were used to create a catalogue of 'otherness'. In such inter-ethnic perceptions, knowledge of the other was created by reference to reciprocal national stereotypes, developing opposites through the 'mirror effect', and encouraging prejudices between peoples.[25] Such schematic images shaped the representation of foreigners in popular opinion. Contemporary observers loved to list the 'spirit' of each ethnic group, to note their type or temperament and native qualities, as well as their atavistic weaknesses. Such indications formed the constitutive elements of 'otherness', a concept based on a feeling of superiority, mixed with condescension and some mistrust. Flaubert had accurately caricatured this idea earlier in an entry in his *Dictionnaire des idées reçues*: 'The French: the first people in the universe.'[26]

The stereotypes of the Spanish, for example, were shaped by their ambivalent proximity. In southwest France, there were Spaniards everywhere, constituting three-quarters of the registered foreigners in the region early in the 1920s. Well known, they were familiar to local people without necessarily being seen as close. Their experiences demonstrate some of the complexities of the processes structuring the sense of 'otherness'. Spaniards were seen as rustic and hardworking. They were employed above all as labourers for heavy work (digging, mining, quarrying and factory work), and for demanding agricultural tasks, such as maintaining vines, as they were recognized as being 'good with the hoe'. More generally, it was said that Iberians were 'untiring pieceworkers, sober and patient'[27]; they were 'slow to tire, sober and thrifty'.[28] But they were still commonly represented as being at the margins of social respectability. They were too easily attracted to the towns, and in the industrial quarters they swarmed into decaying, unhealthy slums. Many little towns had their crowded Spanish quarter, whether 'little Madrid' in Nérac, or 'little Spain' in Auch. Spanish migrants were usually temporary workers, mostly living alone. They were either single men or men who had left their families back home. They went from job to job, changing employers quickly as opportunities presented themselves. For these reasons, they were also seen as unstable, dreamers, untrustworthy and ill-disciplined. They were foreign tramps, unemployed foreigners and worrying foreigners. Their bad reputations went before them, so that when they arrived in towns they provoked common fears. The 'thieving Spaniards' who 'infested' Toulouse station were frequently denounced.[29]

The stereotypes concerning Italians in the 1920s did not seem to have changed significantly since the nineteenth century.[30] They also centred on their apathy, laziness, talkativeness, Mediterranean exuberance, their artistic sensibility – weren't they all musicians, didn't they all play the violin? – their passionate nature, their hot-headed tempers, and their 'hot blood'. One anti-fascist exile who arrived in Toulouse in the mid-1920s was amazed by the 'myths' that still circulated among the French: 'Some of them still see the Italian farmer as a man swift to anger, ready to use his dagger, as a Calabrian brigand, with ribbons in his hat, a blunderbuss on his shoulder, and his belt stuffed with knives.'[31] Italians were crafty by nature: they loved cheating and plotting. These clichés circulated widely. 'In the field of *combinazione*, the Italian is our master.'[32] Italians were also reputed to be treacherous and cowardly. They did not know how to fight, and they fled from the battlefield, a point neatly illustrated by a popular rhyme in Languedoc: 'O, noble, brave Italian race/For whom battle brings disgrace./When a cannon smokes and reeks/They turn tail and shit their breeks.'[33]

On the other hand, they were praised for their willingness to work and their robust, skilful, tough, frugal natures. Most French people, however, had the impression that only those from northern Italy were really hardworking. Other regional stereotypes of Italians circulated, creating a psycho-geographic panorama, based on simplistic clichés.

> *The northerner, the Lombard or Piedmontese, is lively, brave and makes a good soldier. Those from the centre, the Tuscan and the Roman, are a bit lazy: they tend to be artistic and hospitable. The southerners, the Napolitan and Sicilian, sleep in the sun. They are careless about their appearance, and extremely superstitious.*[34]

## 3. Internal borders and social boundaries

These aforementioned hostile images of Italians, however, co-existed with a set of positive images that had largely been created by memories of the wartime experience. Throughout the 1920s, the Germans were referred to as barbarians, while the Italians, who had been France's allies, were often seen more positively. As so many adults were war veterans, the oppositions created by the war were decisive. The trenches were remembered as a symbolic demarcation line, dividing peoples; a concrete manifestation of feelings of inside and outside, with and without, self and other. A hatred of the *Boche* survived, despite the growth of pacifist feeling. The German world was rejected; it was seen as barbaric – a return to an ancient form of demarcation, which opposed the humanist world to the barbarian world. On the other hand, Franco-Italian military fraternity was celebrated. It had been born in the trenches, consecrated by blood sacrifice and had created an indissoluble bond. To cite one example among many: 'France and Italy fought for the same ideal. The blood of their children, shed on the same battlefields, had inextricably bonded their union.'[35] This line of thinking helped define what the relations between the two peoples ought to be and – by extension – how the native French people of the Midi ought to relate to trans-Alpine migrants. A paper edited in Montauban referred to this bond explicitly in an article welcoming the arrival of immigrants to the southwest. 'Now is the time to enact, in our countryside, the union between our *poilus* and the *fanti grigioverdi*, which only previously existed during a few unforgettable days as they stood side-by-side on the battlefield.'[36]

Another issue remains: that of the land, the question of 'roots' in the fields. Since the nineteenth century, regionalist works had developed this theme.[37] The works of Maurras and Barrès exercised a weighty influence: they argued that a historic and biological 'rooting' was the foundation of culture and the best basis for the nation. The writers of rustic novels sang the praises of land and tradition, and developed an entire armoury to connect rurality to rooting. All of them popularized a nostalgia for rural life – understood as the conservatory of identity, where 'the peasant soul creates the French soul' in each little land within France.[38] It was only because the rural base had survived that the Midi had been able to preserve its character, argued these novelists. They celebrated the closeness of man and earth, and idealized the peasantry, who lived amidst the calm of nature and its humble, daily beauty; who enjoyed simple, 'true' pleasures; whose labour was almost sacred; who had inherited an ancestral wisdom and a quiet, chaste sense of morality; and so on. As only the fields were filled with this 'spirit' of the people, as only the peasants possessed this instinct that allowed them to form the base, to root themselves, so it followed that only peasants could provide the true foundation for a society. Landed property was therefore seen as the keeper of continuity and transmission. According to such thinking, it was the natural power of the soil, society's womb, that stabilized and fused peoples. Here, the question of the assimilation of the foreigner or the migrant was not discussed according to any concept of the border as a legal-spatial limit, but instead according to the degree in which they were 'rooted'. The same discourse produced the negative images of migrants crowded into towns, cut off from all roots, unlikely ever to become French.

It should be recalled that these perceptions of the presence or absence of a sense of belonging were articulated in a society that was still mainly rural. Statistical records suggest that the urban population did not form the majority of the French population in 1931. Ruralist arguments, therefore, sharpened the idea of 'otherness' by suggesting that one could only truly belong within a local setting, an idea that could be applied to all of those who were strangers to a particular locality. Village societies worked as models of small communities, shaped by interpersonal links and close relationships.[39] A stranger was anyone who did not belong to this little world, who was not part of a recognized *milieu*, and who had not been made familiar through daily contacts within a specific neighbourhood. More important than any ethnic or national criteria, the stranger was always the other, in contrast to the native, the neighbour, the lads on the corner. One strikingly clear illustration of this theme can be found in answers to an administrative enquiry concerning the willingness of meridional peasants to employ foreign agricultural workers. All the replies expressed a similar view: 'they would want to get to know them first', 'they preferred local labourers', 'they did not trust people they did not know'.[40]

The vagabond, feared and rejected in the 1920s, was constructed as the negative to the positive image of the peasantry. According to one Gascon author, 'tramps are distrusted everywhere in the countryside ... to call someone here a *mec* is a dreadful insult, for it means itinerant, an urchin, a homeless person.'[41] This type of marginal, the bearer of deviancy, was an archetype of social disintegration. The uprooted individual, with no attachments and nothing to hold dear, and without responsibilities or duties, seemed to be at the mercy of all modern disorders. This explains the hostility felt towards travelling people, whether tzigane, gypsy or manouche, whether French or not. It also explains the distinction drawn between migrants who had settled, and who had therefore taken the first step towards assimilation, and those who were itinerants, whether travelling workers or rural artisans. The latter were frequently equated with 'gangs', or with 'thieves who frightened the peasants'.[42] Lastly, this attitude helps explain anti-Semitism, for the Jew was the foreigner *par excellence*, even if the Jew in question was actually an internal French migrant. Here, the 'Jewish question' was understood as the problem of an ethnic group without a nation who, unable to belong anywhere, was fated to suffer millennia-long wandering. In the early 1920s, the regional Catholic press signalled its anti-Semitism by propagating the story of a secret project, organized by the government and the Comité exécutif de Secours israélite, to assist some thirty-five thousand Jewish families from central Europe to settle in the French countryside.[43] At the heart of this rumour was the image of the fields being opened up to 'the Israelite', the epitome of the itinerant.

Some travelling trades were seen in the same way. They were best represented by forest workers or mountain labourers, who were quite numerous in some areas. In the villages alongside forests, the image of the stranger was conflated with the woodcutter or charcoal burner. These were groups with their own distinctive practices, produced by successive waves of migration.[44] They were marked by their mobility, moving from one place to another, following the workyards. Many were recruited through middle-men of their own nationality, who hired them out in teams to local employers. These groups were formed by village solidarities and family ties: fathers and sons, uncles and nephews, brothers and cousins all set out together. Official reports tell us something about the isolation in which these groups lived and worked. They stayed in far-away shacks, with little contact with the surrounding population. Such groups were quite different from the stable, serious and moral family-based immigration that the regional authorities welcomed as a means to resolve the region's demographic decline. Travelling workers were isolated and unstable, and kept in close contact with their homelands. They were far from what the French considered to be the acceptable face of immigration. Travellers appeared anti-social and they aroused suspicion. In reality, however, they followed the long-established routes of a traditional, temporary form of migration. For these migrants, their stay in France was just a temporary position among the many options available to protect the family economies of their own villages. For the French, they were a marginal community, unusual and sometimes disturbing.

One other factor contributed to the hostility shown to foreigners. In the 1920s a xenophobic reaction, aimed specifically against tourists, swept across France.[45] Some politicians supported it, thus giving the movement a certain institutional form. One member of the *conseil-général* of the Basses-Pyrenees played a leading role. He proposed an entry and residence tax to be applied to all non-working foreigners. His suggestion was taken up by many *conseils-généraux* and by some deputies. The movement gradually ran out of steam, as it became obvious that the government was not going to pass any legislation. For a while, however, it received some vigorous press support. Stereotyped arguments circulated, denouncing 'the invasion', 'the tide', and 'the locusts'. Well-off foreigners with a lot of money to spend and those who rented country cottages were particularly targeted. The British and the Americans were the most criticized groups: they were seen as 'tipsy *fellows*', 'old *ladies*', '*lords* on holiday' or as 'itinerant Americans' [all italicized words were in English in the original texts]. The press echoed the standard vocabulary of the xenophobes. It spoke of 'schemers', 'profiteers', 'plutocrats' and a 'parasitic mass': phrases that reveal a clear anti-cosmopolitanism. On the one hand, it suggests a sense of cultural dispossession. These 'multi-coloured savages' were transforming the typical French town into a 'dreadful *cosmopolis*'. The foreigners' arrogance was shocking. They were accused of stimulating inflation, of living comfortably at the expense of the French, and of making the coastal resorts and spa towns uninhabitable. They were rich, lazy, cosmopolitan, itinerant and urban: these terms capture most clearly the negative image of foreigners in France. Such themes suggest a profound rejection of cosmopolitanism and of the ability to cross physical and cultural borders, which was seen as a profoundly destabilizing factor. The foreigners' alleged blurring of guidelines and the social disintegration that their presence heralded all conflicted directly with the values that we have shown as founding the French identity in this period.

## Conclusion

This examination of attitudes to migrants and foreigners shows the deep complexity of these invisible borders with their mixed, shifting contours. Of course, they reflected contemporary mentalities: the cultural system (in the widest sense of the word), the ideological currents, and the socio-political structures. They were influenced by the many different types of identity formation that were circulating in post-war France, including republican, rural, colonial and regional identities, each suggesting different types of border. Yet these invisible borders also appear to fluctuate; they are capable of evolution and, on occasion, of reconstruction. In the context of the Midi in the 1920s, they evoke a France that was at once republican, colonial and still very rural (at least in terms of its values), and very attached to the concept of regional identity – if only in a mythical, folkloric form. These representations made use of the idea of the border as a symbolic barrier between groups, as a concept that defined difference, distinction and therefore segregation. But the invisible borders also suggested a scale of proximities, of constructed or imagined kinships, that could open the way to a sense of a shared culture with some migrant populations. In other words, such borders did not so much oppose 'the French' to 'the foreign', but functioned in such a way as to suggest a spectrum of nuances and ambivalences.

## Notes

1 Claude Raffestin, 'La frontière comme représentation', *Relations internationales*, 63 (September 1990), pp. 295–303.

2 Eugen Weber, *Peasants into Frenchmen: The Modernisation of Rural France* (Stanford: Stanford University Press, 1976).

3 Rogers Brubaker, *Citoyenneté et nationalité en France et en Allemagne* (Paris: Belin, 1997).

4 Eric Vial, 'Les Italiens: une immigration "catholique" en pays "catholique"?', *Réforme*, 2601 (18 February 1995).

5 'Les indésirables', *La Dépêche* (23 May 1925).

6 Claude Liauzu, *Race et civilisation: L'autre dans la culture occidentale. Anthropologie historique* (Paris: Syros Alternatives, 1992); Christian Delacampagne, *L'invention du racisme* (Paris: Fayard, 1983).

7 Tzvetan Todorov, *Nous et les autres. La réflexion française sur la diversité humaine* (Paris: Seuil, 1989).

8 See Eric Savarese, *Histoire coloniale et immigration: Une invention de l'étranger* (Paris: Séguier, 2000); Pascal Blanchard and Sandrine Lemaire, *Culture coloniale: La France conquise par son Empire, 1871–1931* (Paris: Autrement, 2003); Pascal Blanchard (ed.), *L'autre et nous, 'Scènes et types'* (Paris: Syros, 1996); Special edition on 'Imaginaire colonial, figures de l'immigré', *Hommes et migrations*, 1207 (May 1997); Special issue on 'Colonisation, immigration: le complexe impérial', *Migrations société* 81–2 (May 2002).

9 See 'Zoos humains', *Le Monde*, 16–17 (January 2000); and Eric Baratay and Elisabeth Hardouin-Fugier, *Zoos, histoire des jardins zoologiques en Occident* (Paris: La Découverte, 1998).

10 Philippe Videlier, 'Les modes de pensée hérités de la sociologie du XIXe siècle et de la domination coloniale', in *Mémoire et intégration* (Paris: Syros, 1993), pp. 53–63; Christian Marouby, *Utopie et primitivisme: Essai sur l'imaginaire anthropologique* (Paris: Seuil, 1990); and 'Fictions de l'étranger', *Quasimodo*, 6 (Spring 2000).

11 Laure Teulières, *Immigrés d'Italie et paysans de France (1920–44)* (Toulouse: Presses Universitaires du Mirail, 2002).

12 Pierre-André Taguieff, 'Face à l'immigration: mixophobie, xénophobie ou sélection; un débat français de l'entre-deux-guerres', *Vingtième siècle*, 47 (July 1995), pp. 103–31; Jean Benoist and Jean-Luc Bonniol, 'Hérédités plurielles: Représentations populaires et

conceptions savantes du métissage, *Ethnologie française,* 24 (January 1994), pp. 58–69; Pierre Birnbaum, *'La France aux Français': Histoire des haines nationalistes* (Paris: Seuil, 1993).

13   *La Gascogne rurale* (20 May 1923).

14   *La Dépêche* (23 May 1925).

15   Guy Barbichon, 'Migration et conscience de l'identité régionale: L'ailleurs, l'autre et le soi', *Cahiers internationaux de sociologie,* 75 (January 1979), pp. 321–42.

16   See Y. Le Scanff, 'L'origine littéraire d'un concept géographique: l'image de la France duelle', *Revue d'histoire des sciences humaines,* 5 (2001); Pierre Bourdieu, 'Le Nord et le Midi: contribution à une analyse de l'effet Montesquieu', *Actes de la recherche en sciences sociales,* 35 (1980), pp. 21–5.

17   S. Mastellone, 'L'idea di latinita (1914–22)', in *Italia e Francia dal 1919 al 1939* (Milan: Ispi, 1980), pp. 13–20.

18   For example, 'Les Italiens, les Belges et nous', *La Dépêche* (27 April 1926); 'Un regard sur l'Italie', *L'Express du Midi* (28 November 1926).

19   'La France défendra le droit d'asile', *La Dépêche* (14 September 1926).

20   *Rapport du Dr. Durand pour le comité départemental de retour à la terre du Tarn-et-Garoone le 14 avr. 1923* (Archives départementales du tarn-et-Garonne: 7 M 1172).

21   Hubert Lagardelle, *Sud-Ouest, une région française* (Paris: Valois, 1929), p. 82.

22   On the Occitan movement, see Robert Escarpit (ed.), *La Gascogne, pays, nation, région?* (Paris: Edition Entente, 1982); André Armengaud and Robert Lafont (eds), *Histoire d'Occitanie* (Paris: Institut d'études occitanes/Hachette, 1979).

23   This text was later published as Bernard Sarrieu, *L'assimilation des étrangers en France et particulièrement dans le Midi* (Montauban: G. Forestié, 1924).

24   *La Terro d'Oc* (September 1928).

25   Jean-Noël Jeannenay (ed.), *Une idée fausse est un fait vrai* (Paris: Odile Jacob, 2000); Pierre Coslin and Fajda Winnykamen, 'Stéréotypes interethniques et connaissances réciproques', in Claudine Labat and Geneviève Vermes (eds), *Qu'est-ce que la recherche interculturelle?* (Paris: L'Harmattan, 1994), pp. 182–93.

26   Gustave Flaubert, *Le dictionnaire des idées reçues* (Paris, 1881).

27   Joseph de Pesquidoux, *Sur la glèbe* (Paris: Plon, 1922), p. 144.

28   'Les étrangers chez nous', *La Dépêche* (30 May 1924).

29   'Les étrangers chez nous', *La Dépêche* (12 May 1924).

30   See Pierre Milza, 'L'image de l'Italie et des Italiens du XIXe siècle à nos jours', *Les Cahiers de l'IHTP* 28 (June 1994), pp. 71–82; and Pierre Milza, *Français et Italiens à la fin du XIXe siècle* (Rome: Ecole française de Rome, 1981).

31   'La qualité de l'immigration italienne', *Le Midi socialiste* (28 December 1925).

32   'Le Foyer Français', *La Dépêche* (6 March 1926).

33   Cited in G. Bazalgues, 'L'intégration des Italiens à Sète ou la revanche sur le ghetto', in *'Estrangiers', ici des gens d'ailleurs* (Aix-en-Provence:

Edisud, 1985) 80. The editors wish to thank Chris Meredith for his help in translating this rhyme.

34  'Voyage en Italie il y a un demi-siècle', *L'Express du Midi* (28 August 1927).

35  *L'Union centrale agricole* (November 1924).

36  *La Voce dei campi* (May 1926).

37  Anne-Marie Thiesse, *Ecrire la France: le mouvement littéraire régionaliste de langue française entre la Belle époque et la Libération* (Paris: Presses Universitaires de France, 1991); P. Vernois, *Le roman rustique de Georges Sand à Ramuz (1860–1925)* (Paris, Nizet, 1962).

38  E. Labat, *L'âme paysanne* (Paris: Delagrave, 1919).

39  Bernard Poche, 'Sociologie de l'auto-référence', *Espaces et sociétés*, 70–1 (1993) 33–53; and 'Lorsque l'étranger cesse de l'être ou le pouvoir naturalisateur du local', *Espaces et sociétés* 46 (1985), pp. 121–7.

40  *Enquête agricole, 1923,* Archives départementales du Lot (7M 44); Archives départementales du Tarn-et-Garonne (7M 1175).

41  Pesquidoux, *Sur la glèbe*, p. 209.

42  'Une enquête optimiste', *La Dépêche* (18 August 1925).

43  *La Croix du Midi* (4 October 1925).

44  Daniel Loddo and Aimé Mucci, *Il canto de la carbonara. Charbonniers italiens de Grésigne* (Cordae/La Talvera, 1999); Aimé Mucci, *Les forçats de la forêt; L'épopée des charbonniers* (Toulouse: Association cultures et traditions euro-Méditérranéennes/Editions Universitaires du Sud, 2002).

45  Ralph Schor, *L'opinion Française et les étrangers, 1919–39* (Paris, Publications de la Sorbonne, 1985).

# Part III

---

# The Margins Within

# Chapter seven

# Insecurity and no-go areas

*Cathérine Levy (translated by Sharif Gemie
and Margaret Majumdar)*

### Translators' note

*Much of this paper turns around the concept of 'la sécurité' and its opposite,
'l'insécurité'. Readers should bear in mind that both these terms have far
wider meanings in French than their English-language homonyms suggest,
and that these terms became central to the 2002 French election campaigns.*

An essential function of the modern state, from which it draws
much of its legitimacy, is the provision of security, or safety, for
members of society. The concept of security, however, can be
defined in many different ways. Security is a public matter when
it concerns a common interest within the state's borders, in cases
that link the nation to the territory. At the same time, the
inhabitants' security is also a guarantee of their liberty. Security
is therefore a concept that has both collective and individual
dimensions. As a concept, it originated in the French Revolution,
in the form of the right to security. This idea provoked immediate
debate concerning the issues of, on the one hand, security of
possessions and individuals and, on the other hand, the right to
live and work. The first set of concepts implied the creation of a
repressive apparatus, while the second, on the contrary, suggested
the exercise of rights and a relative equality. The history of social
and political struggles that have developed over the past two
centuries can be placed in the context formed by these two
contrasting interpretations of security.

Principles of collective international forms of security and – since
1944 – social security have guaranteed not just political rights, but
also the exercise of social rights which, through a redistribution

of wealth, allow a relative equality between workers and property owners. Indeed, the egalitarian nature of social rights contrasts with the subordination implied in work contracts and property rights. Social rights strengthen integration: they imply 'equal membership of the city'.[1] On the other hand, property rights separate people. Once the balance of power is on the side of the property owners, society will be dominated by the principles of the security of goods, individuals and immediate profit, and the social framework itself will be threatened.

Social rights – like social classes, capital, factories and politics – are situated in the arena in which the confrontation between individual and collective rights unfolds, between what the law proclaims and what it practises. Such rights are applied within state borders. Towards the end of the twentieth century, the consolidation of the European Community modified both the concept and function of borders. While the borders that surround each European state still exist, at least as a representation of the territorial space within which national laws are applied, the same borders no longer exclude those who do not share a common national identity. Instead, new borders within the national territory demarcate differentiated access to rights and to the law. In particular, a third-world workforce still exists, caught within a framework constructed by colonial politics by other means and justified as priorities of a security, financial and economic nature. A similar denial of rights is also applied to all those who live in the precarious condition of 'social insecurity'.

Insecurity, a recurrent theme in the French ideology, is represented as a social fact, to be fought about but never to be understood. Since 1983, political groups inspired by social-democratic ideals have adapted themselves, step by step, to neo-liberalism and its security politics. Proclaiming the wisdom of values such as individualism, competition and the benefits of consumerism, these political groups have contributed to the rise of social violence. Their model of the neo-individual is based on the same values of acquisition and the crushing of rivals that are not so different from those adhered to by the most petty delinquent who, however, does not possess the same legitimacy.

In the form in which it has developed over the past twenty years, insecurity is primarily created by the relationship between work and unemployment. It is not, however, this type of insecurity that has dominated successive governments' attention, nor has it been the subject of their legislative initiatives.

## 1. Social insecurity

In 1944, the state proposed that it would provide its citizens with security that would act as 'a guarantee against the risks which workers and their families face'. This principle formed the foundation for subsequent legislation that, over the years, provided a partial fulfilment of the original proposal.

After 1975 and the shift from 'ordinary' unemployment to mass unemployment, a process started that eroded protection and security; that is, social security. Forms of employment that once appeared atypical – seasonal, temporary, part-time – became increasingly common. New economic discourses and the modernization of social security reflected the same values: they sought to impose the 'European' social model that took shape during the 1990s. Their priority was economic efficiency. Social institutions were not abandoned if they could be converted into sources of profit, such as pension funds or private insurance schemes. Successive policies were based on the argument that profits would create jobs. While waiting for the accomplishment of 'full employment of part-timers', governments created a corresponding social security framework to provide the essential minimum for the popular classes. The implementation of such forms of cut-price protection changed, within a few years, the welfare function that the state owes to society. A new vocabulary was devised to change the manner in which the working class was represented by the state and to justify tougher forms of control over these sectors.

The year 1983 is a key date in modern history because it was then that the 'insecurity phobia' returned, in a manner that looks remarkably familiar today. The similarities are striking. First, a social crisis, involving unemployment and dispersed and defensive struggles around issues such as housing, pensions and *sans-papiers*.[2] Second, an international crisis, with the government involved in conflicts that have not been formally declared 'wars' (in 1983 it was the Middle East, Libya in particular, and in Africa), but that result in the same security risks as if they had. These conflicts provoke terrorist attacks, the reinforcement of border controls, repression, the undermining of civil liberties and human rights, and so on. The key difference between 2002 and 1983 lies in the industrial conflicts of 1983, principally in the automobile industries at Aulnay and Poissy, near Paris, which were mainly fought by migrant workers, stigmatized as 'the enemy within' by Pierre Mauroy.[3] He even labelled them Shi'ites, implying a link with Iran, while – as Maghrebians – they must have been Sunni Muslims. There followed predictable debates about replacing foreigners with French workers, and of the 'cultural distance' between the French and these migrants: an ideological translation of racist principles. Within the working class it became normal to classify people by their geographic or 'cultural' origins, even though women, young people and the old all live grouped together. The histories of colonization and migration have thus become an integral part of both 'national' and working-class history. We see here the continuation of a colonial relationship, in which immigrants have no status beyond their ability to work. Immigrants are the weak link in the working class: they are the first to be attacked, and their experience indicates the future of all other employees.

There is also a continuity from 1983 to the present in the manner in which immigrants are represented: if the African – or more exactly, the Malian – can still be portrayed as the *sans-papier*, a person completely dominated by an exploitative system and therefore *sans-danger* [not a threat], the Maghrebian workers, usually conflated with Algerians, have a quite different connotation. They are the unskilled labourers within the production process. They are capable of revolt, of strikes, they can be 'naturalized', but they are also, and above all, the symbol of the independence struggle, of the Algerian War and of that shared past that has not yet been 'digested'. From the *fellagha* of the 1960s to the Taliban is but a short step . . .

It was in 1983 that the ethic of solidarity that provided the foundation of the social state began to erode. Restrictions to unemployment benefits were introduced, leading to the creation of Plan d'Aide au Retour à l'Emploi (PARE – a 'New Deal' style programme to aid the integration of the unemployed into work). Allowances became increasingly conditional, and both their amount and duration were cut. Solidarity was replaced by individual assistance, judged by merit. 'May the best win' was the motto of the ruling classes. It was imposed as a principle onto the whole of society, for example, as free competition between firms, including those in the public sector that had to be 'opened up' to competition, and also as competition between individuals. As Lordon has argued, 'while Fordism had worked to neutralize competing forces, neo-liberalism liberated them', in the belief that such measures would resolve the crisis.[4]

Security is not only about maintaining property rights but also refers to a sense of physical integrity; that is to say, those qualities that allow people to take care of themselves, house themselves, feed themselves, clothe and educate themselves. France's employment record suggests that these resources are by no means certain. The level of unemployment, as defined officially, rose from 10.8 per cent in 1990 to 12.8 per cent in 1999, while the number of non-standard, insecure jobs has also increased. It has been estimated that six or seven million people are in a materially difficult position that could reasonably be described as insecure or precarious.

Conditions have been made worse by the suppression in 1986 of the requirement of an administrative authorization for all dismissals. An employer is now allowed to dismiss any employee without any restraints, as has happened for instance at EuroDisney and McDonalds. There have been abuses of the right to dismiss employees for economic reasons. This means that even someone with a permanent contract may feel some degree of insecurity. Labour legislation, already weakened by the turn to 'flexibility', now also allows the creation of 'special' categories of jobs. This category is principally composed of temporary posts (60 per cent), acting positions (30 per cent) and training or subsidized posts (10 per cent). The number of these jobs has quadrupled in the last fifteen years.[5] In 1998, 9 per cent of all employees, or about one and three-quarter million people, worked in such posts.[6] More than a third of these workers were forced to accept 'involuntary underemployment'. They continued to look for other jobs and were still registered with the Agence Nationale Pour l'Emploi (ANPE) – the equivalent of the Jobcentre.[7]

This level of job insecurity develops into a new sort of domination, based on a generalized and permanent state of insecurity, forcing workers into submission and into accepting exploitation. Such conditions closely resemble the original, unrestrained capitalism of the early nineteenth century, and can be characterized as 'flexploitation': the rational organization of insecurity.[8]

Rates of unemployment vary both according to social categories and region or area. The old industrial zones, whether they have re-converted or not, have been more severely affected than many city quarters. Special Urban Zones (ZUS) have been created on the edges of some cities.[9] About four and a half million people live in such areas, usually in social housing. They are mostly drawn from the more fragile sectors of the population: the unskilled, with few qualifications if any, and with low incomes. In 1999, unemployment levels in these areas were double the national average (25.4 per cent).[10] One job in five is insecure – temporary, a training course or an acting position – while the national average is one in eight. The rates of economic activity have also generally declined in such areas, while they are rising elsewhere. The young form a particularly significant sector among the unemployed: while youth unemployment is rising everywhere, it is particularly serious in these zones. Here, it rose from 28.5 per cent in 1990 to 38.6 per cent in 1999. It should also be remembered that people under twenty-five cannot claim Revenu minimum d'insertion (RMI – an approximate equivalent of the minimum wage), and that more than one-third of the people who live in the ZUS are under twenty, while the national average is one-quarter. In other words, the young people of such areas, even if they are qualified and even if they are 'French', face discrimination from the start.[11] Immigrants' children find that naturalization, as a result of their birth on French territory, does not change their actual status as immigrants, whether Arab, Maghrebian or Algerian.

Such people continue to be victims of a visually based stigmatization, which 'produces its own territory as a visible sign of an impossible appropriation'.[12] A factor that is at once a cause and a consequence of this stigmatization is the difficulty in travelling, in leaving the zone – first, because of the cost; second, for more complex reasons such as a lack of knowledge of the areas outside the zone, which seem like unknown territory, ruled by other codes; and last because of the police, a truly dangerous factor.[13]

## 2. Differentiated access to social rights: insecurity and public space

The law is interpreted more and more frequently in terms of the allocation of appropriate rights to recognized groups. 'Legislative practices are tending to harmonize the letter of the law with new lifestyles, forms of work, new technology, new forms of family and new social relationships . . . The law is becoming a means to register the lifestyle of a community.'[14] The concept of the law as providing equal rights for all was debated: this was precisely because its practices were seen as inconsistent with its principles. As these rights have become more and more targeted at particular groups, there is no longer a common object around which political debate can define a single identity. Over the years, welfare policy has become shaped around particular cases and special rights, so that the security that the state provides has become a form of differentiation between groups.

An older model of relatively stable social equilibrium, recognized in the French constitution, was based on the idea that a nation's popular sovereignty was exercised through the law. This authority could take an active form, through a conflict or a strike, or it could be exercised through the legal system. Even the power of capital was included within this framework of respect for the law, until the crisis that began in Europe around 1975. The first cracks came when a new order was established that 'registered a stage in the evolution of capitalism in which the power of finance was re-affirmed', and which introduced a form of 'crisis management that gave priority to financial imperatives, which meant ignoring unemployment, and which even counted on [unemployment's] repressive effects on wage demands and security of employment'.[15] Nation-states and multi- and transnational firms wanted to dismantle labour legislation and social legislation. Governments responded to such calls and subsequently protective legislation was significantly reduced.

While the job situation deteriorated, the dominant discourse avoided discussing economic and social causes. Instead, it suggested that these newly precarious situations were the responsibility of the individuals who suffered them. The loss of a job and the difficulties of re-entering the labour market were all the fault of the unemployed. These new, individualistic interpretations grew more common.

From these premises, an argument was constructed that the unemployed should not benefit from the state's generosity unless they gave something back in return; that is, they should prove that they were not profiting from the state. Control measures on recipients of social security were therefore justified. To obtain benefits, recipients had to accept obligations, which were monitored. The unemployed were seen as inherently 'suspect'.

Rules and regulations multiplied. Governments did not consider the causes of unemployment – principally management strategies and market forces – but only its effects, which, inevitably, took different forms in different cases. They were therefore confronted by a variety of situations to which they applied a range of measures. At the same time, successive changes limited both the amount and the duration of benefits, and also increased the range of benefits available, each with particular requirements. A subtle set of distinctions was made between various types of unemployed people, each targeted by this or that measure, designed to re-integrate them into society. It was almost as if each person was given an individual label, designed to stress difference and allocate a place. Such categories prevented unemployed people from taking initiatives, as they were required to stay within the borders of their category. It was not the particular unemployed person, with his or her specific qualities, that mattered, but the recipient and his or her label, such as 'less than six months out of work', 'RMI-ist', 'under 25s', 'single parent', etc. There were therefore invisible, but nonetheless real, borders between each status, outlining a sector within which some protection was offered. Leaving the sector, however, meant entry into a more threatening zone; no longer being a target of prescribed measures meant losing part or all of one's rights. Such classifications, dividing unemployed workers into groups and sub-groups, were acts of 'that political power *par excellence*, which is the power to form groups, to manipulate the objective structure of society': the power to impose a social vision.[16]

Administrative policies imposed an image of society within which the unemployed had become the excluded or the poor, loose labels that contributed to the obliteration of any sense of community of interest. Instead, 'common-sense' representations were imposed, which identified the group by the conditions that they experienced. In fact, the 'poverty' created by a low income is a comparative term: no one experiences 'poverty' in itself, and one can easily be waged and poor. These terms only refer to a conflation of individual experiences, with no reference to the social structures in play. 'The "excluded" is a name for those who have no name, just as "market" is a word for a world that is not a world.'[17] This loss of a designation – an ability to express their ideas by the working class as a united social category – and their consequent loss of visibility, allowed the government to ignore the causes of the crisis: capitalism's economic policies. As Marx noted, such policies created a 'correlation between the accumulation of capital and the pauperisation ... within the very class that produces capital'. The designation of modern capitalism as a 'market' is another example of the same drive to avoid all analysis of social relationships: there is just the market, which, by the simple power of individual competition, will bring about an era of equality and democracy across the world.

The laws and regulations governing the particular treatment of a specific section of society are based on these new representations, which are presented as self-evident, and not on any analysis of social reality. The new policies are essentially compensatory interventions – housing benefits, attendance allowances and subsidized health care – for those unfortunates who, by their 'unemployability', their fecklessness, their incompetence, have found themselves here. Such interventions merely provide limited access to some social rights. To benefit from these compensations, unemployed people must stay within their status, as all benefits are conditional, and the move from one status to another automatically results in the loss of some rights. This results in a confinement or a relegation into a smaller and smaller zone. This zone resembles in part that which was reserved for cheap colonial workers in the 1960s.[18]

Access to benefits is dependent on the administration's decisions. For example, unemployment benefit was originally understood as an insurance payment following the loss of a job. It has gone through a series of transformations, resulting in a decline of both its level and its duration. Today, in the form of assistance for the return to work (PARE), it has become a contract or, in other words, 'precarious', as it depends on the administration's perception of the manner in which the contract is fulfilled. Several authorities are involved: the ANPE, the RMI, the benefits agencies, and the National Fund for Family Allowances (Caisse nationale des allocations familiales).

These agencies are not separate from each other, but overlap. Their role is to monitor the recipients of benefits and to check that they are searching for work in the required manner. They also investigate the recipients' daily lives to check that they are not receiving some outside income. Such activities lead to the refusal of benefits. According to ANPE figures, there were 47,193 such cases in 1990, and 225,408 in 2000. Their numbers increased dramatically after 1995. Such cases are not simply examples of the withdrawal of benefits, but truly of the deprivation of freedom. It is a new method by which to manage 'the dangerous classes', a social control that functions continuously. Within such authority structures 'nothing is ever finished'.[19]

Spot checks into people's daily lives can have serious consequences, in particular the suppression of their income. The Caisse d'Allocations familiales, a specialist in the recovery of unwarranted benefits, claims to recover 'millions' each year, mainly through domestic visits. When confronted with such a visit, individual recipients are often unable to exercise their rights. The presumption of proof is turned round: the administration is not required to demonstrate the justice of its sanction, but recipients have to prove that agency is wrong. Often they are required to provide positive evidence: they must prove that they are seeking work. Sometimes it is a negative point that must be demonstrated. Proving that one is not benefiting from a supplementary income is a particularly complex exercise, as one has to find material evidence to prove that something does not exist.

## 3. No-go areas and the politics of security

Regulatory control bodies are principally concerned with the popular classes: they are considerably less energetic in their surveillance of the regulations concerning wages, hours and conditions of work. Yet there are many delinquent employers. In 2000, there were 537,000 cases reported, involving warnings or prosecutions, of which 49 per cent concerned health and workplace conditions.[20] It should be noted that such data is gathered by the Inspecteurs du travail (Labour Inspectorate), whose numbers have been considerably reduced over the last twenty years, meaning fewer workplace visits and fewer cases being brought against employers.

In 2001, la Caisse d'Assurance Maladie (Medical Insurance Fund) for waged workers found evidence for more than 700,000 workplace accidents sufficiently serious to result in absence from work. This figure has risen by more than 3.2 per cent in a single year. Over the past twelve years there has been a slow, but continuous, rise in workplace accidents. Numbers have dropped in industrial firms, partly because so many firms are closing. They have risen sharply in the service sector, within which two out of every five workers are employed, including areas such as canteens, restaurants and cleaning: all areas in which the proportion of temporary workers is rising.[21] Temporary and short-term contracts have certainly contributed to the rise of workplace accidents: workplace medical services find it difficult to monitor temporary workers who, by definition, are only present for a short period of time. Their brief presence in the workplace also means a far shorter training in workplace safety, or sometimes none at all, because they change their positions so quickly. Worse still, temporary workers are most often given the most difficult and the most dangerous jobs.

In 2001, l'Inspection du travail also uncovered more than ten thousand cases of illegal work. Many different forms are included in this category: hidden work, the employment of unauthorized foreigners, work involving National Insurance fraud, and so on. Few of these cases are followed by prosecutions. Besides, it is unclear whether the variations in the numbers of cases reflect real rises and falls, or whether they are merely a reflection of the shortage of inspection staff. The same observation can be made about the monthly crime figures, which depend on the number of recorded complaints and the levels of police activity.

One of the conditions for the exercise of one's rights of freedom of speech and circulation is the right to security, safety and – in general – protection. Social protection laws are an integral part of one's liberties. They must offer, as a matter of principle, the means by which all residents of a territory can live. The application of justice should restore rights to the victims of crimes, while the police should guarantee the maintenance of public order. The quite distinct functions of justice and policing, however, tend to become confused. This point explains today's confusion between serious crimes and minor offences, and the conflation of criminality with delinquency. Security, in the new interpretation, has been redefined into first, a logical accessory of an uncontrolled social situation, dominated by social insecurity; and second, a means by which to shift the ideological landscape.

The state's authority is no longer limited to the actions of the social security agencies. It is seconded by the police, who act in the cases of foreigners, *sans-papiers*, and on targeted sections of the population, such as the young; those who look like foreigners (in such cases, French nationality is no protection); and those who live in certain areas, such as well-known urban trouble spots. While breaches of labour law rarely lead to prosecutions against firms, controls triggered by facial features or physical appearance often are followed by legal proceedings resulting in expulsion or detention, and sometimes both. These repressive measures are surprisingly frequently exercised against working-class children. On average, only 28 per cent of those stopped by the police experience any further legal proceedings. This proportion, however, rises to 87 per cent when minors are concerned.[22] Today, there are about a hundred police officers for every one youth worker, and these figures give a clear indication of the type of protection and security that the state is implementing.

This situation grew worse after 11 September 2001. The European Commission proposed an 'extensive' definition of terrorism, and the French government passed the 'security in daily life' law. This measure introduced some immediate changes into penal and immigration legislation, by which 'petty delinquents, asylum seekers and anti-globalization protestors can all be equated with terrorists'.[23] Travelling without a ticket or gathering in a building entrance can be punished by a prison sentence. The state's definition of security is therefore reduced to the surveillance and repression of precisely those sectors of the population whose lives are least secure. 'In order to protect security, the police act in countless cases in which the judicial situation is not clear and, frequently, they function as a crude restraint in the lives of citizens already strictly defined by regulations.'[24]

Insecurity was a central issue in the presidential and legislative elections of 2002 and has become a recurring theme in many subsequent bills. A project by the Garde des Sceaux (the approximate equivalent of the Lord Chancellor) proposes the creation of 3,300 new posts of 'local judges': people with no official status, half-way between a Wild West sheriff and a notable. These judges will enact quick justice for grassroots France [La France d'en-bas]: immediate court appearances, provisional detention (which will become the norm rather than the exception), penalties for those aged ten and above, detention for those aged thirteen and above, judgements to be decided *in absentia*, etc. A project from the Ministry of the Interior works in a similar manner: 18,000 new police officers, whose priorities will be recovering stolen mobile phones and cars, and acting against delinquent and anti-social behaviour. In sum, they will be directed against petty delinquency. The danger in these projects is that they will make scapegoats out of those with whom 'delinquency is almost automatically associated'[25] – the migrants, whether real or imaginary, the travellers and minors. This is the real meaning of a 'zero tolerance' crime policy.

These projects will be completed by the construction of new prisons and centres of detention. Places for 11,000 new prisoners will be created. In February 1999 there were 51,200 people held in French prisons: only 2,000 of them were women.[26] Most were young: half were under thirty, with prisoners most likely to be aged between twenty-one and twenty-five. Patterns of imprisonment follow structures of social inequality: the 'popular' classes are most represented. Three-quarters of male prisoners left school before they were eighteen, whereas the average age for the completion of full-time education is twenty-one. Of those with previous work experience, one-half had been manual workers, but one in seven had never worked. Forty-seven per cent of prisoners' fathers were manual workers. Their mothers were most likely to be without jobs (54 per cent) or to be workers in service industries.

Some other features marked out the masculine prison population. They came from big families (more than half of them had four brothers or sisters); 24 per cent were born abroad, while only 13 per cent of the total French population were not born in France; they came from fragile families: half of male prisoners left their families before they were nineteen, while the national average is twenty-one. More than half were single men. Among those who were not, their partners' work patterns resembled those of their mothers.

Other detention centres were proposed for foreigners without the right to stay in France. There are already many such detention centres near airports and coastal ports, in which migrants are denied all legal rights, contrary to international conventions.

## Conclusion

'Insecurity phobia' is based on the same principles as similar scares in the past: the violence of capitalism has a direct effect on

*At the Border*

the working class, which then blames a section within itself for this violence – and this section is regulated by colonial-style administrations. In this manner, colonial history is being reproduced within the borders of France, in zones where the migrants, the unemployed and their children are being relegated or enclosed. In the current international context they are all labelled as 'potential enemies', or at least as suspects. They are regulated by forms of monitoring that are illegal and discriminatory. While there are countless administrative mistakes and blunders, these are tolerated, because the administration's agents act with impunity. This impunity leads to a lack of respect, which, in turn, leads to 'la haine'. Violations of civil liberties should result in legal proceedings, initiated by a third party. In the absence of such procedures, a desire for revenge accumulates.

Public spaces, roads and areas of circulation are also zones for stopping, resting and self expression. 'The street' is a place from which demands are made: it is the space for demonstrations, delegations and petitions; it allows a political discourse of popular demands. Political actors who aim to express the *vox populi* in political terms must grasp the key elements of such agitation, so different from the silence of the majority. When public space is under police control, however, it becomes reduced to a mere road, a means of circulation from one private place to another.

Public safety has been reinterpreted to become a means to demonstrate how well the state protects goods and persons by the mobilization of the forces of law and order. Public space becomes just a space for circulation within the limits imposed by police controls. 'Police rule' demonstrates, in reality, the point at which the state, whether due to powerlessness or due to the internal logic of all judicial order, can no longer guarantee the objectives it desires at all costs.'[27]

## Notes

1   E. Balibar, 'Communisme et citoyenneté, réflexion sur la politique d'émancipation à la fin du 20ème siècle', Paper given at the conference *En Mémoire de N. Poulantzas.*

2   *Sans-papiers*: migrants present on French territory who do not possess the legal right to work, and who often lack other critical documents.

3   See the comments by E. Hobsbawm in *Nations et Nationalisme*, 'One cannot deny the power of feeling which lead groups of "us" to create

ethnic or linguistic identities against the threat of "those foreigners", above all at the end of the twentieth century when the insane wars have unleashed a great reinforcement of patriotic enthusiasm . . . and when xenophobia has become the most common mass ideology in the world', (p. 313).

4   F. Lordon, 'Violences néolibérales', *Mouvement* (autumn 2002).

5   See the data in 'Interim et CDD, parcours, usages, enjeux', one of the 'dossiers thématiques' issued by INSEE-DARES-Liaisons sociales, April 2001, in which new forms of 'precarious' employment are analysed.

6   *Enquête emploi de l'INSEE,* 1998.

7   ILO provides the following definition: 'Employees who work less than the normal hours of work, and who are seeking further supplementary employment.' More than half of temporary workers and about 40 per cent of trainee workers are underemployed.

8   Pierre Bourdieu, *Choses dites* (Paris: Minuit, 1987).

9   ZUS: inter-urban areas that have been designated as priority areas for local authorities because of their problems. In 1996, 751 such zones were identified. Alongside the ZUS, and partially overlapping with them, are the Zones de Redynamisation Urbaine, and the Zones Franches Urbaines. These allow special fiscal measures to benefit employers, urban job creation schemes, and other measures concerning commerce, environmental renewal, etc.

10  INSEE, 835 (March 2002).

11  The inhabitants of the ZUS and other urban zones who are targeted by urban renewal programmes such as 'la politique de la ville' find that they are stigmatized if they have non-French names, and also by their faces, and even by their postal codes.

12  A. Sayad, *La double absence* (Paris: Seuil, 1999), p. 357.

13  A return ticket for a half-hour journey from Sevran to Paris costs about 10 euros. Val Fourré is only accessible by train and bus, and Dammarie les Lys by RER and bus. It should not be forgotten that about eight million people live in the suburbs.

14  J. Rancière, *Lignes* (mai 2002).

15  G. Duménil and D. Lévy, *Crise et sortie de crise* (Paris: PUF, 2000).

16  P. Bourdieu, *Choses dites* (Paris: Minuit, 1987), pp. 164–5.

17  A. Badiou, *Lignes* (May 2002), p. 33.

18  One could also cite, before them, the experience of the Algerian migrant workers. The first of them, defined as 'sellers of their label force', arrived in mainland France in 1871.

19  G. Deleuze, *Pourparlers* (Paris: Minuit, 1990).

20  *Statistiques d'activité de l'Inspection du Travail* (Ministère du Travail, 2002).

21  Premières synthèses, le risque d'accident du travail varie avec la conjuncture économique, août 2001.

22  Data from PJJ (Protection judiciaire de la jeunesse – Judicial Protection of the Young), which is based in the Ministère de l'Education Nationale and the Ministère de la Justice. 'The numbers of

condemnations of children in courts have doubled in ten years, from 35,000 in 1990 to 70,000 in 2001. Prison sentences have also doubled in the same period, reaching four thousand in 2001. About 70% of under-age prisoners re-offend.'

23  Statement by E. Syre-Marin, President of the Magistrates' Union, November 2001.

24  Walter Benjamin, 'Critique de la violence', *Ouevres*, Vol. I (Paris: Gallimard, 2000), p. 211.

25  Sayad, *La double absence*, p. 400.

26  'L'histoire familiale des détenus', *INSEE première* 708 (April 2000).

27  Benjamin, *Critique de la violence*, p. 217.

# Chapter eight

# The Maghrebian community in France: defining the borders

*Dawn Marley and Judith Broadbridge*

The borders of a society are not only geographical or physical: they may also be cultural and linguistic, and exist within a society. Certain groups within a national society may be isolated, to a greater or lesser degree, due to these borders. Ever since the creation of the *République, une et indivisible*, official French discourse has denied the existence of such internal, invisible borders in France. All French citizens are equal, states the constitution; there can be no 'minorities' or 'communities', simply a national community, composed of individuals who are all absolutely equal. Nevertheless, everyone knows that some French citizens are more equal than others, and that those whose parents or grandparents were immigrants from outside Europe are not usually as equal as those whose ancestors really were the *Gaulois*. This gap between official discourse and social reality is referred to by Michèle Tribalat as 'complete schizophrenia'.[1] She points out that the lack of official data on ethnic minorities in France does not prevent most people from having a clear idea about what different groups are like and of how easily they tend to adapt to the French way of life. Although French citizens may claim to agree with the idea that they are all equal, regardless of origins, in reality certain groups are not viewed in the same light. This chapter is concerned specifically with the group of French citizens whose origins lie in the Maghreb. This Arabic word, meaning 'west', is commonly used in France to refer to the three countries of North Africa formerly under French colonial rule: Algeria, Morocco and Tunisia. Inhabitants of these countries are collectively known as '*Maghrébins*' or '*Arabes*' in France, as are their descendants, even when they have been born and brought up in France and know no other home. Whilst legally there is no discrimination against any French citizen, regardless of ethnic origin, in practice people of Maghrebian origin are routinely treated differently to other French citizens: Muslims in general, and Maghrebians in particular, are often viewed in a hostile light. Hargreaves accounts for this hostility thus:

> *At least three sets of factors are involved: the unhappy legacy of decolonization in North Africa, the heightened visibility of anti-western Islamic states in international politics, and feelings of personal insecurity linked to the processes of globalization and economic restructuring with which France and other industrial countries have been grappling since the 1970s.*[2]

The aim of this chapter is to examine the objective and subjective boundaries of this community, and in particular to examine the role of language in defining and perpetuating a community identity. The primary focus of our study will be the findings of a sociolinguistic questionnaire survey among university students at a number of French universities. In the light of this study, we will consider the continuing existence of the Maghrebian community in two ways. First, we will consider its 'ethnolinguistic vitality'. This concept, developed by Giles et al., proposes a means of assessing the extent to which a minority language is likely to survive, taking into account both objective and subjective factors.[3] Second, we will consider the influence of Maghrebian culture on 'mainstream' French culture and the reflected impact of this on the Maghrebian community in France. We will also comment on the importance of religion as an element of cultural identity for Maghrebians, and the relationship between religion and language. As a result, we will comment on the way in which the borders of this community have evolved, from being based on a very clear 'national' allegiance, to a more tenuous linguistic and cultural base. It will become clear that the borders are by no means clear, and it is difficult to determine how they will evolve in the future.

Before looking in any more detail at the Maghrebian community in France, it is important to place the study in a wider sociolinguistic context, examining the role and status of the relevant languages both in France and in the Maghreb, and looking at language policy and attitudes on both sides of the Mediterranean.

## 1. Non-indigenous minority languages in France

The French language, perhaps more than most national languages, plays a particularly significant role within French national identity. In the early part of the twentieth century, it came close to being the only mother tongue of French residents, after centuries of being promoted to the detriment of regional languages. The other languages of France had, on the whole, been unable to maintain their position after the introduction of free education, exclusively in French, in the 1880s. Already changes in society over the nineteenth century – improved transport, growth in industry and rural exodus – had all contributed to the increased use of French as a *lingua franca* in all classes of society, and the concomitant decline of the other languages of France. Once free compulsory education was introduced, this decline was dramatic.

However, regional languages did not quite disappear, and by the late 1960s there were signs of a 'comeback', accompanied by another threat to the national supremacy of French: the arrival of exogenous languages: those of the immigrant workers who arrived *en masse* in the 1950s. Following the Second World War, the French government believed that the quickest way to rebuild the country would be to employ immigrant labour. The preferred sources of this labour force were the neighbouring countries that had provided workers after the First World War – Italy, Belgium, Spain, and even Portugal and Poland. However, the numbers coming from these countries were insufficient to meet the demands of France's growing economy, and by the 1950s the majority of immigrant workers were coming from France's overseas colonies, primarily Algeria, and to a lesser extent Morocco and Tunisia. This phenomenon is well documented in French, and a very accessible account is provided in English by Hargreaves.[4]

Initially the presence of so many non-French speakers was not perceived as problematic, because it was assumed that they would return to their home countries. During the 1950s and 1960s workers tended to come as single men, staying for a limited period and returning. However, more and more workers took advantage of the programme of 'regroupement familial' (family reunification), and by the end of the 1970s there were large numbers of Maghrebian families settled in France. Although the French government tried, in the 1950s, to discourage family reunification for Maghrebian immigrants – whilst encouraging it for European immigrants they were increasingly unsuccessful in this.[5] It became clear that there would not be a mass 'return' and that France would have to adapt to the permanent presence of a large, partially non-French speaking community.

Two decades later, in 1999, a number of languages whose origins lie outside the Hexagon were incorporated into the list of 'languages of France' – Yiddish, Romany, Western Armenian, Berber and Dialectal Arabic. These languages were among the seventy-five mentioned in a report by Bernard Cerquiglini, then director of the Institut National de la Langue Française, as regional or minority languages of France, to be protected under the terms of the European Charter for Regional or Minority Languages (1992). These five languages are included in the list because they are 'languages used by nationals of the state that differ from the language or languages used by the rest of the state's population but which, although traditionally used within the territory of the state, cannot be identified with a particular area thereof' (article 1.c). They are deemed to come under the remit of the charter because they are not protected anywhere else.[6] Dialectal Arabic and Berber are the vernaculars of the Maghreb, yet have no official status: in Tunisia it is claimed that almost 100 per cent of the population are Arabic speakers, while in Algeria and Morocco it is estimated that anything up to 50 per cent of the population are native speakers of Berber languages, also known as Tamazight. Tamazight languages are indigenous to North Africa, and are very distantly related to Arabic, the language introduced by the Arab invaders in the seventh century. None of these vernaculars is used as a written language, and no Tamazight script is known in the Maghreb.[7] Thus the mother tongues of the Maghreb, with no official status in their home countries, are now protected by law in France.

The inclusion of these languages seems to suggest that they are statistically important in France – a suggestion it is difficult to confirm, given the lack of a language question on the census until 1999. In the absence of these figures, Dominique Caubet suggests that there could be as many as two million Arabic speakers in France, and a million Berber speakers.[8] Caubet also suggests that the popularity of the *baccalauréat d'arabe maghrébin* (she estimates that about 2 per cent of students taking the *baccalauréat* take the optional exam in *arabe maghrébin*) is an indication of the vitality of this dialect.[9] Despite the fact that the *baccalauréat d'arabe maghrébin* exists, this language does not enjoy high prestige, either in France or in the Maghreb, as we shall see later. People whose mother tongue is Maghrebian Arabic or Berber, and who acquire French at school, will generally develop a 'subtractive' bilingualism.[10] This means that, far from being perceived as an advantage, their bilingualism is perceived as a handicap. It may even be the case that such individuals would deny being bilingual.[11] These people may be aware that 'Arabic' is a language with a rich literary tradition and that it is held in high esteem throughout the Arab and Muslim world. However, if they have heard this language they will probably not have understood it, and they will almost certainly be unable to read it, hence they may not even see the connection between Standard Arabic and their dialect. Obviously if the home language is Berber there is not even the prestige of Standard Arabic as a potential source of pride, since they are very definitely not varieties of the same language. For many speakers of Maghrebian vernaculars, their home language is simply a '*dialecte*' or '*patois*' and French is the only 'real' language.

Such an attitude is not uncommon in France, a country that for centuries has sought to undermine minority languages. In Perpignan, for example, elderly speakers of Catalan would be inclined to say that French is the only language they know, because they are conscious that 'real' Catalan, the language of Barcelona, is not the same as the variety they speak. Moreover, many elderly people still have painful memories of being humiliated, as children, for not speaking French well.[12] Numerous studies among children of immigrants suggest that they frequently do not mention that they know a language other than French, and when they do, they often do not know what it is called. During a sociolinguistic study in Perpignan, for example, one of the authors met young people who claimed to speak '*le marocain*'. That this is a common practice seems to be confirmed by the instructions in the 1999 supplement to the census. The section on transmission of family languages asks informants which language(s) their parents used to speak to

them when they were children. There are a number of examples
to help informants to respond, among them the following:

> *For foreign languages, do not give the nationality but the language. Examples:*
> *don't say Algerian, Moroccan, Senegalese, but Arabic, Kabyle, Wolof, etc.*

## 2. Attitudes towards French and Arabic in the Maghreb

While the official status of languages in the Maghreb is quite
different to that in France – in all three countries 'Arabic' is the
official national language and French has no official status –
attitudes are by no means as clear-cut. Since independence (1956
for Tunisia and Morocco, 1962 for Algeria) all three countries
have pursued policies of Arabization, with varying degrees of
success. For a variety of reasons beyond the scope of this paper,
it was not possible simply to replace French with Arabic, and even
today, over forty years on, French maintains an important role in
a number of key areas, such as higher education, trade and industry
and the economy.[13] It would be useful at this stage to mention
briefly the fact that 'Arabic' is a word that covers a continuum of
languages, from the language of the Koran and Classical Arabic,
through Modern Standard Arabic (MSA), to regional dialects.
The constitutions of the Maghreb do not specify which variety of
Arabic is the national language, but in practice it is taken to mean
MSA, often referred to popularly as 'Classical Arabic', because of
its closeness to the classical written form.[14]

Very generally speaking, language attitudes in the Maghreb may
be summarized thus: Arabization is essential, and is good for the
country, but French is also very useful. Arabic is a beautiful language
and ultimately superior, but French gives access to the wider
world. The Arabic of Arabization is MSA, the written variety used
throughout the Arab world for education, administration, the
media and the majority of official functions. It is not, however,
spoken as a mother tongue by anyone in the Arab world; everyday
oral communication is generally conducted in Dialectal Arabic.
These dialects vary enormously across the Arab world, and the
dialects of North Africa are particularly far removed from the
standard and virtually incomprehensible to other Arabic speakers.
Dialectal Arabic then, far from being revered, is more often than

not dismissed as 'not a real language', and is not considered overtly to be prestigious, although some sociolinguistic studies suggest that there is a certain covert prestige.[15] As for Berber, or Tamazight, the indigenous languages of the region, they are regarded as even less prestigious. A recent resurgence of language loyalty and a growing Berber cultural movement are still regarded with suspicion by many, despite the fact that the Berber languages are the indigenous languages of the region.

Most Maghrebians are convinced, ideologically, of the need for Arabization, and believe that Arabic is the language that best expresses their national identity. However, despite the fact that the education system has for some time been fully Arabized across the Maghreb, and thus knowledge of French is reduced, studies consistently show that attitudes towards French remain favourable.[16] Although French is no longer needed in many areas of public life in the Maghreb, it continues to represent a means of access to the world outside the Maghreb. There are two areas in particular in which knowledge of French is perceived as desirable: science and technology, and the modern consumer society. French remains a prestige language, and is still regarded as more suitable than Arabic for certain domains of modern life. It should be noted in passing, however, that this role is being increasingly challenged by English. Satellite television and the internet have led to far greater exposure to English than in the past, and in strictly utilitarian terms, English is undoubtedly a more useful language for 'getting on' in the world. At present, French maintains its place in the Maghreb, but its future as first foreign language is no longer assured.

Dialectal Arabic and Berber languages have no official status anywhere in the Maghreb, and some researchers have expressed the belief that one of the hidden objectives of Arabization is to eradicate the vernaculars, in the same way that the promotion of the French language has led to the virtual disappearance of other vernaculars in France.[17] As far as Berber is concerned, the plethora of Berber (or Tamazight) cultural associations in recent years, not only in the Maghreb but worldwide, may yet prevent these languages from rapid extinction. As far Dialectal Arabic, it remains the mother tongue of at least half the population of the Maghreb (probably of almost all Tunisians), but it too may be threatened in the long term, as a new 'intermediate' Arabic appears to be evolving: less formal than Standard Arabic, but more formal than pure dialect.[18] The possibility that Dialectal Arabic might die out would probably not worry too many Maghrebians, since the standard attitude towards it is that it is not a real language, but simply a 'means of communication'. However, Dialectal Arabic, like Tamazight, has the advantage of being a truly living language, and expressing national identity in a way that MSA, being a pan-Arab language, cannot. Although people may profess a disdain for their vernacular, the truth is that these languages are the only ones that really allow them to be themselves, and if they were to be superseded by MSA, the language and culture of the Maghreb would be infinitely diminished.

## 3. The 2002 study on language among students of Maghrebian origin

Against the sociolinguistic background described above, this study was conducted among sixty-seven students at three French universities, Toulouse, Nancy and Pau, in the course of 2002, with the aim of finding out how students of Maghrebian origin perceive their own identity, and the extent to which language plays a role in this. The sample was fairly evenly divided between male and female, with 52.2 per cent (thirty-five) male and 46.3 per cent (thirty-one) female. The age range was wide for a student sample, due to a relatively high number of mature students.

Table 1. Date of birth

| | |
|---|---|
| 1970–5 | 23.9 per cent (16) |
| 1976–80 | 35.8 per cent (24) |
| 1980–5 | 38.8 per cent (26) |

### a. Place of birth and nationality

The following series of tables indicates that the majority of the sample could be classified as 'second-generation immigrants', because a large majority were born in France or arrived there at a very young age, and an even larger majority are French nationals. In other words they are, for the most part, legally French, and all but a small minority were completely educated and socialized in

France, through the medium of the French language. One might therefore assume that they would consider themselves to be French rather than Maghrebian, and yet this is far from being the case.

Table 2. Place of birth

| France | 65.7 per cent (44) |
|---|---|
| Morocco | 22.4 per cent (15) |
| Tunisia | 6 per cent (4) |
| Algeria | 3 per cent (2) |
| Other | 3 per cent (2) |

Table 3. Date of arrival in France

| From birth | 62.7 per cent (42) |
|---|---|
| Before age 5 | 11.9 per cent (8) |
| 1999 or more recently | 11.9 per cent (8) |
| 1990s | 4.5 per cent (3) |
| 1980s | 4.5 per cent (3) |
| No response | 4.5 per cent (3) |

Table 4. Nationality

| French | 68.7 per cent (46) |
|---|---|
| French/Moroccan | 1.5 per cent (1) |
| Moroccan | 14.9 per cent (10) |
| French/Tunisian | 4.5 per cent (3) |
| Tunisian | 3 per cent (2) |
| French/Algerian | 1.5 per cent (1) |
| Algerian | 1.5 per cent (1) |
| No response | 4.5 per cent(3) |

The following series of tables shows that the parents, by and large, were first generation immigrants: the majority arriving in the 1960s and 1970s. More than a third of respondents, however, put a question mark next to this question, suggesting that their parents arrived in France before they were born, and they have never taken an interest in when it was. In all probability it would have been during the 1960s and 1970s, given the age range of the respondents. Just over a quarter of the parents have French nationality, although none of them were born in France.

Table 5. Parents' country of birth

|  | Mother | Father |
|---|---|---|
| Morocco | 38.8 per cent (26) | 40.3 per cent (27) |
| Tunisia | 16.4 per cent (11) | 14.9 per cent (10) |
| Algeria | 37.3 per cent (25) | 37.3 per cent (25) |
| Other | 1.5 per cent (1) | 1.5 per cent (1) |
| No response | 6 per cent (4) | 6 per cent (4) |

Table 6. Parents' arrival in France

|  | Mother | Father |
|---|---|---|
| From birth | 1.5 per cent (1) | 1.5 per cent (1) |
| 1999 or later | 4.5 per cent (3) | 3 per cent (2) |
| 1950s | 1.5 per cent (1) | 6 per cent (4) |
| **1960s** | **20.9 per cent (14)** | **22.4 per cent (15)** |
| **1970s** | **26.9 per cent (18)** | **23.9 per cent (16)** |
| 1980s | 9 per cent (6) | 6 per cent (4) |
| No response | 35.8 per cent (24) | 37.3 per cent (25) |

Table 7. Parents' nationality

|  | Mother | Father |
|---|---|---|
| **French** | **29.9 per cent (20)** | **26.9 per cent (18)** |
| Moroccan | 31.3 per cent (21) | 32.8 per cent (22) |
| Tunisian | 9 per cent (6) | 10.4 per cent (7) |
| French/Algerian | 1.5 per cent (1) | 1.5 per cent (1) |
| Algerian | 17.9 per cent (12) | 19.4 per cent (13) |
| Other | 1.5 per cent (1) | 0 |
| No response | 9 per cent (6) | 9 per cent (6) |

### b. Language usage

The following tables detail the language habits within the families of these students, and their intentions for language use with any children they may have in the future. Inevitably, in this type of questionnaire it is difficult to decide the extent to which responses reflect reality; equally, it may be said that even if they do not reflect actual language usage, they can be valuable anyway, as they indicate language behaviour in an idealized situation. Thus it is interesting to note that well over half the informants claim to use Arabic to speak to their parents. It should not be surprising that their parents address them in Arabic, since this is in most cases the parents' first language. However, one might expect that the students, who have grown up in France, would normally respond in French. It is thus probable that many of those who claim to use Arabic in fact use mainly French, but claim to use Arabic even if it is only occasional. It is therefore significant that they should report on usage of Arabic, given the low status of the language in France and the prevailing notion that French is the language of social acceptance and ascendance. Even more significant in this respect is the clear majority who declare their intention to use Arabic with their own children in the future. A study based on participant observation, or even language diaries, may have revealed a minimal use of Arabic, but in this attitude survey, the claim of using Arabic is important because it indicates a degree of language loyalty that the informants feel even if they do not always act on it.

Table 8. When you were a child, which language(s) did your parents use to address you?

|  | *Mother* | *Father* |
| --- | --- | --- |
| French | 7.5 per cent (5) | 1.5 per cent (1) |
| **Arabic** | **37.3 per cent (25)** | **37.3 per cent (25)** |
| Berber | 14.9 per cent (10) | 13.4 per cent (9) |
| **French/Arabic** | **29.9 per cent (20)** | **38.8 per cent (26)** |
| Arabic/Berber | 9 per cent (6) | 9 per cent (6) |
| Other | 1.5 per cent (1) | |

Table 9. In which language(s) do you speak to your parents?

|  | *Mother* | *Father* |
| --- | --- | --- |
| French | 22.4 per cent (15) | 22.4(15) |
| **Arabic** | **56.7 per cent (38)** | **58.2 per cent (39)** |
| Berber | 10.4 per cent (7) | 10.4 per cent (7) |
| **French/Arabic** | **3 per cent (2)** | **3 per cent (2)** |
| Arabic/Berber | 6 per cent (4) | 6 per cent (4) |

### c. Attitudes

We asked students about their perception of their own identities, asking them to say which of the following was closest to how they felt. It is very clear that despite all the factors that might lead them to feel French, very few claim to feel totally French.

Table 10. Which language(s) do you intend to use to speak to your own children?

| | |
|---|---|
| French | 7.5 per cent (5) |
| Arabic | 7.5 per cent (5) |
| **Arabic/French** | **58.2 per cent (39)** |
| Arabic/Berber/French | 16.4 per cent (11) |
| Other* | 10.4 per cent (7) |

* 'Other' generally involved English; in two cases, only English, in the remainder a combination of English, French and Arabic.

Table 11. Identity

| | |
|---|---|
| Totally French | 3 per cent (2) |
| French first, but also Maghrebian | 9 per cent (6) |
| **Maghrebian first, but also French** | **29.9 per cent (20)** |
| **Both French and Maghrebian** | **35.8 per cent (24)** |
| Neither French nor Maghrebian | 20.9 per cent (14) |
| Totally Maghrebian | 20.9 per cent (14) |
| Other | 3 per cent (2) |

Cross-tabulations with place of birth, or with languages used with parents, do not lead to the conclusion that being born in France or speaking Arabic in the home affects the sense of identity of these young people. Eighteen of those born in France claimed that they felt both French and Maghrebian, while ten felt Maghrebian first and then French, and only two felt totally French, whereas eight felt totally Maghrebian. Whichever languages were spoken in the home, the majority claimed to feel either Maghrebian first, then French, or equally Maghrebian and French. This suggests then that it is neither the *'droit du sol'* nor the mother tongue that influences the sense of identity of young people of Maghrebian origin.

We asked one further series of questions on attitudes towards language and culture. Students were asked if they agreed or disagreed with a series of statements, detailed in the table below.

Their responses indicate a high level of awareness of the importance of conserving both the language and culture of their parents' country. They are rather less concerned about the need to write the language, which is hardly surprising given that many of their parents are probably illiterate, and they have not grown up with an awareness of the written form of their parents' language. Perhaps because of this, they do not consider that schools should be concerned with teaching these languages. Moreover, they may have had an experience of the *Enseignement des langues et cultures d'origine* (ELCO) programme, a well-intentioned but ultimately unsuccessful programme designed to help children of immigrants learn the language and culture of their parents' homelands. They disagree strongly with the idea that French is the only language worth knowing in France, apparently rejecting the idea that cultural and linguistic assimilation is essential for everyone who lives in France. Perhaps most interestingly, a large majority consider that language is an important element in the Maghrebian community in France; they consider that speaking a Maghrebian language is part of what distinguishes their community from the rest of the French population.

Table 12. Attitudes to language use

|  | Yes | No | Don't know |
|---|---|---|---|
| It is important to conserve our ancestors' culture | 89.6 per cent (60) | 1.5 per cent (1) | 6 per cent (3) |
| It is important to learn to speak our ancestors' language | 89.6 per cent (60) | 4.5 per cent (3) | 6 per cent (4) |
| It is important to learn to write their language | 67.2 per cent (45) | 10.4 per cent (7) | 22.4 per cent (15) |
| If you live in France it is a waste of time to speak languages other than French | 10.4 per cent (7) | 88.1 per cent (59) | 1.5 per cent (1) |
| It is the responsibility of schools to teach mother tongues | 13.4 per cent (9) | 62.7 per cent (42) | 23.9 per cent (16) |
| Language is an important element in the Maghrebian community in France | 88.1 per cent (59) | 6 per cent (4) | 6 per cent (4) |

## 4. Language shift and cultural integration

The preceding analysis suggests that this group of 'second-generation' Maghrebians in France is in a transitional zone, linguistically and culturally. Studies of language shift among immigrant communities in Western countries suggest that typically language shift is rapid, with the first-generation using primarily the language of their home country, but their children, who grow up in the new country, introducing the majority language into the home once they start school.[19] In Fishman's terms this can be summariszd as 'Resolution 1: B → A=A'.[20]

It is, he asserts, only one of three possible patterns, when one language enters another language territory. However, it is the 'predominant American immigrant experience' and is also the expected pattern in immigrant communities in western Europe. The ability to communicate well in French is absolutely essential to achieving any kind of success in France, and it would in fact be astonishing to discover that young people at university were not predominantly French speakers. Judging from the language usage patterns reported by these young people, it would be logical to assume that the next generation will have only a residual knowledge of Maghrebian vernaculars. However, language shift and language loss are not inevitable in such cases.

> *Minority groups can experience the fact that a shift towards the majority language does not always imply better chances for educational achievement and upward social mobility. A group may 'give away' its language without getting social-economic advantages in return. It is no longer discriminated against because of language, but because of colour, culture, etc. On the basis of such experiences, minority group members may develop strategies to foster use of the minority language and to improve proficiency in the minority language, which is then revitalized.*[21] (Appel and Muysken, 1989: 45)

It is undoubtedly the case that people of Maghrebian origin are discriminated against regardless of proficiency in French. This is underlined in a recent survey by the market research group TNS Sofres, in which young people claimed that racism in France is predominantly directed at Maghrebians (although interestingly the majority of those surveyed claimed not to share these widespread racist feelings).[22] One reaction to this could be to make greater efforts to maintain the minority language, and the questions on attitude do suggest that young people believe it is important to preserve the language and culture of their parents, even if their usage suggests otherwise.

## 5. The ethnolinguistic vitality of Maghrebian languages in France

If we look at this study in the light of the model of linguistic vitality proposed by Giles et al., it would appear that there is little hope of the languages being maintained beyond the third generation.[23] This model suggests that there are four sets of factors that may influence language maintenance: status factors, demographic factors, institutional support factors and cultural (dis)similarity. Giles et al. suggested that each of these factors could be assessed, giving an overall assessment of ethnolinguistic vitality, and thus a fair indication of the strength or otherwise of the group under consideration. We will therefore examine the likelihood of Maghrebian languages being maintained in France, according to this model.

In terms of status, the Maghrebian languages look very weak, since even in their home countries they have low status. Given that the vast majority of first generation immigrants were (or are) illiterate and in low-paid jobs, the general economic and social status associated with the language is low, and there is little widespread awareness in France of any socio-historical status for the language. (In different circumstances, for example, where migrant groups are well educated, parents can bring children up with an awareness of the 'glorious past' of their language.)

Demographic factors are similarly relatively weak: most people of Maghrebian origin live in towns, and although they often live in areas with a high proportion of other Maghrebians, they nevertheless need French for most everyday activities. A number of authors refer to the fact that France boasts a high number of mixed marriages, i.e. between 'native' French and French people of Maghrebian origin.[24] Such a trend almost inevitably means a further shift away from the use of Maghrebian languages, since the 'native' French partner is unlikely in most cases to speak the Maghrebian language, and French would of necessity be the family language.

Institutional support factors do exist, but are limited and marginal. There is little in the way of Arabic/Berber media, but in any case print media would be of little use, since most first-generation immigrants tend to be illiterate. There are radio stations catering for immigrants, or their descendants, but no television. This gap is largely filled now by satellite television: satellite ownership is widespread among the Maghrebian community, for whom Arabic language channels represent an important source of entertainment and information. The stations being watched are either from the 'home countries' and thus help to reinforce the sense of community with those countries, or from Egypt or the Middle East. As far as education is concerned, Arabic is taught in France – Classical Arabic is taught at some universities, and Maghrebian Arabic is taught in schools, although it is not viewed as being on a par with other school languages such as English or Spanish.[25] Once again, these factors are weak.

Finally, in terms of cultural (dis)similarity, the difference between French and Arabic or Berber is enormous, a factor that would normally be expected to reduce the rate of language shift, and certainly helps to explain why so many first-generation Maghrebian immigrants find French so difficult to learn. In fact, the media often seem to make much of the fact that children of immigrants are 'torn between two cultures', and the great difference between them may mean that there is sometimes more intense loyalty than there would be for a culturally more similar language, such as Italian.

The overall assessment of ethnolinguistic vitality can be expressed in the following tabular form, based on the model in Giles et al.[26]

Table 13. A model of ethnolinguistic vitality

| Status | Demography | Institutional Support | Cultural (Dis)similarity | Overall Vitality |
| --- | --- | --- | --- | --- |
| low | low | low | high | low |

Nevertheless, Giles et al. add something of a disclaimer to their model, in saying that additional factors can intervene to increase or reduce vitality. It is clear that language loss or maintenance can be affected by many factors, not all of them linguistic. In this particular case, there are two factors that may well have an impact on language maintenance. The first is the current popularity of Maghrebian culture in France; the second is the suspicion with which Islam, the religion of North Africa, is currently viewed in France. Although in general terms these factors may have very different impacts on the way the Maghrebian community is viewed, in linguistic terms they may have the same impact: for very different reasons, they may reinforce language loyalty among young people who might otherwise have abandoned the Maghrebian language completely. Each factor will now be assessed.

## 6. Maghrebian culture in France

One factor that may help to explain the professed desire to maintain the languages and culture of the Maghreb is the recent '*engouement*' ('craze' or fashion) for Maghrebian culture in France. Since the late 1990s, Maghrebian-inspired fashions have been very much to the fore in French culture, particularly in dance and music trends, although there are also examples dating back considerably further. Probably the most well known example of this is *raï*, a music form originating in Oran, in Algeria, which became extremely popular in France in the late 1980s, with Cheb Khaled among others. Equally, comedians such as Smaïn (Algerian) and Michel Boujenah (Tunisian Jewish) were already highly popular in the late 1980s. Since then, many other musicians of Maghrebian origin have found success in France, not only among Maghrebian immigrants, but among all young French people. A large number of comedians of Maghrebian origin, both Muslim and Jewish, have also been successful in recent years. Caubet has suggested that this could be a source of pride for young people of Maghrebian origin, since these 'heroes' are shared with other young people and not limited to the immigrant 'ghetto'.[27] She also suggests that it could equally induce a sense of language loyalty and pride towards their mother tongues. Although a knowledge of Arabic is certainly not essential to enjoying the music and comedy – which is precisely why it appeals to a wide audience – nevertheless the fact that these artists are known to be Arabic (or Berber) speakers could indeed contribute to a more positive appreciation of these languages on the part of young people.

### 7. Religion as an element of cultural identity

Another important element that helps to explain both the degree
of discrimination suffered by Maghrebians in France, and the
loyalty to the language and culture of the Maghreb, is the attachment to Islam, the religion of over 99 per cent of the Maghreb
today. A major reason for the discrimination suffered by people
of Maghrebian origin is their obvious religious difference. Even
when Maghrebians look completely European (and they often do),
their Arabic names indicate that they are Muslims and therefore
different. The religious difference was not viewed as an issue in
the peak years of Maghrebian immigration to France, partly because
French industry desperately needed the manpower, and partly
because everyone assumed that the immigrants would simply
stay a few years and then go home. However, once the workers'
families started coming and settling in France, it became another
matter, and by the 1980s the 'problem' of Islam began to rear its
head. It became particularly acute in 1989, when the so-called
'headscarves affair' erupted, to be followed by the Gulf War in
1991. Kaltenbach and Kaltenbach refer to the headscarves affair
as the moment when France realized that Islam was a domestic
issue.[28] The Gulf War represents the moment when French Muslims
realized that they may have a clash of loyalties, and that even if
they did not perceive it that way, other French people would assume
that they did. Subsequent events, in France and internationally,
have further contributed to the cultural identity problem of French
Muslims. The issue was evoked frequently in the late 1980s and
early 1990s, as exemplified in an interview with Nasser Ramdane,
one of the leaders of a protest movement among French high
school students in 1990–1. In the interview, entitled, 'Etre arabe
et français aujourd'hui', Ramdane claimed that although he felt
close to his parents' culture, France was his country.[29] 'Let's say
I feel "*beur*" (second-generation Maghrebian). I'm both Arab and
French.' When asked if he was a Muslim, he replied that Islam,
like all religions, was interesting, but was not exactly a 'cool' lifestyle.
His answers would probably be similar to those of many young
people who have grown up in France in a Maghrebian family.

For many French citizens of Maghrebian origin, being a Muslim
is something they would never have thought about normally, but
the ongoing headscarves affair and other domestic issues, in

conjunction with 11 September 2001 and its aftermath, mean that they often find themselves obliged to think seriously about their religious and cultural identity. In recent years, there appears to be a resurgence of interest in Islam among young people, in many cases brought about by a desire to find a clear sense of identity. Many people claim that Islam gives them a sense of identity and purpose that they were lacking in mainstream French society. If people of Maghrebian origin do decide to practice Islam, it may well have an impact on their language use and attitudes, particularly if the family language is Arabic, the sacred language of Islam. Using Arabic on a daily basis is another way of identifying with the Islamic community, and expressing an Islamic identity. Thus, a renewed interest in religion among young people may also be responsible to a certain extent for a renewed interest in North African language maintenance.

## Conclusion

This study suggests that despite the negative image of Dialectal Arabic and Berber in France and in North Africa, there is strong language loyalty amongst young people of North African origin in France. The young people in this survey mostly said that they will use Arabic or Berber with their children, albeit mixed with French, and on the whole they saw themselves as Maghrebian and French. This study does not indicate that there is a real movement to halt the shift away from Arabic and Berber, but it does suggest that young people feel proud of their origins, and that they see these languages as an important part of an identity they wish to maintain. Despite the official denial of minority identities in France, it is very clear that young French citizens whose parents immigrated from the Maghreb do not see themselves as 'typical' French citizens. They are very conscious of having a Maghrebian identity, and even though their community languages appear to have a low degree of ethnolinguistic vitality, language loyalty nonetheless appears to be an important element in their perception of group identity. The boundaries of the group, however, are not set only by language, but also significantly by the way in which the group is perceived by the rest of society. On the one hand there is the positive appreciation of certain elements of Maghrebian culture, such as music, whilst on the other hand there is the negative reaction towards the religious aspect of this culture. In the current climate, it is hard to see how this community can ever be totally assimilated into the national community. Even when young people of Maghrebian origin no longer speak Maghrebian vernaculars at all on a daily basis, and when their cultural practices are actually identical to those of their French peers, the invisible boundaries of perceived cultural, linguistic and religious difference will still be there, marking the community as distinct.

## Notes

1  Michèle Tribalat, *Faire France. Une enquête sur les immigrés et leurs enfants* (Paris: La Decouverte, 1995), p. 12.
2  Alec Hargreaves, 'The challenges of multiculturalism: regional and religious differences in France today', in William Kidd and Siân Reynolds (eds), *Contemporary French Cultural Studies* (London: Arnold, 2000), pp. 95–110 (p. 106).
3  Howard Giles, R. Y. Bourhis and D. M. Taylor, 'Towards a theory of language in ethnic group relations', in Howard Giles (ed.), *Language, Ethnicity and Intergroup Relations* (London: Academic Press, 1977), pp. 307–48.
4  Olivier Milza, *Les Français devant l'immigration* (Paris: Editions Complexe, 1988); Alec Hargreaves, *Immigration, 'race' and ethnicity in contemporary France* (London: Routledge, 1995).
5  Hargreaves, *Immigration*, pp. 15–16.
6  Anne Judge and Stephen Judge, 'Linguistic policies in France and contemporary issues: the signing of the charter for regional or minority languages', *International Journal of Francophone Studies*, 3:2 (2000).
7  For a fuller discussion of these languages, see Dawn Marley, 'Uniformity and diversity: fact and fiction in Moroccan language policy', in Kamal Salhi (ed.), *French In and Out of France. Language Policies, Intercultural Antagonisms and Dialogue* (Peter Lang, 2002), pp. 335–76.
8  Dominique Caubet, 'L'arabe dialectal en France', in *Haut Conseil de la Francophonie, Arabofrancophonie* (Paris: L'Harmattan, 2001), pp. 199–212 (pp. 200–1).
9  Caubet, 'L'arabe dialectal en France', p. 201.
10 René Appel and Pieter Muysken, *Language Contact and Bilingualism* (London: Arnold, 1989), p. 102.
11 Fabienne Melliani, *La langue du quartier, Appropriation de l'espace et identités urbaines chez les jeunes issus de l'immigration maghrébine en banlieue rouennaise* (Paris: L'Harmattan, 2000).
12 Dawn Marley, 'Ethnolinguistic minorities in Perpignan: a question-naire survey', *Journal of Multilingual and Multicultural Development*, 14:3 (1993), pp. 217–36.

13  But see: Dawn Marley, 'Uniformity and diversity: fact and fiction in Moroccan language policy'.

14  For further discussion of the varieties of Arabic see, for example, Fouzia Benzakour, Driss Gaadi and Ambroise Queffélec (eds) *Le français au Maroc* (Bruxelles: Editions Duculot, 2000).

15  See, for example, Paul B. Stevens, 'Ambivalence, modernisation and language attitudes: French and Arabic in Tunisia', *Journal of Multilingual and Multicultural Development*, 4:2–3 (1983), pp. 101–14; Dawn Marley, 'Language attitudes in Morocco following recent changes in Moroccan language policy', *Language Policy* 3 (2004), pp. 25–46.

16  Abdelali Bentahila, *Language Attitudes Among Arabic-French Bilinguals in Morocco* (Clevedon, Avon: Multilingual Matters, 1983); Ahmed Boukous, *Société, Langues et Culture au Maroc. Enjeux Symboliques* (Rabat: Faculté des Lettres et des Sciences Humaines, 1995); Mohamed Elbiad, 'The role of some population sectors in the progress of Arabization in Morocco', *International Journal of the Sociology of Language*, 87 (1991), pp. 27–44; Ouafae Mouhssine, 'Ambivalence du discours sur l'arabisation', *International Journal of the Sociology of Language*, 112 (1995), pp. 45–61; Marley, 'Language attitudes in Morocco'.

17  Boukous, *Société, Langues et Culture*; Mohamed Benrabah, *Langue et pouvoir en Algérie* (Paris: Séguier, 1999).

18  Boukous, *Société, Langues et Culture*, 35; Mansour Sayah, 'Linguistic issues and policies in Tunisia', in Kamal Salhi (ed.), *French In and Out of France. Language Policies, Intercultural Antagonisms and Dialogue* (Peter Lang, 2002), pp. 411–32 (p. 413); Moha Ennaji, 'A syntactico-semantic study of the language of news in Morocco', *International Journal of the Sociology of Language*, 112 (1995), pp. 97–111 (pp. 108–10).

19  Appel and Muysken, *Language Contact and Bilingualism*, p. 41.

20  Joshua A. Fishman, 'Language maintenance and ethnicity', *Canadian Review of Studies in Nationalism*, 1980, pp. 229–48.

21  Appel and Muysken, *Language Contact and Bilingualism*, p. 45.

22  TNS Sofres, Les jeunes et le racisme, enquête pour l'association Festival contre le Racisme (2002), *http://www.sofres.com/etudes/pol/190302_jeunesetracisme_r.htm*

23  Howard Giles, R. Y. Bourhis and D. M. Taylor, 'Towards a theory of language in ethnic group relations', in Howard Giles (ed.), *Language, Ethnicity and Intergroup Relations* (London: Academic Press, 1977), pp. 307–48.

24  Emmanuel Todd, *Le destin des immigré* (Paris: Seuil, 1994); Hargreaves, *Immigration, 'race' and ethnicity*.

25  Dominique Caubet, 'Quelques aspects de la présence maghrébine dans la culture urbaine en France', *Ethnologues*, Vol. 22, 1 (2000); Dominique Caubet, 'L'arabe dialectal en France', in Haut Conseil de la Francophonie, *Arabofrancophonie* (Paris: L'Harmattan, 2001), pp. 199–212.

26  Giles, Bourhis and Taylor, 'Towards a theory of language', p. 317.

27  Caubet, 'Quelques aspects', pp. 252–3.

28  Jeanne-Helene Kaltenbach and Pierre-Patrick Kaltenbach, *La France, une chance pour l'Islam* (Paris: Editions du Felin, 1991).

29  Hamid Barrada and Ariane Poissonnier, 'Etre arabe et français aujourd'hui', *Afrique Magazine*, 77 (1991), pp. 52–7.

# Chapter nine

# Solidarity in pariahdom? Oppression and self-oppression in gay representations in France

*Owen Heathcote*

With its tradition of the *poète maudit* and of explicit, often violent, literary eroticism, French literature and culture often seem to be crossing borders of acceptability and transgressing norms of 'good taste'. As John Phillips writes in *Forbidden Fictions*:

> *French culture has long been perceived by the English-speaking reader as somehow more 'erotic' than Anglo-Saxon culture. This impression is partly due to the large numbers of pornographic publications that have been imported from Paris since the sixteenth century, first into England and later into the United States, but also to the peculiarly French association of pornography and subversion.*[1]

The border crossing of French cultural productions is an integral part of a longstanding tradition associated with sexual explicitness and sexual violence and, perhaps even more significantly, with the belief that such violent sexual border crossing is intellectually and culturally stimulating. In France, such border crossing is seen as an important and even necessary challenge to established norms. Thus, contrary to what might be expected in Anglo-Saxon communities, the sexually violent, and for some even abhorrent, writings of the Marquis de Sade are published in the most prestigious collection of Gallimard's *La Pléiade*. Thus, too, from Gilles de Rais to Pierre Guyotat and from Monique Wittig to

Catherine Breillat, Virginie Despentes and Catherine Millet, sexual
explicitness goes hand in hand with sexual violence in what is often
claimed to be the subversion of both literary and cultural models.[2]
Such works are, supposedly, literary and counter-literary, discursive
and counter-discursive, and cultural and counter-cultural. It would
seem, then, that sexual perversion goes hand in hand with literary
subversion. Or, perhaps the reverse, that literary subversion goes
hand in hand with sexual perversion.

Although it is not always clear whether the subversion of literature
aims to reflect and promote new perspectives on sexuality or
whether new perspectives on sexuality need for their expression
new forms of literature, the result is, as Christiane P. Makward
and Madeleine Cottenet-Hage write of Monique Wittig: '. . .
fantasies of ecstasy and terror, of penetration, destruction and
fragmentation, of killing and resurrection; this produces the literal
staging of drives of every description. A truly "polymorphously
perverse" imaginary displays its hallucinating visions'.[3] Whether
Wittig's point of departure is literary or sexual iconoclasm, the
result is the same: a series of countercultural myths that leave few
*a priori* in place. Monique Wittig is but one writer among many
who seem to take a delight in moving and upsetting our mental
and cultural furniture.[4]

Although some critics, such as Philippe Sollers, welcome such
literary-sexual border crossing and even judge writers on the extent
to which they are 'dangerous for every form of authority', others
are more sceptical of writers' ability to transgress, at least in any
concrete or permanent fashion.[5] Christian Authier, for example,
has argued that 'we are sinking beneath the weight of iconoclastic
productions and unsettling artists. From rave parties to advertising,
from erotic literature to pornographic films, everyone sees themselves as rebellion incarnate'; while Pierre Jourde, in his critique
of Philippe Sollers and the new vogue for sexual explicitness in
women's writing, has commented that 'In most cases, a genre is
used to give the impression of content. As if the genre alone were
an automatic source of meaning, because it deals in supposedly
authentic material (the confession) or the physical (sex).'[6] For
Jourde, then, mere sexual explicitness is not enough to create
new thinking or to challenge old. Authier, on the other hand, is
of the opinion that sexuo-literary iconoclasm has been co-opted
by the literary-critical establishment and has even become part 'le

nouvel ordre sexuel', that is the new sexual conformism: 'When erotic escapades and pornography invade mass culture and become the "official" culture rather than a counter-culture, what is being challenged?'[7]

None of the works discussed by Pierre Jourde in his *La Littérature sans estomac* (2002) falls into the category of 'gay writing'; that is, literature by, for, or about gay male sexuality. There has, however, not been a shortage of gay sex(uality) in the French cultural tradition. By using gay sex both to shock and to subvert, writers such as Sade have established interesting precedents for more recent authors, film producers and artists. Jean Genet, Pierre Guyotat and Pierre et Gilles, for example, have all developed their own versions of the *poète maudit* tradition with a more explicit and often violent homoerotic agenda. In fact, explicit gay sex, whether in written or visual form, is often, *of itself,* seen as intrinsically subversive. The portrayal of subversive gay sex may be useful in certain contexts where norms need to be subverted. There is, however, the danger that it can be seen as intrinsically violent and threatening, especially in an age so deeply affected by AIDS. It could be argued, then, that there is not much difference between straight and gay sex. Gay sexual explicitness has simply become a literary equivalent of the *Loft Story* syndrome, with its emphasis on *le coquin* [naughty], *les scènes chaudes* [hot scenes] and *le croustillant* [spicy], and thus redolent of media hype, salaciousness and voyeurism.[8] If this is indeed the case, should we see the sexual violence of a Genet or a Guyotat simply as the gay equivalent of the masochism of *Histoire d'O,* or of the sadism in *Baise-moi*?[9] Or, should we perhaps regard the masochism and the sadism evident in some gay writing as a comment on the oppression of the gay community rather than on gay sex? Furthermore, does the predictability and repetitiveness of the 'new sexual explicitness' identified by Jourde apply in equal measure to gay as well heterosexual cultural production?[10] Or does gay sexual violence, as Philippe Sollers and Didier Éribon have argued, represent a sexual-literary-cultural subversion that can make a unique contribution to gay identity and the gay community?

In order to offer preliminary answers to the foregoing questions, this chapter examines a number of examples from recent gay novels, films and iconography. It begins with a brief examination of the literary criticism of Didier Éribon, one of the foremost gay theorists and political activists in France, who strongly emphasizes the violence at the heart of gay literary production and gay subjectivity.[11] As Éribon dwells largely on oppression and self-oppression in the work of authors, such as Proust, Gide and Genet, the second section examines more recent productions, including those by the well-known writer Guillaume Dustan and works by lesser-known contemporary novelists, such as Benoît Duteurtre, Christophe Honoré, Jean-Bernard Liger-Belair and Gilles Pétel. Violence and its relation to oppression and self-oppression do not only concern the novel but also visual productions, such as film and photography. The third section of this chapter looks at two films – Barbet Schroeder's *La Vierge des tueurs* (1999) and Sébastien Lifshitz's *Presque rien* (2000) – and the 2001 exhibition by Pierre et Gilles entitled 'Arrache mon cœur'. The following analysis, which focuses not so much on the sexual explicitness of the works in question as on their depiction of sexual (or other) violence, poses two questions. First, is sexual violence in gay cultural productions constitutive or deconstitutive of identity? And if deconstitutive, does it question hypostasized identity politics or does it 'simply' serve to express the distress of 'the downcast gay'? Second, to what extent is the gay community, often symbolized by the Paris gay scene, a vehicle for further violence? And is this violence the inevitable result of oppression or self-oppression, or, possibly, symptomatic of a generalized, *fin-de-siècle* sexual anarchy?[12]

## 1.

Basing his comments on the work of Proust, Gide and Genet, Didier Éribon sees the gay character as a martyr, outcast and pariah. In his tellingly titled *Une morale du minoritaire* (2001), Éribon claims, for example, that 'What lies at the heart of Genet's works is the description of those processes whereby an individual is made "abject" by the social order.'[13] According to him, the literary abjection reflects actual real-life abjection since 'Gay subjectivities [are] produced by social subordination ("shaming").'[14] He seems to be speaking, then, for all gays when he states in the same book that 'we are children of abuse' and in his *Réflexions sur la question gay* (1999) that his 'starting point was the problem of abuse, which is so important for gay lives, whether now or in the past'.[15]

Éribon is of the opinion that the gays' sense of inferiorization, injury and insult can be countered by resistance and that out of pariahdom comes an empowering 'solidarité entre les parias' [solidarity among the pariahs].[16] His emphasis, however, is less on resistance and empowerment than on 'the symbolic violence inflicted by dominant representations'.[17] It is difficult here to differentiate between the violence of dominance and the violence of subversion, because the outward oppression is clearly internalized to the point of being constitutive of gay representations, gay subjectivity and gay identity and also because Éribon's models, such as Genet, are only outlaws in as much as they are always already outcasts. When seen through Éribon's lens of abjection and injury, all discourse about gay subjectivity and gay representation becomes 'both a discourse of resistance and a discourse of submission' but with, alas, the emphasis ultimately on submission rather than resistance and on self-oppression rather than oppression.[18] Reality, fortunately, contradicts this rather bleak vision of homosexual self-entrapment. As Authier states in his critique of Éribon: 'This virtually paranoid vision of the homosexual condition in France in the year 2000 may well hold for certain groups of gay activists or gay communities, but, fortunately, seems to bear little relationship to France as a whole.'[19] To move out of the impasse of Éribon's theoretical and political positions, then, it is necessary to turn to other, more critical, more empowering and more future-orientated representations of gay subjectivities and the gay community.

## 2.

For a less nebulous example of 'la solidarité entre les parias', it may be helpful to turn to Guillaume Dustan's considerably more joyous references to what Frédéric Martel once famously or infamously referred to as 'le bonheur dans le ghetto' [fulfilment in the ghetto].[20] As Dustan writes on returning to Paris at the beginning of his exuberant and infinitely less self-apologetic *Je sors ce soir*: 'I get my eye in, feeling I can relax now I'm back once again with my brothers in the ghetto. They are all homos. They are all guys I can stare at without risking getting my head knocked in.'[21] Dustan retaliates to the homophobia with a different verve and insouciance than Éribon: his own, desiring look. He also

responds with a different self-assertive violence, arraying himself
with an increasing selection of sexual toys and moving deeper
and deeper into sexual sadism with an appreciative partner: 'It's
good to be a bit nasty. I've never felt better, he said, looking at
me, eyes moist.' However, this 'voyage au bout du sexe' [a long
day's journey into sex] is far from liberating.[22] According to Authier,
Dustan's unreflective hedonism, endorsement of 'strong individuals' and disregard for the other, is perilously close to fascism.[23]
Lawrence R. Schehr is furthermore of the opinion that Dustan's
work is both misogynistic and dangerous in its advocacy of
'barebacking'. If Schehr's observation that any critical distance
established by Dustan in relation to his own violence is abolished
in 'a pure flow of language and libido of writing bareback' is
correct, then there is as great a complicity between violence and
Dustan as between violence and Éribon.[24] Although ostensibly
very different writers, both closely link gayness to abuse – whether
that is abuse of the self or abuse of the other.

Before moving on to other writers' representations of oppression
and self-oppression, it is useful to try to determine what inhibits
both Eribon and Dustan to provide a radical critique of violence;
that is, what factors have they got in common that encourage
complicity with the very stigmatization they would otherwise
denounce? One factor might well be that, however seemingly
critical of that stigmatization, Éribon is both politically and viscerally
caught up in the 'we' of the stigmatized he identifies. Differently
but with the same result, Dustan too is caught up in pleasurable
self-admiration. Before referring to 'his brothers in the ghetto',
he sees the hell that is that ghetto but still plunges in: 'It is
Dante's hell. I dive in.' And once in, any detachment gives way
to pleasurable self-regard: 'Once out, I look at myself.'[25] Both
Éribon and Dustan, then, prefer identification to critique. There
is therefore a danger that this loss of difference and distance
does, when possibly confused with the love of the same in
homosexuality, reproduce the 'circle of sameness' and 'economy
of the same' that Irigaray and others have associated with a
masculine discourse.[26] Both Dustan and Éribon allow time and
history to be flattened in favour of age-old and infinitely repeated
discourses of oppression and self-oppression. Every time Dustan
goes out into clubs and bars, he repeats the monotonous circularity
of the dance. And each time Éribon excavates the literature of

homosexuality, he retrieves not only evidence of a perennial *génie gai*, but also the reiterated repression of that *génie*, combined with its internalization of its victimhood. Unlike Judith Butler, who sees 'hate-speech' as eminently iterative and hence as eminently *interruptible*, both Éribon and Dustan are, in their very different ways, seemingly unable or unwilling to interrupt the cycle of stigmatization. Butler's argument regarding hate-speech poses some interesting questions. First, how can 'hate-speech' about gays be interruptive? Second, how can what Butler calls 'discursive transitivity' be 'specified in its historicity and its violence?' Third, if Butler is correct in claiming that 'no speech act *has* to perform injury', then how can such injury be reduced or prevented rather than simply confirmed and repeated?[27]

One way of reducing a sense of injury is to forestall it and to be one's own most lucid and well-informed critic. This can apply both to the category of homosexuality itself and the attendant creation of the so-called 'gay ghetto', such as the Marais district of Paris.[28] On the latter theme, the novels *Baisse tendancielle du taux de plaisir* (2002) and *Gaîté parisenne* (1996) by, respectively, Jean-Bernard Liger-Belair and Benoît Dutreure, are instructive.[29] Like Guillaume Dustan, the main character in *Baisse tendancielle du taux de plaisir* regards the Marais as a kind of hell. But while the former plunges into it, the latter remains much more detached. He refers ironically to the Marais as a 'Mykonos-sur-Seine' (*Baisse*, 41) where pleasure is mechanized, a zoo with rules (*Baisse*, 47), and a transgression institutionalized (*Baisse*, 49). Although the main character lives and loves in the Marais (*Baisse*, 40), he cites Dustan's remark that the Marais is 'one of the most exotic zoos in the world' with a kind of mocking relish (*Baisse*, 39), absorbing the quote into a kind of literary intertext. He makes a similarly disrespectful reference to Genet: 'I . . . who am producing some bad Genet without wishing to do so' (*Baisse*, 84). By distancing himself from both Dustan's *Je sors ce soir* and from Genet, Liger-Belair, or at least his hero, distances himself from the repetitive, uncritical stances of both Dustan and Éribon, showing them to be as recuperable and as *ringards* as the historico-cultural context in which they operate. By also situating his character's most erotically charged experiences in trains rather than in the Marais, Liger-Belair shows that the Marais is but one, relatively unfulfilling, source of gay sexual pleasure. For him, pleasure is available in the

most seemingly innocent and unpromising situations. Handsome
young men are everywhere, not just in the self-oppressive confines
of the infernal ghetto but more excitingly on the journeys of
those who leave the ghetto behind and take the TGV with its
angelic carriage attendant, or the road to Jerusalem, where awaits
another angel, 'the handsome Gabriel' (*Baisse* 23). As the narrator
refuses both angels and chooses 'torture' instead, Liger-Belair
suggests that the ghetto has encouraged not liberation but
masochism. This masochism, however, is sufficiently acknowledged
to prepare a potential 'modification' into a less inhibited lifestyle
by the end of the book.

Benoît Duteurtre's *Gaité parisienne* is equally critical of the ghetto,
but not just the current ghetto. The novel takes a long look at
the Paris gay scene, from its beginnings in the bars and clubs of
the 1950s through to the construction of the Forum area in the
early 1980s and finally to the virtually post-ghetto culture of the
*fin-de-siècle*, where young gay men, represented by the 'vacant
beauty' of the student Julien, are more interested in career than
community and more in business than in politics: 'The four words
– *harmonisation, credit, legislation, international* – matched his youthful
yuppie tones as if he were intoning the creed.' (*Gaité* 64) This
move from a pre-gay – even pre-homosexual – to a post-gay world
is, however, not exclusive to the young. The older Nicolas, who
narrates the story, runs a cultural journal entitled *Anti-pouvoir*
which, somewhat paradoxically, has the backing of the Ministry
(*Gaité* 60). To show that the very refashioning of the Marais and
of gay identity is symptomatic of the power of commerce and
fashion over activism and community, Duteurtre sets the world of
Dustan's *Je sors ce soir* and *Plus fort que moi* in a very different time
frame and a very different social context. In addition, by letting
Nicolas's first attempt to seduce Julien end in fiasco rather than
in ecstasy, Duteurtre aims to deconstruct the image of both the
gay predator and the gay hedonist. He furthermore argues that
the terms oppression and self-oppression can no longer be used
by gay men because gays are already co-opted into commerce and
the establishment and all of Paris, not just the closed world of
clubs and parties, is there for the taking. Once Nicolas has seen
through the hollowness of Julien, himself imperfect given his
'sexe *tordu*' (85), he can move on, like the narrator of *Baisse
tendancielle du taux de plaisir*. The pleasure of moving out of, or

beyond, the ghetto, is that Paris itself becomes an inexhaustible source of pleasure. Duteutre turns the Marais [marsh] into the *marée* [tide], filling Nicolas with new light, life and energy (*Gaité* 208).

Duteutre and Liger-Belair not only place the Parisian gay ghetto in a broader social, cultural and historical context than in Dustan, but also gay or homosexual identity. Considering Guy Hocquenghem's argument that 'homosexuality is a fabrication of the normal world' and Leo Bersani's suggestion that '[a]n intentionally oppositional gay identity, by its very coherence, only repeats the restrictive and immobilising analyses it set out to resist', it seems only appropriate that recent French fictions have moved away from the paranoia of homosexual pariahdom in favour of more open yet more inclusive sexual arrangements.[30] Given the increasingly high profile and relative acceptability of bisexuality, both in wider French society and within the hitherto unwelcoming gay community, it is interesting to note that the protagonists of both *Gaité parisienne* and *Baisse tendancielle du taux de plaisir* combine or alternate close relationships with women and with men, and in Gilles Pétel's *La Déposition* (2002) combine, over a period, relationships with both sexes.[31] In none of these novels, however, does the protagonist actually identify himself as a bisexual. Nicolas in *Gaité parisienne* is 'freed from all yearning for love (in general) and from homosexuality (in particular)' (*Gaité* 123), if only because it enables him to be more sexual than (just) homosexual and become 'another trendy broad' (*Gaité* 95). In Liger-Belair's novel, the travelling hero is turned on by sportsmen in lycra, both despite and because of the fact that their physical unselfconsciousness betrays them as 'het, in a word'. (*Baisse*, 90) Similarly, Vincent in *La Déposition* dreams of being 'loved by a man who would really go for women' (*Déposition* 153). The question of whether these characters should be seen as homosexuals, 'situational homosexuals', 'closeted homos', heterosexuals, 'closeted het' (*Gaité* 161), bisexuals or unacknowledged bisexuals is less important in these novels than the characters' desire for, and pleasure in, men. As the young narrator writes in *La Déposition*: 'I still don't think that homosexuality was the root of the problem ... I've never been fussed by going to bed with a man.' (*Déposition* 77) However disingenuous this remark may seem, it is at least one way of pre-empting pariahdom. As for violence in *La Déposition*, the narrator's

lover-uncle or uncle-lover, Vincent, is killed towards the end. The
narrator, however, is *not* responsible for his death. In fact, the title
of the novel suggests that it serves as a statement disavowing
involvement in violence, whether that arising from oppression or
self-oppression.

## 3.

The novels by Duteurtre, Liger-Belair and Pétel suggest that both
oppression and self-oppression can be sidelined or parodied. They
do this, however, against a background of considerable violence.
Although the narrator of *La Déposition* may be innocent of Vincent's
death, the likely killer is a gay (or non-gay) pick-up, since Vincent
was in the habit of taking home rent boys. In other works too,
such as Christophe Honoré's *La Douceur* (1999), it is boys who
are suspected of being 'pédés' [queer] who are responsible for a
seemingly gratuitous, shockingly cruel murder of one of their
fellows.[32] Films also frequently accompany gayness by, or associate
it with, violence, ranging from the pain and melancholy felt by
Mathieu (Jérémie Elkaïm) in Sébastien Lifshitz's *Presque Rien* (2000)
to the serial murder by the teenage hitman Alexis in Barbet
Schroeder's *La Vierge des tueurs* (1999).[33] Violence also looms large
in Pierre et Gilles's 2001 photographic exhibition entitled 'Arrache
mon cœur' at the Galerie Jerome de Norimon in Paris. According
to Jonathan Turner, their images take on 'an unexpectedly dark
turn', exploring 'sex, death and the dark side of beauty'.[34] The
central image in this exhibition shows a naked male holding to
his chest a dripping mock-up of a copiously bleeding heart. The
popular gay magazine *Têtu* used a similar image for the cover of
its March, 2002 issue. It shows a young, semi-naked male, with a
large clot of 'blood' splashed on to his chest. The splash of blood
is held in position by lamé threads, which not only turns the
blood into jewellery, but is also reminiscent of congealed sealing
wax, confirming that any suggestion of violence has been converted
into a sexual package. Inside the magazine, the same model
reappears in a series representing 'tous les fantasmes de la psyché
érotique gay', 'à épingler sur les murs de votre chambre, sur vos
classeurs d'écolier, dans votre casier à la salle de sport . . .', [every
fantasy of the gay erotic psyche; for pinning up in your bedroom,
in your school exercise books, in your sports locker].[35] Violence

then persistently and insistently accompanies recent textual and visual gay male representations. Should we interpret the violence as further examples of paranoia and pariahdom or as the disavowal of both oppression and self-oppression?

At first sight, it seems that the melancholy of *Presque rien* and the violence of *La Vierge des tueurs* simply replicate and perpetuate the stereotypical linking of gayness and violence. Both Stéphane Rideau as the rough-cut, sexy Cédric in *Presque rien* and the young killers Alexis and Wilmar in *La Vierge des tueurs* seem to be new versions of the sexual outlaw charted by Éribon and Bersani.[36] And the reader could easily associate the murder of Antoine in Honoré's *La Douceur* with 'abnormal' sex. None of these young loners, however, is a 'gay killer'. There is no suggestion that Cédric is other than self accepting and well adjusted as a gay youth and explicit homophobia is remarkably absent from this film, in which the gayness of the characters is, as Lifshitz claims, almost incidental.[37] In both *La Vierge des tueurs* and *La Douceur* as well, the violence is neither gay motivated nor gay targeted. In *La Douceur*, the killing seems inexplicable. In *La Vierge des tueurs,* violence is part of a gang culture. The main character Wilmar kills Alexis as retribution for shooting his – presumably heterosexual – brother. Thus, in all these productions, violence is de-gayed. It is arbitrary, or part of the *dominant* culture, or both, as in the case of *La Vierge des tueurs.* Despite his rugged independence, Cédric at times acts passive and tender, and while Alexis is violent on the streets, he demonstrates a sense of peace when at home with Fernando. These productions, then, are about violence and about gayness but not about the relations between the two. As such, they do not offer a new version of oppression producing self-oppression in the form of the 'gay outlaw' and the gay pariah.

The images in Pierre et Gilles' 'Arrache mon cœur' and *Têtu* also disassociate gayness and violence. These images may seem, like *Presque rien* and *La Vierge des tueurs,* to respond to the appeal of 'gay rough trade' in order to sell. The models, however, are hardly categorizable in terms of sexual orientation or sexual practices. Indeed, although these images may seem to be more bloody versions of that other gay icon, Saint Sebastian, that 'blood' is less realistic than stage blood and the pose adopted by the models is more self-consciously contrived than that adopted in various representations of Saint Sebastian.[38] The violence is, therefore,

doubly, if not triply, 'de-gayed': the models' orientation is unknown
and considered irrelevant and the violence is unreal and independent of any actual or suggested gay sex. Rather than examples of
Éribon's oppression and self-oppression, these images are camp
or kitsch parodies of gay pain or gay melancholia. Like images
of Saint Sebastian, these images depict bodies that remain,
underneath a superimposed wound, intact and unblemished. These
bodies, then, are not those of homosexual martyrs. On the contrary,
despite (or because) of the merely artificial wounding, the images
are re-gayed with unapologetic, unstigmatized homoerotic energy.
Perhaps counteracting the images of emaciated bodies of AIDS
sufferers, the pictures of Pierre et Gilles and *Têtu* offer pictures
of readily available, highly sexed, 'full-blooded' masculinity. This
'full-blooded' masculinity, however, is available to gays rather than
restricted to so-called 'real men'.

   It can be said, therefore, that the character Cedric in *Presque
rien* and the images of Pierre et Gilles and *Têtu* are all part of a
reworking of potentially self-oppressive gay masculinity, converting
almost literal stigmatization into an artificial adjunct, in order to
offer an otherwise unimpaired male body for pleasurable
consumption.[39] Rather than an image of the stigmatized gay, such
images not only unhook gayness and stigma – since the model
has no sexual orientation and since the wound is itself artificial
and removable – but also show that *all men, including so-called
heterosexuals,* are available for 'gay' consumption. Taking this a stage
further, it can even be suggested that the wound is not that of
gayness but of heterosexuality, which the male model can and will
shed in order to become fully available for gay pleasure and gay
fulfilment. This eminently artificial and removable wound is,
therefore, the last 'fig leaf' of modesty before all men acknowledge
the gayness that lies beneath the obviously detachable and
undesirable stigma of 'normality'. By parading himself as a parody
of the Christic Bleeding Heart, the gay model is not the martyr
but (the) Man.

## 4.

What conclusions can be drawn from the foregoing examination
of oppression and self representation in gay representations in
France? First, the more obviously iconoclastic representations are

in their creation and perpetuation of the figure of the 'gay outlaw' unhelpful, no matter whether they confirm or contest the notion of gay identity and gay community. These representations fail to go beyond pariahdom, although they often adopt pariahdom only as a strategy for fragmenting hypostasized sex and gender categories and for attracting attention to gay oppression and resistance. Only if gayness is divorced from violence, as in films such as *La Vierge des tueurs* and novels like *La Douceur*, can gay representations go beyond pariahdom. Second, and linked to the foregoing, it appears that more ostensibly hegemonic portrayals of seemingly conformist gays can offer a more far-reaching critique of sex and gender categories because they enable gays to move seamlessly between so-called straight and gay worlds, thereby queering and co-opting supposedly straight men into their orbit of desire. Third, this co-option of straight by and into gay is, perhaps paradoxically and certainly disturbingly, most obviously achieved by the highly visible and highly commercialized commodification of desirable, 'decorative' men, as in *Têtu* and the pictures by Pierre et Gilles. It is no longer in a culture of violent or violated pariahdom, but in what Susan Faludi sees as our 'ornamental culture' where 'manhood is displayed, not demonstrated', that universalized male-to-male desire is more readily represented and realized.[40] Fourth, the de-gaying and re-gaying of desirable men in a generalized 'homo-ness' is accompanied by a parallel conversion of the old 'bad boy' violence into a highly obtrusive but eminently removable fashion accessory – the swabs of imitation blood – that enables the 'bad boy' to show that he is really a nice, gay-available boy underneath.[41] For the notion of gay as pariah to become as outdated as insisting the emperor is not only clothed but straight, it is essential that guys become gays by removing rather than by adding their make-up, and that violence becomes mere intertextual *clin d'œil* and masquerade, both of which will make gay maleness the new, natural, universalized masculinity.[42]

## Notes

1   J. Phillips, *Forbidden Fictions: Pornography and Censorship in Twentieth-Century French Literature* (London: Pluto, 1999), p. 1.

2   Breillat's films *Romance* (1999), *A ma Soeur* (2000) and *Sex is Comedy* (2002) and Virginie Despenters and Coralie Trinh Ti's film *Baise-moi* (2000) have provoked as much controversy for their sexual explicitness

as Catherine Millet's book *Vie sexuelle de Catherine M.* (Paris: Seuil, 2001).

3  C. P. Makward and M. Cottenet-Hage (eds), *Dictionnaire litteraire des femmes de langue francaise: De Marie de France a Marie NDiaye* (Paris: Karthala, 1996), p. 626. This and subsequent translations of French texts are by the author.

4  M. Stocker, *Judith Sexual Warrior: Women and Power in Western Culture* (New Haven/London: Yale University Press, 1998), p. 213.

5  *Le Monde* (5 July, 2002), p. vii.

6  C. Authier, *Le Nouvel Ordre sexuel* (Paris: Bartillat, 2002), p. 208; P. Jourde, *La Litterature sans estomac* (Paris: L'Espirit des Peninsules, 2002), p. 19.

7  Authier, *Le Nouvel Ordre*, p. 210.

8  Expressions such as these were repeatedly used in the commentary on the second series on the French TV channel M6 in June 2002.

9  P. Réage, *Histoire d'O* (n.p.: Jean-Jacques Pauvert, 1975).

10  Jourde, *La Litterature*, p. 18.

11  E. Showalter, *Sexual Anarchy: Gender and Culture at the Fin de Siecle* (London: Bloomsbury, 1991).

12  Eribon has become one of the best-known gay critics in France as a result of his analyses of Genet, Proust and Wilde; his broadcasting; and his work at the Ecole des Hautes Etudes in Paris. For his most recent contribution to the field of gay literary criticism, see *Dictionnaire des cultures gays et lesbiennes* (Paris: Larousse, 2003). Eribon has also published on Michel Foucault. For one of his most recent publications on Foucault in English, see 'Michel Foucault's histories of sexuality', *GLQ*, 7 (2001), pp. 31–86.

13  D. Eribon, *Une morale du minoritaire: variations sur un thême de Jean Genet* (Paris: Fayard, 2001), p. 69.

14  Eribon, *Une morale du minoritaire*, p. 292.

15  Eribon, *Une morale du minoritaire*, p. 86; D. Eribon, *Réflexions sur la question gay* (Paris: Fayard, 1999), p. 18.

16  In answer to a question posed after his talk on 'La Genie gay' at the Louvre on 24 November 2001. As a solution, Eribon prefers resistance to a Foucauldian notion of counter-discourse. See, for instance, his *Papiers D'identité: interventions sur la guestion gay* (Paris: Fayard 2000), p. 82.

17  Eribon, *Réflexions*, p. 112.

18  Eribon, *Papiers*, p. 86.

19  Authier, *Le Nouvel Ordre sexuel*, 117. On the extent and nature of the 'gay community', see L. Bersani, *Homos* (Cambridge: Harvard University Press, 1995), pp. 113–81.

20  F. Martel, *Le Rose et le noire: les homosexuels en France depuis 1968* (Paris: Seuil, 1996), pp. 179–210.

21  G. Dustan, *Je sors ce soir* (Paris: P.O.L., 1997), 18. Born William Baranes in 1965, Guillaume Dustan achieved celebrity in 1996 with his first novel *Dans ma chambre*. He has since produced several other novels, as well as a number of short films, including *Nous* and *Back*. He is

also the editor for Balland of the collection 'Le Rayon', formerly 'Le Rayon Gay'.

22  G. Dustan, *Plus fort que moi* (Paris: P.O.L., 1998), pp. 148 and 154.

23  Authier, *Le Nouvel Ordre sexuel*, p. 104.

24  R. Schehr, 'Writing bareback', *Sites*, 6:1 (2002), p. 201.

25  Dustan, *Je sors ce soir*, pp. 17–18.

26  S. Sellers, *Language and Sexual Difference: Feminist writing in France* (Basingstoke and London: MacMillan, 1991), p. 9.

27  J. Butler, *Excitable Speech: A Politics of the Performative* (New York and London: Routledge, 1997), pp. 15, 47 and 163.

28  Various scholars have argued that the category homosexuality depends on and helps to sustain the category hetereosexuality. See, for example, G. Hocquenghem, *Le Desir homosexual* (Paris: Fayard, 2000). Marais, which is a 'gay ghetto' as opposed to a 'gay neighbourhood', has in recent years been increasingly commercialized. Some critics have argued that as a result, it has become depoliticized. See, for instance, D. Rushbrook, 'Cities, queer space, and the cosmopolitan tourist', *GLQ*, 8 (2002), pp. 183–206.

29  J. B. Liger-Belair, *Baisse tendancielle du taux de plaisir* (Paris: Pauvert, 2002); B. Dutreure, *Gaîté Parisienne* (Paris: Galliamard, 1996). Future references to the novels will be given in the text. Previous works by Liger-Belair include *L'Ombre nécessaire* (1990) and *Le Roti* (1999). Duteurtre also wrote *Sommeil perdu* (1985), *Les Vaches* (1987), *L'Amoureux malgré lui* (1989) and *Tout droit disparaître* (1992).

30  Hocquenghem, *Le Desir*, 26; Bersani, *Homos*, p. 3.

31  Bisexuality, however, is still far from accepted in France. See, for example, 'Bisexualité: une identité en marche?, *Tetu*, 82 (October 2003), 66–74; Gilles Petel, *La Deposition* (Paris: Stock, 2002). Further references to this novel are given in the text. For earlier work by Petel, see *Le Métier dans le sang* (1996), *Le Mur de Broadway* (1998) and *Le Recensement* (2000).

32  C. Honore, *La Douceur* (Paris: Editions de L'Olivier, 1999). Further references to the novel are given in the text. Some of the characters in this novel reappear in Honore's *Scarborough* (2002). For more information on Honore, see *La Matricule de anges*, 40 (September–October, 2002), pp. 14–23.

33  Schroeder's film is based on the novel *La Virgen de los Sicarios* (2001) by the Columbian author Fernando Vallejo. For a good review of the film, see *Liberation*, 27 March 2002, p. 42.

34  J. Turner, 'Heart of darkness', *Blue*, 38 (April 2002), p. 50.

35  *Têtu*, 65 (March 2002), cover and pp. 92–3.

36  Bersani, *Homos*, pp. 113–81.

37  P. J. Smith, 'Presque rien', *Sight and Sound*, 11:10 (October 2001), 57. Its title suggests most clearly the relative unimportance of homosexuality in the film.

38  On the enduring importance of Saint Sebastian in gay culture, including the work of Pierre et Gilles, see *Triangul'ère: Art et Culture Gay*, 3 (2002), pp. 1048–107.

*At the Border*

39  Pierre et Gilles made the poster-illustration for *Presque rien*. It depicts the half-naked actors Jeremie Elkaim and Stephane Rideau haloed by star-studded spangles that eliminate any trace of violence.

40  S. Fauladi, *Stiffed: The Betrayal of Modern Man* (London: Vintage, 2000), p. 35.

41  Bersani, *Homos*, p. 10.

42  Monique Wittig has argued along similar lines for lesbian culture. See her, 'The mark of gender', in *The Straight Mind and Other Essays* (New York: Harvester Wheatsheaf, 1992), pp. 76–89.

# Index

Abdelhamid Ben Badis, Sheikh 63
Adt family, Einsheim 45
Agence Nationale Pour l'Emploi
    (ANPE) 141, 145–6
agricultural policy, farm lobby
    37–8
Algeria 58, 73–4
    *Algérie Française* (1830–1954)
        60–2
    Front de Libération Nationale
        (FLN) 65–7, 68, 69, 73
    and Mediterranean 60–2, 69–74
    and Ottoman Maghreb
        (1525–1830) 58–60
    post-independence 68–9
    traditional patterns of territory
        62–5
    *see also* Maghreb; Maghrebians,
        France
Algerian Communist Party (PCA)
    65–6
Algerian Nationalist Movement
    (MNA) 65, 66
*Algérie Française* (1830–1954) 60–2
Algiers, central plaza (*Al-
    Qaisariya*) 73
Alleg, Henri 67
Alsace-Lorraine, annexation of 50,
    54, 79–80, 82
American threat to French
    culture 32
Amicale du Camp de Gurs 106
AMORE47 104

Annéville (Stahlheim), Moselle
    89
ANPE *see* Agence Nationale Pour
    l'Emploi
anthropology 4
    and ethnic stereotypes 121
anti-colonialism, Algeria 62–3,
    64–5
anti-fascist movement 92
anti-globalization movement 31
anti-Semitism 129–30
Appel, René 166
Arabic languages
    status in the Maghreb 156,
        158–60
    *see also* Maghrebians, France
Arabization, Maghreb 158, 159
Arabs *see* Maghreb; Maghrebians,
    France
architecture, French–German
    border (1871–1914) 88–9
Argelès-sur-Mer concentration
    camp 100, 102–3, 105,
    106–7
'Arrache mon cœur' exhibition
    (Pierre et Gilles) 184, 185–6
Association des amis pour la
    mémoire de l'odyssée des
    réfugiés républicains
    Espagnols de Lot et Garonne
    (AMORE47) 104
Association of Muslim Ulama of
    Algeria (AUMA) 63, 68

Association pour la taxation des transactions pour l'aide aux citoyens (ATTAC) 31, 39n3
Auboué, Meurthe-et-Moselle 86, 87
Augustus, Emperor 9
AUMA *see* Association of Muslim Ulama of Algeria
Austrian Empire 51, 52
Austro-Prussian war (1866) 52
Authier, Christian 176, 176–7, 179, 180
Avricourt stations, Moselle/Meurthe-et-Moselle 88–9

*Baisse tendancielle du taux de plaisir* (Liger-Belair) 181–2, 183, 184
Barcarès concentration camp 102–3
Barcelona Declaration 71–2
Barrès, Maurice 128
Becker, Nicolas 49
Beduin, Algeria 63
Bennigsen, Rudolf von 53
Berber (Tamazight) languages status in the Maghreb 159
*see also* Maghrebians, France
Berlin Wall, Germany 3, 6
*beys/beyliks*, Ottoman Maghreb 59
bilingualism, Maghrebians, France 157
Birnbaum, Pierre 99
bisexuality 183
Bismarck, Otto von 45, 52, 53, 54
Bonnet, Serge 84, 87
Bordeaux, Spanish memorials 112
'border region', meanings of 4
border studies 2–6
borders
in the age of nationalism 13–15
definitions/terminology 6–9
in medieval/early modern Europe 11–13
in a post-modern era 15–17
in the Roman Empire 8–11

Bourbon dynasty 48
Butler, Judith 181

Caisse d'allocations familiales (CAF) 146
Caisse d'assurance maladie (Medical Insurance Fund) 146
Caisse nationale des allocations familiales (CNAF/National Fund for Family Allowances) 145–6
capitalism, and poverty 145
Catalan language 157
Çelik, Zeynep 73
cemeteries, military 84
census, minority languages 157–8
Ceynart, Lieutenant-Colonel de 47
CFDT *see* Confédération française démocratique du travail
CGTU *see* Confédération générale du travail unitaire 92
Chaulet, Pierre 66–7
Chirac, Jacques 35
Christianity 13, 119–20
Civil War, Spain 101–2
*see also* Spanish exiles
climates, and character 122–3
CNAF *see* Caisse nationale des allocations familiales
coal, French–German border (1815–70) 43, 44
colonialism, images of 'the Other' 120–1
commemorative practices *see* Spanish exiles
communism 92–3
concentration camps
Second World War 85
Spanish exiles 100, 102–4, 104–7, 115n30
Concordat (1801), Moselle region 83
Confédération française démocratique du travail (CFDT) 87

Confédération générale du travail unitaire (CGTU) 92
conflicts
 international/industrial (1983) 139–40
 *see also* wars
Constitutional Council 37
Cottenet-Hage, Madeleine 176
Council of State 37
culture
 American threat 32
 homoerotic 177–87
 Maghrebians, France 169
 memorial culture, Spanish exiles 104–8, 112–13, 115n30, 116n48
 patrimonial 99
customs posts, French–German border (1815–70) 43
customs union (Zollverein) 49

defence, French–German border (1815–1914) 45–8, 81
demographics, 1920s fear of decline 120, 121–2
*Déposition, La* (Pétel) 183–4, 184
detention centres *see* concentration camps; prisons/prisoners
*deys*, Ottoman Maghreb 59
Dialectal Arabic 156, 158–9, 159–60
doctors, 1920s racism 121–2
Donnan, Hastings 4, 6, 8
*Douceur, La* (Honoré) 184, 185
Dustan, Guillaume 179–81, 181, 188n21
Dutreure, Benoît 181–3

EC *see* European Community
economics
 Algeria 70
 French–German border (1815–70) 43–5
 government policy 29
ELCO *see* Enseignement des langues et cultures d'origine programme

elections (2002) 34–5, 36–7, 90–1
employers, delinquent 146–7
employment *see* unemployment
ENA *see* North African Star
English language, Maghreb 159
Enlightenment 33, 120, 122–3
Enseignement des langues et cultures d'origine (ELCO) programme 165
equality, French republican model 33–4, 119, 153
Éribon, Didier 177–8, 178–9, 180–1, 188n12
eroticism, violent 175–7
 homosexual 177–87
ethnic stereotypes, 1920s 120–2, 125–7
'ethnolinguistic vitality' 154, 167–9
EU *see* European Union
Euro-Mediterranean Partnership 71–2
Europe 26–7
 in the age of nationalism 13–15
 medieval/early modern 11–13
 post-modern 15–17
European Charter for Regional or Minority Languages (1992) 156
European Commission 148
European Community (EC) 30, 138
European Union (EU) 29, 31, 32
 and Mediterranean 71–2
Europeanization 29–32
exceptionalism 26
exiles *see* immigrants/migrants; Spanish exiles

Fanon, Frantz 67
farm lobby 37–8
fascism 92
FFREEE 105, 106–7, 113
Fifth Republic 27–8, 29–30, 31, 36
films, homoerotic 178, 184–7
Fils et Filles de Républicains Espagnols et Enfants de l'Exode (FFREEE) 105, 106–7, 113

First World War 84, 84–5, 92
  post-war attitudes to Germans
    and Italians 127–8
FIS *see* Islamic Salvation Front
Flaubert, Gustave 125
'flexploitation' 141
FLN *see* Front de Libération
  Nationale, Algeria
*fonction publique* 37
Forêts 43
fortifications
  Berlin Wall, Germany 3, 6
  French–German border 46–7,
    81
  Hadrian's Wall, UK 10–11
'France d'en bas, La' (grassroots
  France) 33–4
zero tolerance policy 148–9
Franco-Italian alliance (1915) 92
Franco-Prussian trade agreement
  (1865) 45
Franco-Prussian war (1870–1) 54,
  79, 84
Franco-Pyrenean border *see*
  *Retirada, La*
Frankfurt, Treaty of (1871) 54, 79
French Communist Party (PCF)
  64, 86, 92, 94
French language 155, 157
  status in the Maghreb 158–60
French–German border
  (1815–70) 40–3
  defence 45–8
  industry and trade 43–5
  legacy of 54–5
  under Napoleon III 51–4
  perceptions of 48–51
French–German border
  (1871–1914) 79–83
  migrants 91–4
  mines as markers 86–7
  political identity 90–1
  stations and housing 88–9
  wars 83–5
Front de Libération Nationale
  (FLN), Algeria 65–7, 68, 69,
    73
frontiers, terminology 7–9

*Gaité parisienne* (Dutreure) 182–3
Garde des Sceaux, zero tolerance
  policy 148
Gaullism 29–30, 31
gay ghettos 179–80
  Marais district 181–3, 189n28
gay sex(uality) *see* homoerotic
  culture
Gemie, Sharif 108
Genet, Jean 177, 178–9, 181
German Confederation 43, 47–8,
  49, 53
Germans, post-war hatred of 127
Germany
  Berlin Wall 3, 6
  *see also* French–German border
    (1815–70); French–German
    border (1871–1914)
ghettos *see* gay ghettos
Giles, Howard, 'ethnolinguistic
  vitality' 154, 167–9
globalization 3, 29–32
government *see* elections (2002);
  policy-making, French model
Guenée, Bernard 12
Gurs concentration camp 105,
  106
Guytotat, Pierre 177

Hadj-Ali, Abdelkader 64
Hadrian's Wall, UK 10–11
Hargreaves, Alec 154
*harkis*, Algeria 66
'hate-speech' 181
'headscarves affair' (1989),
  French Muslims 170
'hexagon', stereotype of 118
historians, research focus 5
Hobsbawm, Eric 150n3
Holocaust 85, 100
homoerotic culture
  films 178, 184–7
  literature 177–84, 186–7
  photography 177, 184, 185–6
Honoré, Christophe 184, 185
Horne, John 85
housing, French–German border
  (1871–1914) 89

Hugo, Victor 50
human zoos 121

identity, national
    Maghrebians, France 164
    roots of 118–22
    *see also* Spanish exiles
identity, political, French–German
    border (1871–1914) 90–1
immigrants/migrants
    Algerian 63–5, 70
    French–German border
        (1815–1914) 44, 91–4
    hostility towards *see* racism;
        xenophobia
    increase in migration 3–4, 16
    'otherness' 117, 120–1, 125–7,
        128–9
    and roots of national identity
        118–22
    *see also* Maghrebians, France;
        Midi (1920s); Spanish exiles
industry, French–German border
    (1815–70) 43–5
*insécurité, l'* *see* security/insecurity
Inspecteurs du travail (Labour
    Inspectorate) 146, 147
institutions, state 37
internment camps *see*
    concentration camps, Spanish
    exiles
Islam 62–3, 67, 68–9, 170–1
Islamic Salvation Front (FIS)
    68–9
Italian migrants
    French–German border
        (1871–1914) 91, 92, 93–4
    post-war acceptance 127–8
    stereotypes 126–7
itinerants, fear of 129–30

Jews 99–100
    anti-Semitism 129–30
    Holocaust 85, 100
Joeuf, Meurthe-et-Moselle 94
Jospin government 29
Jourde, Pierre 176, 177
*jus soli/sanguini* principles 119

Kabyles, Algeria 63

Labour Inspectorate *see*
    Inspecteurs du travail
labour legislation 141, 143
Lamartine, Alphonse de 50
land
    and 'rooting' of society 128–9
    tribal land, Algeria 61–2
language
    border/frontier terminology
        6–9
    'ethnolinguistic vitality' 154,
        167–9
    language shift 166–7
languages 155–8
    hostility towards 34
    loss of diversity, Algeria 67
    of Maghrebians, France 154,
        156–7, 160–9, 171, 171–2
    status in the Maghreb 156,
        158–60
'Latinity' concept, 1920s 122–7
Le Pen, Jean-Marie 35–6, 39n4,
    90, 91
legislation
    anti-terrorist 148
    labour 141, 143
    Moselle region 83
    and social rights 142–3
    zero tolerance policy 148–9
liberalism 31, 138
*lieux de mémoire* ('realms of
    memory') 97–101
Lifshitz, Sébastien 184, 185–6
Liger-Belair, Jean-Bernard
    181–2, 183, 184
literature
    homoerotic 177–84, 186–7
    sexually explicit/violent
        175–7
    Spanish exiles 108
*Loft Story* syndrome 177
Lorraine *see* Alsace-Lorraine,
    annexation of;
    French–German border
    (1871–1914)
Louis-Philippe, king of France 48

Luxembourg, Grand Duchy of 43, 53, 81

Machiavelli, Niccolò 11
Madelin, Alain 31
Maghreb
  (Algeria/Morocco/Tunisia)
  Ottoman Maghreb (1525–1830)
  58–60
  status of languages 156, 158–60
  *see also* Algeria
Maghrebians, France 64, 140, 153–5
  culture 169
  language 154, 156–7, 160–9, 171, 171–2
  religion 170–1
Makward, Christiane P. 176
maps
  depiction of borders 58–9
  French–German border (1815–1918) 41
Marais district, gay ghetto 181–3, 189n28
*marche-symbole* (symbolic march), Pyrenees 107–8
marches (border zones), medieval 12
Mars-la-Tour 84
Mauroy, Pierre 140
Maurras, Charles 128
Medical Insurance Fund *see* Caisse d'assurance maladie
medieval Europe 11–13
Mediterranean, and Algeria 60–2, 69–74
Mégret, Bruno 90
memorials
  Spanish memorials, Bordeaux 112
  war memorials, French–German border 84, 85
memory, national *see* Spanish exiles
meridional (southern) character 122–7
Metz 41 (map), 46, 47, 88

Meurthe(-et-Moselle) 41 (map)
  *see also* French–German border (1871–1914)
Middle East Peace Process 71–2
Midi (1920s) 117–18, 131–2
  meridional (southern) character 122–7
  social boundaries 127–31
migrants/migration *see* immigrants/migrants
military cemeteries 84
military conflicts *see* wars
military studies (1820s) 46–7
mines/miners, French–German border (1815–1914) 41 (map), 44, 85, 86–7
Ministry of the Interior, zero tolerance policy 148–9
MNA *see* Algerian Nationalist Movement
Mohammed Abduh, Sheikh 62
*mondialisation see* globalization
Montois-la-Montagne, Moselle 87
Morocco/Moroccans *see* Maghreb; Maghrebians, France
Moselle *see* French–German border (1815–70); French–German border (1871–1914)
Movement for the Triumph of Democratic Liberties (MTLD), Algeria 65, 66
Moyeuvre-Grande, Meurthe-et-Moselle 86, 94
Muslims
  medieval Europe 13
  *see also* Algeria; Maghreb; Maghrebians, France
Musset, Alfred de 49
Muysken, Pieter 166

Nancy 41 (map), 82, 84, 89
Napoleon III 51–4
Napoleonic model of state–society relations 33
National Assembly 28
National Fund for Family Allowances *see* Caisse

nationale des allocations
familiales (CNAF)
national identity *see* identity,
national
nationalism 13–15
neo-liberalism 31, 138
*No pasarán, album souvenir* (film)
112–13
Noiriel, Gérard 100–1
Nora, Pierre 97, 98–9
North Africa *see* Algeria; Maghreb
North African Star (ENA) 64
North German Confederation
53
'nos ancêtres les gaulois'
formula 118
Novéant station 88

Occitanism, 1920s 124–5
Ortlieb, Gilles 87
'otherness', foreigners/migrants
117, 120–1, 125–7, 128–9
Ottoman Maghreb (1525–1830)
58–60

PARE *see* Plan d'Aide au Retour à
l'Emploi
Paris, treaty of (1815) 42
Parisian centralization 27
passports, French–German border
(1815–70) 43
patrimonial culture 99
*Pax Romana* 123
PCA *see* Algerian Communist
Party
PCF *see* French Communist Party
Pétel, Gilles 183–4, 184
Phillips, John 175
photography, Pierre et Gilles 177,
184, 185–6
Plan d'Aide au Retour à l'Emploi
(PARE) 140, 145
*poète maudit* tradition 177
police, targeting working-classes
148, 148–9, 151n22
policy-making, French model
26–8
continuity 36–8

equality and uniformity 28,
33–4, 119, 153
Europeanization and
globalization 29–32
political legitimacy 34–6
reinventing the state 28–9
politics
elections (2002) 34–5, 36–7,
90–1
*see also* policy-making, French
model
population, 1920s fear of decline
120, 121–2
pornography *see* eroticism,
violent
post-modernism 15–17
poverty *see* unemployment
power, medieval Europe
12–13
*Presque Rien* (film, Lifshitz)
184, 185–6
prisons/prisoners 149
*see also* concentration camps
property
property rights as separatist
138
*see also* land
Prussia *see* French–German
border (1815–70)
public space, and political
agitation 150
Pyrenees *see Retirada, La*

racism 72, 140, 166, 170
ethnic stereotypes, 1920s
120–2, 125–7
*see also* xenophobia
railways/railway stations,
French–German border
(1815–1914) 41 (map),
43–4, 44, 88–9
Ramdane, Nasser 170
'realms of memory' (*lieux de
mémoire*) 97–101
reception centres *see*
concentration camps, Spanish
exiles
*Reconquista*, Spain 13

refugees
  political 14–15
  *see also* immigrants/migrants;
    Spanish exiles
regionalization 34
religions
  Christianity 13, 119–20
  Islam 62–3, 67, 68–9, 170–1
religious differences, immigrants
  119–20
republicanism *see* policy-making,
  French model
research *see* border studies
Réseau Express Régional (RER)
  16
Resistance, Second World War 85,
  92
*Retirada, La* (the retreat), Spain
  101–4, 107–8, 114n15
Revenu minimum d'insertion
  (RMI) 142, 145–6
Rhine Province 42–3, 48–9, 50,
  53–4, 56n13
rights *see* security/insecurity
RMI *see* Revenu minimum
  d'insertion
Roberts, Hugh 67
Roechling, Karl 50
Roman civilization, and 'Latinity'
  123–4
Roman Empire 8–11
'rooting', as foundation of society
  128–9
Roth, François 80
ruralism 128–9

Saar region (*Saargebiet*) *see*
  Sarre/Saar region
Sade, Marquis de 175
Saint-Cyprien concentration camp
  100, 102–3
*Salafiyya* movement 62–3
Salih, Ruba 17
Sarre/Saar region (*Saargebiet*) 41
  (map), 42, 43, 44, 45, 49
  annexation 54–5
  loss of Sarrelouis 46
Sarrieu, Bernard 124

Sartre, Jean-Paul 67
Schehr, Lawrence R. 180
Schenkenberger, Max 49
Schroeder, Barbet 184, 185–6
Sebastian, Saint 185–6
Second Chamber 28
Second Republic, Spain 103–4
Second World War (1939–45)
  83–4, 85, 92
security/insecurity (*la
  sécurité/l'insécurité*) 137–9,
  149–50
  politics of 146–9
  social insecurity 139–42
  social rights access 142–6
Seille river 82
Senate 28
*Sénatus Consulte*, land
  appropriation, Algeria 61
sex(uality) *see* eroticism, violent
'shameful treaties of 1815' 48–9,
  51
smuggling 15
social rights *see* security/insecurity
Société d'Etudes Occitanes,
  Toulouse 124
Sollers, Philippe 176
Spain
  Civil War 101–2
  *Reconquista* 13
  *Retirada, La* (the retreat)
    101–4, 107–8, 114n15
  Spanish exiles 96–7, 112–13
  exile and internment 101–4
  memorial culture 104–8,
    112–13, 115n30, 116n48
  memory-environment, family
    life 108–12
  and 'realms of memory'
    97–101
  stereotypes of 125–6
Special Urban Zones (ZUS)
  142, 151n9, 151n11
St Martin, Republic of, West
  Indies 4, 18n5
Stahlheim *see* Annéville
state *see* elections (2002); policy-
  making, French model

stations, French–German border
(1871–1914) 88–9
Strasbourg, diocese of 13–14

Taguieff, Pierre-André 121
Tamazight *see* Berber (Tamazight)
languages
terminology, borders/frontiers
6–9
terrorism, repressive measures 148
*Têtu* (gay magazine) 184, 185–6
Thiers, Louis Adolphe 49
Thil concentration camp 85
Third Republic 88, 102, 118
Tiercelet mine 85
Toulouse *see* Midi (1920s)
tourists, hostility towards 130–1
towns, medieval distortion of
borders 11–12
trade, French–German border
(1815–70) 43–5
tramps/travellers, fear of 129–30
treaties
'shameful treaties of 1815'
48–9, 51
Franco-Prussian trade
agreement (1865) 45
of Frankfurt (1871) 54, 79
of Paris (1815) 42
of Versailles (1919) 15, 55
Tribalat, Michèle 153
Tunisia/Tunisians *see* Maghreb;
Maghrebians, France

UK, Hadrian's Wall 10–11
Ulama Association 62–3
*umma*, Islamic 68, 68–9
unemployment
and social insecurity 139–42
and social rights 143–6
Union Populaire Italienne 92
*Univers concentrationnaire* 102

vagabonds, fear of 129–30
Versailles, Treaty of (1919) 15, 55
*Vierge des tueurs, La* (film,
Schroeder) 184, 185–6
violence *see* eroticism, violent

war memorials, French–German
border 84, 85
Warnier Law (1873), land
appropriation, Algeria 61
wars
Austro-Prussian war (1866)
52
First World War (1914–18)
84, 84–5, 92, 127–8
Franco-Prussian war (1870–1)
54, 79, 84
Second World War (1939–45)
83–4, 85, 92
Spanish Civil War (1936–9)
101–2
welfare benefits 140–1, 143–6
Wendel (industrial firm) 44,
86, 91
Wilhelm I, king of Prussia
51–2
Williams, Derek 9–10
Wilson, T. M., 5, 6, 8
Wittig, Monique 176
working classes
police targeting 148, 148–9,
151n22
repression of 149–50
*see also* unemployment
workplace accidents 146–7
world wars *see* First World War;
Second World War

xenophobia 93, 142, 154
fear of itinerants 129–30
Germans, post-First World War
127
and 'rooting' in the land
128–9
and Spanish exiles 102
and tourists 130–1
*see also* racism

zero tolerance crime policy
148–9
Zollverein (customs union) 49
zones, medieval 12
zoos, human 121
ZUS *see* Special Urban Zones